Probabilistic Data Structures for Blockchain-Based Internet of Things Applications

Probabilistic Data Structures for Blockchain-Based Internet of Things Applications

Neeraj Kumar
Arzoo Miglani

CRC Press
Taylor & Francis Group
Boca Raton London New York

CRC Press is an imprint of the
Taylor & Francis Group, an **informa** business

Contents

Foreword

I am delighted to write this foreword, not only because the authors are my colleague but also because I believe in the collaboration of two different technologies to enrich the real-world problem. This book combines two interesting topics, i.e., probabilistic data structure and blockchain technology. When I first heard about the concept of this book, I was pleased as this book is coming up with a new concept. Reading this book readers will find develop a reason on usage of probabilistic data structures for blockchain technology that too in easy and most understandable language. To make the concepts more clear, examples have been taken by the authors. Moreover, for preparing questions and classroom activities, each chapter contains a set of MCQ's and some questions. Even if you don't have any good computer science experience, this book explains concepts from basics.

The blockchain technology is growing rapidly. The biggest challenge that blockchain technology faces is the storage issue. Some believe blockchain technology is not getting much popularity because of data deduplication which leads to high space requirements and query processing on blockchain data takes a lot of time. I believe this book is one of the best investments to answer those minds. This book aims to discuss techniques to analyze big data on blockchain databases with less storage and minimized time complexity making use of probabilistic data structures. Probabilistic data structure eases query execution keeping a huge amount of data in mind. Also, the practical execution of probabilistic data structure and blockchain is shown using Python language. This book is introduced for technology practitioners, software developers, researchers, professional developers, students, teachers, and decision-makers.

Preface

With the popularity of Internet of Things (IoT) technology, a huge amount of data is being generated which is characterized by all V's, (i.e., velocity, volume, and variety) and referred to as big data. End-users demand high security and privacy along with real-time response for executing of various queries on the huge volume of the stored data. To solve the problem of security, Blockchain (BC) technology emerges as a distributed data storage structure that provides transparency to all the users on the network. However, to reduce overall communication and computational cost, efficient processing along with fast validation and verification of data is the need of the hour. The conventional data structures result in inefficiency for handling big data in terms of storage and response time. Other existing query methods on data, such as MapReduce and SQL are not suitable for delay-sensitive and streaming data from IoT applications. In this context, approximation and probabilistic algorithms are found to be effective to reduce space and computation time complexity. Unlike conventional data structures, Probabilistic data structures (PDS) are based on hashing techniques to store data in a compact form. Less memory requirements, large scale data processing, real-time processing, unstructured data storage, reduced delay are some popular qualities for the adoption of PDS among researchers.

This book will provide an in-depth theoretical and practical knowledge of PDS and blockchain concepts. The working of each probabilistic data structure in this book will be illustrated using code snippets and illustrative examples. Also, this a first attempt to introduce the applicability of PDS in blockchain to technology practitioners. Although the literature does not support much work that integrates PDS with blockchain but this book will provide new directions to the readers on the subject cited above. This book also provides references for the applications of PDS to blockchain. It will also have the implementation codes in Python language for various PDS so that the readers can gain confidence using hand-on experience. Simple syntax, presence of third-party module, user-friendly environment, extensive library support, versatility in providing data-science applications are some of the reasons for adopting Python as an implementation language over other existing languages for implementation of the concepts presented in this book.

The whole book is organized in four sections with 17 chapters, each section preceded by an overview related to it. The first section gives a brief overview of IoT technology and revolution of big data because of the popularity of IoT. Section 2 is dedicated to the fundamental concepts of blockchain technology which first covers cryptographic concepts that are widely used in blockchain and also in PDS. Section 3 covers PDS and algorithms used to estimate membership query, cardinality, similarity, and frequency along with the realization of each PDS with Python language. Section 4 tells about the usage of PDS in blockchain based IoT applications for better storage and computational complexity.

Biography

Dr. Neeraj Kumar

Prof. Neeraj Kumar received his Ph.D. in CSE from Shri Mata Vaishno Devi University, Katra (Jammu and Kashmir), India in 2009, and was a post-doctoral research fellow in Coventry University, Coventry, UK. He is working as a Professor in the Department of Computer Science and Engineering, Thapar Institute of Engineering and Technology (Deemed to be University), Patiala (Pb.), India. He has published more than 400 technical research papers (which are cited more than 10000 times with current h-index of 55) in top-cited journals, such as IEEE TKDE, IEEE TIE, IEEE TDSC, IEEE TITS, IEEE TCE, IEEE TII, IEEE TVT, IEEE ITS, IEEE SG, IEEE Netw., IEEE Comm., IEEE WC, IEEE IoTJ, IEEE SJ, Computer Networks, Information sciences, FGCS, JNCA, JPDC and ComCom. He has guided many research scholars leading to Ph.D. and M.E./M.Tech. His research is supported by funding from UGC, DST, CSIR, and TCS. His research areas are Network management, IoT, Big Data Analytics, Deep learning and cyber-security. He is serving as editors of the following journals of repute.

- ACM Computing Survey, ACM

- IEEE Transactions on Sustainable Computing, IEEE

- IEEE Systems Journal, IEEE

- IEEE Network Magazine, IEEE

- IEEE Communication Magazine, IEEE

- Journal of Networks and Computer Applications, Elsevier

- Computer Communication, Elsevier

- International Journal of Communication Systems, Wiley

Also, he has been a guest editor of various International Journals of repute, such as - IEEE Access, IEEE ITS, Elsevier CEE, IEEE Communication Magazine, IEEE Network Magazine, Computer Networks, Elsevier, Future Generation Computer Systems, Elsevier, Journal of Medical Systems. Springer, Computer and Electrical Engineering, Elsevier, Mobile Information Systems,

International Journal of Ad hoc and Ubiquitous Computing, Telecommunication Systems, Springer and Journal of Supercomputing, Springer. He has also edited/authored 10 books with International/National Publishers like IET, Springer, Elsevier, CRC. Security and Privacy of Electronic Healthcare Records: Concepts, paradigms and solutions (ISBN-13: 978-1-78561-898-7), Machine Learning for cognitive IoT, CRC Press, Blockchain, Big Data and IoT, Blockchain Technologies across industrial vertical, Elsevier, "Multimedia Big Data Computing for IoT Applications: Concepts, Paradigms and Solutions" (ISBN: 978-981-13-8759-3), Proceedings of First International Conference on Computing, Communications, and Cyber-Security (IC4S 2019) (ISBN 978-981-15-3369-3). One of the edited text-book entitled, "Multimedia Big Data Computing for IoT Applications: Concepts, Paradigms, and Solutions" published in Springer in 2019 is having 3.5 million downloads till 06 June 2020.It attracts attention of the researchers across the globe. (https://www.springer.com/in/book/9789811387586)

He has been a workshop chair at IEEE Globecom 2018 and IEEE ICC 2019 and TPC Chair and member for various International conferences, such as IEEE MASS 2020, IEEE MSN2020. He is senior member of the IEEE. He has won the best papers award from IEEE Systems Journal and ICC 2018, Kansas-city in 2018. He has been listed in the highly cited researcher of 2019 list of web of science (WoS). In India, he is listed at 13 position among highly cited researchers list. He is adjunct professor at Asia University, Taiwan, King Abdul Aziz University, Jeddah, Saudi Arabia and Charles Darwin University, Australia.

Mrs. Arzoo Miglani

Arzoo Miglani is currently pursuing Ph.D. from Thapar Institute of Engineering & Technology (TIET), Patiala. She had worked with DIT University, Dehradun for 2 years as an assistant professor and with TIET for 1 year. She has done her ME in Information Security from TIET in 2015. She has completed her B.tech from GJU, Hisar in 2009. She is GATE qualified. Her research area includes Wireless Sensor networks and network security, blockchain and content centric networking.

Part I

Background

1

Overview of Internet of Things

1.1   Understanding the Concept of Internet of Things

The rapid growth in electronics and communication technologies has lead to advancements in our society. Digitization started with the introduction of mainframe computing that uses a large sized computer to connect people. Next, came the era of microcomputers which facilitates every individual to afford their own computational device. The first instance of the Internet called Advanced Research Projects Agency Network (ARPANET) came in the late 1960s with the interconnection of four university computer systems. Later, the TCP/IP protocol suite development expanded the network size. However, during the 1990's, the computing framework became more personal until the introduction of the World Wide Web (WWW). In 1991, the world's first website came online. The early days of the Internet were only popular for WWW, an interconnected network of HTML documents. This kind of web was just a source for military and scientific purposes. Next, this static HTML pages framework was upgraded to Web 2.0 that involves user participation and interactions (social network sites, blogs, e-commerce, etc.). Since then the number of Internet connected devices has been increasing at an exponential rate. Currently, the web era we are a part of is Web 3.0 (also known as smarter web) which is moving beyond and toward Internet of Things. Fig. 1.1 shows the evolution of computing technologies.

The technology "Internet of Things" (IoT) was first introduced back in the year 1999. However, this technology gained popularity after the year 2008. Besides academic research, IoT is an area of interest for the industrial sector as well. In today's scenario, sensors are embedded in everyday things, such as lamps, watches, and mobile phones to name a few. With the usage of IoT, the life of a human being becomes easy and comfortable. Depending on the IoT application, various sensors, such as temperature sensor, humidity sensor, Radio Detection and Ranging (RADAR), infrared, and radio-frequency identification (RFID) are used. The IoT is an emerging computing topic where everyday used physical objects are connected to the Internet (via Wireless Sensor Networks (WSN), bluetooth, RFID, near-field communication, LoRa, etc.) with minimal or no human input. Also, these devices are programmed to be controlled remotely with authorized access. The gateway layer connects IoT devices to the external world for remote control. Infact, WSN is a technology used within an IoT system, which enables aggregation of small sensor nodes to perform multiple tasks, including collection, aggregation, processing, and analyzing data [199], [190], [201]. Smart devices in IoT networks involve machine-to-machine (M2M) communication to achieve tasks without any human intervention. Apart from (M2M), RFID, near-field communication (NFC), vehicle-to-vehicle (V2V), vehicle-to-grid (V2G) are some of the other technologies involved in realizing the idea of IoT. The IoT can range from wearable accessories to large electric machines, each embedded with a sensor chip. For example, the Apple watch contains sensors that provide tracking support, physical activity data, and heart rate data to be analyzed. Likewise, large electric machines, such as washing machines and refrigerators can be made fully automated with IoT enabled implementation. The future Internet will have heterogeneous devices connected together with new capabilities. Notably, IoT has proved to be the front-runner for strengthening the concept of ubiquitous computing [127]. As the popularity of IoT is increasing, it is spreading into every aspect of life. Infact, the advancements in hardware techniques (such as improving bandwidth by using radio cognitive based network) and better connectivity services have made IoT more popular [202]. Other than personal use, IoT provides services to the community as well. It covers many commercial and industrial fields including healthcare, sports, transportation, entertainment, smart home, etc. Fig. 1.2 depicts the layerwise architecture of IoT for collection, transmission, and processing of data.

The year 2008 was the inflection point for IoT as the number of Internet-connected devices exceeded the world's population. To date, the world is deployed with 38 billion Internet connected devices and it is predicted that over 75.44 billion smart devices will be connected with the Internet by the year 2025 [1] (as presented in Fig. 1.3). The continuous contribution given by academia government, and private industries has definitely achieved new service requirements for IoT. Moreover, IoT technology has changed the scenario of storage from hard-disk with limited storage space to cloud storage with unlimited space.

1.1.1   Components of IoT

The different components of IoT are actuators, sensors, connectivity, data processing, platform, and user-interface as shown in Fig. 1.4.

- IoT sensors and devices: A device can be comprised of multiple sensors for sensing tasks. There is a variety of sensors available today including proximity detection sensors, humidity sensors, RFID tags, pressure sensors, temperature sensors, etc. These sensors collect information from surroundings and send it to the data processing layer. It is important to design techniques to convert this collected data into usable knowledge. Unfortunately, these devices are battery constrained. Moreover, changing batteries at a regular intervals for these devices is not a feasible solution

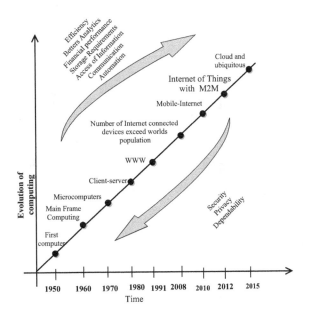

FIGURE 1.1
Evolution of computing.

for many applications, and hence durable batteries that last many years are required.

- User-interface: It provides a user-friendly medium that could be easily accessed by the end-user. The user-interface helps to check all activities happening on the IoT system. For example, users might use interface to check the video recording of the camera installed in the house. One popular way to achieve this is to develop applications with some predefined rules that trigger automatic alarms or notify via e-mails or text on the mobile phone on detection of any unusual activity. Also, the IoT devices are characterized by limited power, small memory, and little processing capability. However, due to the generation of bulk of data by IoT machine, IoT system has to face various challenges including security, data privacy, data management, and interoperability to name a few.

- Data processing: With the advancements in IoT and big data revolution, the importance of data processing techniques has been increased. After

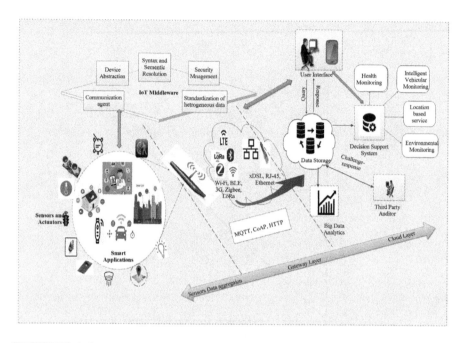

FIGURE 1.2
Layer architecture of IoT for data collection, transmission, and processing.

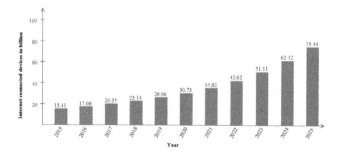

FIGURE 1.3
IoT connected devices worldwide.

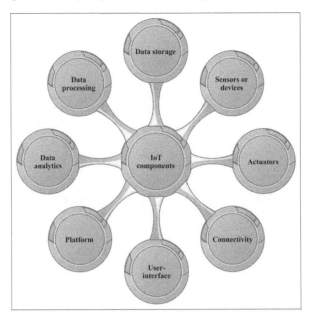

FIGURE 1.4
Major components of IoT.

the data is generated by sensors, it is sent to the user's device or to cloud for analyzing data. Data processing can range from something very simple (such as- detecting whether the current temperature reading on AC or heater is within a defined range) to very complex (detecting an unwanted person in the house and triggering alarms). However, the data should be processed in real-time (without delay) in order to improve the efficiency of system.

- Connectivity: Clearly, to transfer collected data to the cloud server, a medium is required. However, depending on the system the data is sent in real-time or batches at any time. The things of IoT networks are interconnected through a public or private network. The various medium of communication involves cellular network, Wi-Fi, Bluetooth, wide area network (WAN), zigbee, LoRaWAN, satellite to name a few. Notably, Message Queuing Telemetry Transport (MQTT) is a specific M2M/IoT connectivity protocol, used for connecting with remote locations with premium network bandwidth. However, each one of the networks has its own properties including efficiency rate, data transfer rate, range, bandwidth, etc. Moreover, the identification of any entity in network is the foundation of IoT. Both of the Internet Protocol Version 4 (IPV4) and Internet Protocol Version 6 (IPV6) are supported by IoT. Due to shortage of IPV4 addresses, objects on IoT are sometimes referred with IPV6 addresses.

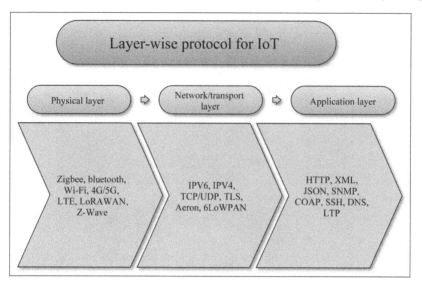

FIGURE 1.5
Layer-wise protocol for IoT.

Infact, IPV6 is the key communication enabler for future IoT. Feature of IPV6, i.e., scalability, security, and connectability, etc. makes it a perfect solution for IoT. For short-range communication, IEEE 802.15.4 and IEEE 802.11 are proposed by the Institute of Electrical and Electronics Engineer (IEEE). Refer to Fig. 1.5 for categorization of layerwise protocol for IoT. Hence, depending on the specification of the system, choosing the best connectivity option is important.

- Platform: With the increase in Internet-connected devices, it is hard to manage and store an enormous amount of data generated by IoT devices. In particular, cloud based infrastructures are used to store and process IoT data. Additionally, many data management tools are also available and provide automatic features to manage the bulk of generated data.

1.2 Big Data Revolution

A new trend that has been growing exponentially over the past few years is the "Big Data." Big data is a new era in the field of data utilization. It refers to a collection of large datasets having structured and unstructured data that is analyzed further to take intelligent decisions. The big data is assumed to be increased to 163 ZB by 2025 as per a report by International Data Corporation (IDC) [2]. Big data is characterized by 3 V's ,i.e., volume, velocity, and variety. Although other research has introduced veracity, value, variability as additional characteristics [85]. Big data is used by many organizations to solve business problems and to bring innovations. New data sets from IoT system, satellites, social media, online gaming, etc. is a leading factor for the big data revolution. The dataset is so complex and voluminous that conventional software can't handle them [205]. Additionally, in this abundance of generated data, there lacks the insight of useful data. However, data analytics are trying to develop sophisticated languages to analyze these huge data. However, as an advantage, an increase in data leads to an increase in accuracy and more confident decision making [178], [194].

Additionally, big data analytics is a process of searching databases, data mining, and concluding some results in order to improve organization performance. These analytics demand tools that can deal with structured, unstructured, and semi-structured data, and converts it into a more understandable form. However, privacy, confidentiality, availability, speed, authentication, efficient storage, and handling redundancy are some of the big data strategies to work upon in order to make improvements in the system.

1.2.1   Big data and IoT

In particular, data generated from IoT devices have contributed a major role in big data landscape. An increase in the number of IoT connected devices demands advanced technologies to meet customer requirements. Also, this popularity of IoT has made analytics of big data more complicated due to the collection of data through heterogeneous devices in the IoT environment. The basic concept behind IoT is to connect all physical devices in the world (i.e., at home, workplace, in moving vehicles) via the Internet and then processing the information from collected data in order to take meaningful decisions. IoT generates data from different sources (variety) which may contribute to structured and unstructured data. Furthermore, the amount of IoT data can vary from gigabytes (GB) to zettabytes (ZB) (volume) and generated data may be collected in batches or streams (velocity) [192], [50]. Hence, with this enormous amount of data generated by IoT devices, we require an advanced data processing system. IoT data analysis can provide big insights into hidden analysis for a variety of areas, such as- health analysis, malware detection, business market analysis, and prediction, etc. Some of the IoT big data applications are shown in Fig. 1.6. Data mining, machine learning, deep learning, statistical analysis, etc. are some of the latest data analysis techniques to analyze data independently [101], [211]. Over and above, IoT analytics are still not fully developed as most of the IoT generated data is still unexploited. Additionally, with the massive increase in data generation by IoT devices, a major concern is data storage and how to query such a large set of data in single pass [150]. In particular, big data analysis tools are utilized by researchers to solve the above mentioned challenges. Fig. 1.7 presents factors leading to big data revolution.

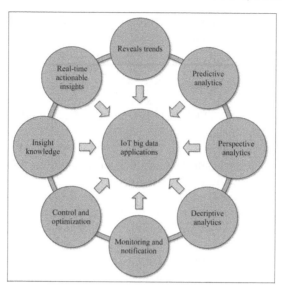

FIGURE 1.6
IoT big data applications.

The convergence of IoT and big data creates new opportunities in various sectors. The data generated from IoT sensors is then fed to big data framework for exploration and analysis. The aim of integrating big data with IoT is to analyze large amounts of data and to process it in real-time. Big data systems are adopting the Platform-as-a-Service (PaaS) model to handle IoT data in a flexible and scalable way. In some cases, IoT analytics and processing are also collaborated with edge computing services which decentralizes IoT processing at the edge of the network [162]. However, selected data from edge nodes is still transferred to the cloud. Clearly, more the IoT system grows, the more it will create demand on business with respect to big data capabilities. The following steps are taken for IoT big data processing:

- First, a large amount of structured, unstructured, and semi-structured data generated by IoT devices is collected by the big data system. The data complexity is characterized mostly by 3 V's, i.e., volume, velocity, and variety. Refer to Fig. 1.8.

- Next, a big data framework stores the collected data in a shared distributed database.

- Further, the stored data is analyzed using big data analytic tools, such as-Hadoop, MapReduce, RDBMS, etc.

- Finally, reports of analyzed data are generated.

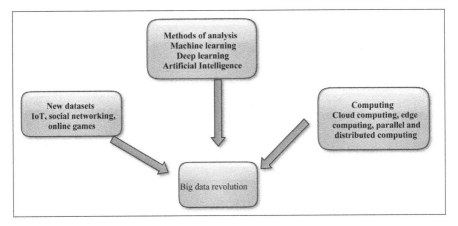

FIGURE 1.7
Factors leading to big data revolution.

Big data analytics can prove beneficial to IoT for variety of reasons including:

- Examine data

- Reveal trends

- Find hidden co-relations

- Reveal new information

- Find unseen patterns

- Queries on data

- Classification and clustering of data

Unfortunately, currently available software are not able to handle the emerging big data well. Also, the collaboration of IoT and big data, however, has created challenges for the research industry including data storage and analytics tool. Additionally, this increased data requires increased security that puts a new challenge for big data security professionals. The data passing over Wi-Fi and bluetooth must be sent with leak proof technologies. Moreover, the analytics department should design ways to handle redundant data generated by IoT devices.

Moreover, today's data-driven and decision-making scenario is forcing processing and analytics to happen as fast as the data is being generated. In this context, the stream processing of data can be effective. Traditional data is collected in batches and involves batch processing. Batch processing, however, processes huge volumes of data but with a long period of latency. For instance, the data may be processed every 12 hours or 24 hours. Unfortunately, the data

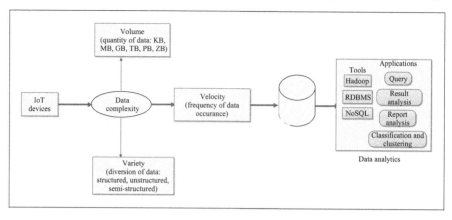

FIGURE 1.8
IoT big data processing.

is not fresh by the time it is processed and analyzed. In contrast, stream processing of data is often more time sensitive over batch processing. Streaming data refers to data that is continuously generated by various data sources and collected simultaneously. For example, data generated from traffic light has no start or finish. Processing real-time streaming data as soon as it is collected can lead to an efficient system. Notably, the streaming data framework always assumes that data is being continuously generated and always moving. Most of the IoT data can be characterized as streaming data. Health sensors, traffic light sensors, temperature sensors, etc. are good studies for data streaming. Data streaming enables data to be analyzed in real-time and provides decisions for a wide range of activities. Therefore, to achieve real-time analytics, many researchers have adopted stream processing of data over batch processing. Hadoop MapReduce is the best and popular platform for batch processing whereas Apache Kafka, Apache storm, Apache Samza are some open source platforms for stream processing of data. Also, Apache flink is a popular open source data flow engine to achieve data distribution and fault tolerance over data streams with distributed computations. It offers almost zero latency as data is streamed in real-time. Notably, due to poor Internet connectivity and bandwidth limitations, earlier years of research refrains streaming data to reach the destination in a continuous fashion. However, streaming data faces challenges for scalability, data durability, and data storage. Therefore, in order to make real-time decisions on streaming data, a new paradigm is required that can process the data at a very high throughput speed. Table 1.1 shows the difference between batch and stream processing of data.

One of the solutions to address streaming data problems is by using probabilistic data structures (PDS) as they have the capability to handle scalable and dynamic data efficiently. PDS are useful for applications that demand real-time response in performing queries on large data sets. Also, PDS

TABLE 1.1
Comparison of batch and stream processing of data.

Batch processing	Stream processing
• No time lines defined	• More time sensitive
• Latency in minutes to hours	• Real-time decision in order of seconds or few minutes
• Involves complex analytics	• Involves simple analysis
• Always process large volumes of data	• Handles individual records

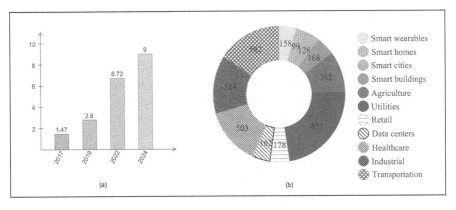

(a)   (b)

FIGURE 1.9
(a) Market size for edge computing worldwide 2024; (b) Application wise market share ($) of edge computing for year 2019.

optimizes time and space complexity for various queries, such as- membership, cardinality search, and frequency count, etc. The future chapters will discuss PDS and its types in detail.

1.3   Understanding edge computing

Edge computing is defined as a distributed computing architecture that supports data processing close to the place where things are located and generates the data. Edge computing is taking computing era towards more distributed architectures. Edge computing was introduced because of the exponential growth of IoT devices that further communicates with cloud [123]. This technology brings data storage, processing, and computations closer to the devices instead of relying on thousands of miles away from central location. As per a report from Gartner, 75% of the data will be produced outside the cloud by the year 2020 [3]. In an edge computing scenario, sensors and devices transfer data to a nearby edge computing device (such as- a gateway, switch, router, and micro datacenter, etc.) that processes the data rather than sending it to a remote data center. The main purpose of designing edge computing is to address the cost of bandwidth while data travels long distance from data generation point to cloud storage. With this, data can be processed easily in real-time with significantly reduced latency in order to improve application performance. Security and privacy services can also be improved by storing sensitive data closer to the device. Also, with the local processing of data, a significant amount of money can be saved. The increasing growth and wide adoption of IoT within organizations are expected to rely more the edge computing market. It is expected that market size for edge computing world wide can reach 9 billion by the year 2024 as shown in Fig. 2.1 (a). Also, Fig. 2.1 (b) represents application wise market share of edge computing for year 2019 in $. Over and above, edge computing promotes new possibilities for IoT applications, in particular for using ML services for tasks such as- object detection, language processing, etc. This implies that there could be more efficient processing of data and less centralization of attributes. Many IoT applications including smart grid, Internet-of-Vehicles (IoV), Internet-of-Drones (IoD), autonomous vehicles, etc. can take benefits of edge computing. Some of the benefits of edge computing are depicted in Fig. 1.10.

- **Reduced latency**: In contrast to cloud network, edge network is closer to IoT devices which implies a shorter round trip for storing, processing, and communication.

- **Better battery life for IoT devices**: As edge computing will open communication channels for a shorter time which means battery life of battery constrained IoT devices can be extended.

- **Better data management**: Edge computing is a future of data management as rather than managing data at a centralized location, this technology enables distributed management by multiple edge devices.

- **Improved security and privacy**: Edge computing also provides some security and privacy benefits. As already discussed, due to the inherently centralized nature of the cloud, it is vulnerable to Distributed Denial-of-Service (DDoS) attacks. In contrast, edge computing distributes storage and processing across various devices and data centers, which eliminates the possibility of a single server to get down. Also, edge computing reduces the size of transmitting data to a central data center. Most importantly, storing data near to where device is located improves privacy of the system as well.

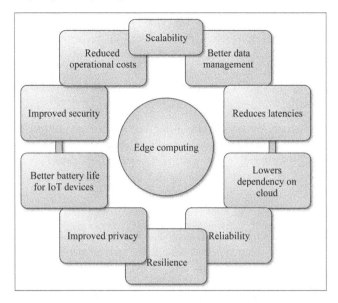

FIGURE 1.10
Key advantages of edge for IoT.

- **Scalability**: Clearly, with decentralized processing, less load is placed on the central network. Edge computing provides a less expensive way to scalability so that companies can extend their computing capacity with edge data centers. Additionally, the usage of edge computing devices reduces substantial bandwidth demand on the core of the network.

- **Resilience**: Edge computing provides more communication paths over a centralized model which also assures resilience of data communications. If there is a failure at one device of the edge, other resources can still produce continuous operations. With so many computing devices and data centers of the edge connected to the network, data can be routed via multiple pathways to assure the availability of data to users.

- **Reduced operational costs:** Obviously, the bulk of data generated by IoT sensors is not relevant for IoT. In this context, edge computing offers data to be filtered before sending it to the cloud which reduces data transmission costs. Also, edge computing reduces requirements for abundance of cloud storage which in return reduces infrastructure costs.

- **Autonomous operations:** Many IoT applications demand to be autonomous in their operations. Edge computing enables local storage and computations. Hence, the system can still function even if not connected to the Internet.

Hence, the exponential growth of IoT devices that demand real-time computations continues to drive towards edge computing services. However, this collaboration of edge computing with IoT needs new investments, infrastructure, and management platforms.

The following are the challenges faced while deploying edge computing in the IoT environment:

- **Heterogeneity:** As discussed computing platforms might have different operating systems and hardware specifications. Also, communication technology can be heterogeneous with respect to data rate and transmission range. Therefore, one of the challenges in edge computing is to design a portable software space for different environments. Also, another concern is to develop a language that supports hardware heterogeneity.

- **Standard protocols:** In IoT framework, heterogeneous devices and sensors connect with edge server through communication protocols. Due to the reason for having different interfaces, a specific communication protocol is demanded. Hence, the development of standard protocol in IoT system is challenging due to an increase in development of new devices.

- **Availability:** Availability refers to the provision of resources and services anytime for subscribed IoT nodes. Ensuring the availability of hardware and software resources is challenging for an increasing number of IoT devices.

- **Security and privacy:** Clearly edge computing provides relief to cybersecurity department as IoT data do not travel much. Although dynamic characteristics of the environment at edge make network unprotected. Many executable applications are running at edge of network so maintaining the confidentiality of data is important.

Activity

Multiple Choice Questions

1. ARPANET stands for?

   A. Advanced Real Projects Air Network

   B. Advanced Research Preparation Agency Network

   C. Advanced Recruitment Process Agency Network

   D. Advanced Research Projects Agency Network

2. The huge number of devices connected to the Internet of Things has to communicate automatically, not via humans. What is this called?

   A. Skynet

   B. Bot 2 Bot

   C. Machine-2-machine computing

   D. Intercloud

3. MQTT is —- protocol?

   A. Machine-to-machine

   B. Internet of Things

   C. Machine-to-machine and Internet of Things

   D. Machine things

4. Version 6 of IP address has how many bits?

   A. 64

   B. 128

   C. 32

   D. 256

5. MQTT stands for

   A. MQ Telemetry Things

   B. MQ Transport Telemetry

   C. MQ Transport Things

   D. MQ Telemetry Transport

6. What are the three V's of Big Data?

   A. Volume

    B. Velocity

    C. Variety

    D. All of the above

7. — is the process of examining large and different variety of data sets?

    A. Big data analytics

    B. Machine learning

    C. Deep learning

    D. None of the above

8. Which type of data Hadoop can deal with is?

    A. Structured

    B. Unstructured

    C. Semi-structured

    D. All of the above

9. What connects IoT devices to cloud to aggregate data, translate them between protocols and to process data before sending it somewhere?

    A. IoT sensors

    B. IoT standards

    C. IoT gateways

    D. IoT processors

10. Which one of the following is a challenge of IoT edge computing?

    A. Increased security risks

    B. Inconsistent industry standards and regulations

    C. Lack of support for new devices

    D. All of the above

1. d	2. c	3. c	4. b	5. d	6. d	7. a
8. d	9. c	10. d				

2

Smart Applications

2.1 Internet-of-Energy

The global electricity consumption of users is predicted to rise by 30% by the year 2040 (compared to 2017) as reported in [30]. This ever-increasing demand is due to urbanization, increasing appliances craze, and population growth. In order to satisfy this demand, the issue of environmental pollution due to CO_2 combustion has been raised as a critical issue. To design a complete IoT based smart homes and smart cities, an intelligent electricity distribution approach is required. Adopting renewable energy resources, Electric Vehicle (EV's), smart grids are some of the most effective solutions to deal with this problem. With the usage of distributed energy resources, the energy system is shifting towards decentralization. Additionally, the concept of local energy market is also getting popularity which involves local trading of electricity among different nodes of the network. Similarly, the smart grid provides an autonomous platform for generation, distribution, storage, and transmission of electricity. A smart grid framework maintains stability by balancing electricity generation and consumption among different utilities [117]. To collaborate a smart grid with distributed energy resources, microgrids are effectively used. With the usage of microgrids, it becomes easy for energy traders and consumers to trade energy locally which clearly minimizes transmission power loss. Over and above, EV's and Vehicle-to-Grid (V2G) technology are an important part of smart grid that contributes to developing a green eco-friendly environment. EV's enable better storage and energy balancing services in collaboration with wind and solar plants. Similarly, V2G technology facilitates EV's to act as an energy storage medium so that energy could be transfer back to the grid during peak hours for load balancing purposes. The owner of EV's gets paid in return for discharging electricity.

Clearly, the usage of all the above-mentioned technology is shifting the energy market framework towards a distributed and decentralized network from a centralized network. This dynamic interconnection of different energy components including power stations, microgrids, EV's, smart grids and people with the Internet is referred to as the Internet of Energy (IoE). In particular, IoE is the accomplishment of IoT, big data, artificial intelligence (AI), and computing technology for distributed energy management systems to optimize existing energy infrastructure. IoE has revolutionized the energy market in order to achieve a self-managed intelligent power infrastructure. Similar to IoT, IoE is based on sensors and automated real-time monitoring techniques to collect energy information from different utilities.

Therefore, the collaboration of energy market with intelligent edge devices for real-time processing of data is taking the energy market towards a different future. However, IoE comprises multiple forms of energy which lead to security and privacy issues in the network which demands a new energy system. Additionally, communication protocols and standards are facing issues for controlling and maintaining IoE devices. Data management, payment mechanism, Peer-to-Peer (P2P) energy trading, demand response management, cyberattacks, and dynamic pricing are some of the other issues faced by IoE.

2.2   Autonomous Vehicles

The increase in the human population directly affects the number of vehicles an individual possesses which clearly creates a burden on current transportation infrastructure. The strength of vehicles is estimated to reach 2 billion globally by 2030 as reported in [177]. The increasing number of vehicles causes various issues in the current transportation system, such as- parking difficulty, increased road accidents, high commuting time, increased pollution, etc., which creates demand for a reliable transportation system [196], [141]. In addition, autonomous vehicle faces many other challenges including software heterogeneity, verification, and validation of data and latency [187]. Recently, the integration of cognitive computing with IoT has achieved greater popularity as self-learning models are included in smart things with an aim to simulate human thought processes. This technology is referred to as cognitive Internet-of-Things (CIoT). Among various applications of CIoT, autonomous vehicles are a new craze among developers. Due to recent advancements in computer vision technology, automobiles industry, and cognitive computing, autonomous vehicles are getting a lot of attention from industry as well as academic research.

Autonomous vehicles aim at automatic acquiring, collection, management, and distribution of traffic information among different transportation utilities including vehicles, access points (AP's), and Road Side Units (RSU's). Improved safety, time savings, improved traffic flow, autonomous parking, new business opportunities, customer-centric experience, and accident reduction are some of the key objectives to be achieved by autonomous vehicles. Autonomous vehicles consist of programmed controlled AI agents to supervise, take decisions, and self-manage without human intervention. Autonomous vehicles are supposed to perform tasks including sensing neighborhood environment, control speed, and implement driverless driving without any human control. Additionally, requirements for physical road signals, vehicle insurance, and traffic police will get reduced with autonomous vehicle usage [158]. Autonomous Vehicles: Autonomous vehicles are connected via a dedicated short-range communication (DSRC) protocol. These vehicles are equipped with a wide variety of sensors and actuators (piezoelectric sensors, microwave doppler RADAR sensors, inductive loop sensors, IR sensors, acoustics sensors, etc.) to process real-time traffic data for better operation and decision-making. These sensors help to provide information regarding speed, lane occupancy, object detection to accomplish tasks including traveling time delay, and traffic flow prediction. In particular, camera sensors are meant to support the surrounding view, RADAR sensors help in object detection whereas LIDAR sensors are used for collision avoidance. Also, software define networking (SDN) brings flexibility, programmability, and some other extensive advancements to autonomous vehicles [43], [42], [198]. In addition to this, autonomous vehicles are connected with GPS based taxis and cellular record data. Autonomous vehicles demand lots of data collection and processing. All data shared among connected cars, access points, and Road Side Unit (RSU's) is uploaded to a cloud server for processing and decision-making. Nevertheless, there is considerable cost of maintaining the collected data from different sources. Therefore, the nature of this collected data (volume, variety, velocity, quality) should be considered.

2.3 Healthcare

Medical care and health care are worth mentioning applications for IoT. With IoT, doctors can now monitor a patient's health continuously. Also, the patient's interaction with doctors has become more efficient. Many devices, such as- fitness bands, glucometer, motion detector, heart rate monitoring cuffs, etc. have increased the personalized attention of the user towards their health. These devices are utilized to notify calorie count, exercise check, breathing check, appointments, stand up goals, and electrocardiogram (ECG) etc. Also, there has been craze of of wireless body area network where multiple sensor nodes are deployed randomly in the human body [180]. In case of major disturbance or routine activity change, an alert message is sent to family and concerned doctors. Additionally, telesurgery has a huge capability to deliver healthcare services to remote locations based on high source data delivery [96]. Cost reduction, improved treatment, faster disease diagnosis, proactive treatment, and error reduction are some of the key advantages of IoT based healthcare. Moreover, IoT can identify time for refilling supplies of devices. Gateways, health database, mini-medical servers ae some important components for providing on-demand services to authorized stakeholders. Recently, there is an exponential growth in usage of Healthcare 4.0 diagnostic systems across the globe. Here, records of patients are stored in electronic health record (EHR) repository that is located either at centralized or distributed places to monitor and access the data from anywhere [105], [193], [44], [104]. In this context, e-health cloud framework has evolved for exchanging, sharing important information among various medical institutions, medical researchers, and hospital systems, etc. [145]. Some of the IoT healthcare applications are:

- Glucose level sensing

- ECG monitoring

- Blood pressure monitoring

- Oxygen saturation monitoring

- Wheelchair management

- Medication management

- Rehabilitation system

- Cough detection

- Melanoma detection

- Remote surgery

Healthy children, GoogleFit, Period calendar, Noom walk, OnTrack diabetes, Eyecare plus, Asthma tracker, and Daily yoga are some of the popular smartphone appliances for general healthcare. Notably, research objectives in IoT based health care involve network architecture, interoperability, heterogeneity, security, policies, and guidelines, etc. [210]. In particular, due to sensitive nature of health care data, it faces security and privacy issues [103]. Similar to standard communication scenarios confidentiality, integrity, authentication, availability, data freshness, authority, resiliency, fault tolerance are the security requirements to achieve secure IoT based healthcare solutions. However, due to computational, memory, and energy limitations of IoT based sensors refrains the implementation of complicated security protocols in healthcare systems. Additionally, mobility, scalability, and dynamic security updates are some of the other challenging factors to achieve security requirements.

2.4   Smart Farming

The next era of computing will be totally IoT-based. The agriculture industry is another field disrupted by IoT. As per a recent statistics from the United Nations report, the world population is expected to reach 9.7 billion by the year 2050 [4]. In order to feed such a massive growth in population, the agriculture industry has adopted IoT. Notably, having lack of knowledge regarding climate can affect the quality of crop production. Many times, farming and agriculture activities fail due to bad prediction which lead to huge loss to farmers. Farming area is considered as a crucial sector for ensuring food security.

With IoT, challenges including unpredictable weather conditions, climate changes, a environmental changes are tackled efficiently to meet the growing demand of food. IoT-based agriculture market is expected to reach USD 20.9 billion by the year 2024 when compared to USD 12.7 billion in 2019 [5]. By employing Global Positioning System (GPS) and smart sensors on farming field and collaborating with big data analytics, farmers would be able to manage agriculture efficiently. IoT facilitates easy collection and management of huge data collected from sensors devices and with cloud computing services data can be easily accessed from anywhere and anytime.

Smart farming is a high-technology system for growing food in a sustainable way. Smart farming eliminates the need for physical work among farmers to increase the productivity. IoT based smart farming monitors crops conditions and field's various factors including humidity, soil, moisture, temperature, etc. in real-time. Moreover, plant-monitoring, animal-monitoring, pest control, supply chain management, infrastructure management, and control system management, etc. are some other applications of IoT-based smart agriculture [87]. Additionally, excess use of water and electricity can be saved with the help of sensors and interconnectivity for optimal plant growth. This eliminates the need for physical presence while disturbing weather conditions. Refer Fig. 2.1 for applications of IoT based agriculture.

Besides large-scale farming, IoT-based smart farming is also designed for family farming and organic farming. Recently, aerial drones are also used to improve agricultural activity. With visual imagery data collected while flying, insights including plant health indices, yield production, plant health measurement, field water pond mapping, weed pressure mapping, nitrogen content in wheat, etc. can be provided to farmers.

2.5 Smart Education

In recent years, smart education has gained attention from both academia and industry. IoT can affect every aspect of students, learning by providing a better learning experience. The aim of a smart learning environment is to achieve self-learning, self-motivated services so that learners can attend educational courses at their own place and use personalized learning content. Some of the advantages of IoT-based smart education are discussed as follows:

- IoT is providing a key role in teaching and assessment. As IoT has a core functionality of the device-to-device (D2D) management and

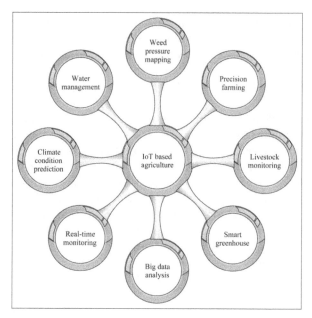

FIGURE 2.1
Applications of IoT based agriculture.

interconnectivity, it easily manages devices, and provides student inter-action for a better learning experience. Therefore, IoT provides learning from home and distance-based learning programs are running successfully.

- An automatic connection between different educational unit will automat-ically reduce overall expenditure.

- IoT system can be used to track the overall security of the institution. Ac-tivities, such as- fire safety, tracking students' movements, outsider entry can be easily tracked with IoT-based sensors. Also, vehicles of the institute can be managed and security can be provided to them.

However, digital learning involves a vast number of e-devices which demands device management and decision-making.

2.6 Smart Industry

Increased competition among industries and increasing demand for production are putting stress on machines thus causing the risk of failure. Furthermore, raw material is getting costlier, forcing industries to optimize their operation and to reduce energy and manufacturing waste. Moreover, industries require secure real-time monitoring of machines, and workers. In this context, IoT-based smart industries are proved to be helpful to address the discussed problem.

The smart industry also known as industry 4.0 facilities inter-connectivity for smart factories, working machines, and industrial infrastructure in order to streamline smart business operations and to create intelligent self-optimized industrial facilities [131]. 2019 is regarded as an inflection point in the maturity of industry 4.0 [6]. Digitization, inter-connectivity, new technology, and advanced manufacturing are driving factors for the smart industry revolution. Smart industry network interconnects products, machines, manufacturing units, companies, production plants, etc. at a highly granular level. This technology is basically based on the concept of automation, connectivity, cloud, big data, machine learning, simulations data analytics, augmented reality, and data exchange in manufacturing. Smart industry changes the way factories and workplaces operate, making them more safe, efficient, flexible, and environmentally friendly. Smart factory, smart airport smart railway, automotive industry, and smart construction are some of the key IoT applications for smart industries. IoT enables machines to get connected inside the factory and also to cloud server enforcing optimal planning and flexibility in manufacturing. With smart industry, linear and sequential supply chain operations are shifting towards an interconnected and open system of supply chain operation. Asset efficiency, better quality, lower cost, safety, detection of fault occurrence, and sustainability are the benefits of smart industry. Notably, The data reliability in Industrial Internet of Things (IIoT) has to be higher as compared to smart home and smart city applications [67]. For some application of industries low latency and low jitter is expected from wireless communication in an industrial environment. Fig. 2.2 transform happened because of smart industry.

Notably, the collaboration of IoT with the smart industry is shifting the scenario from the value chain approach to a network-centric approach. However, the issue of interoperability is one of the serious concerns in designing an automated human-to-machine and machine-to-machine co-operation.

2.7 Smart City

Many IoT based applications are designed to improve the lifestyle of city residents by gathering information. The demand for smart cities is increasing daily with increase in population level as it is difficult to manage these limited resources among the huge population [195]. A smart city is referred to as an innovative city that is based on information and communication technologies to improve the quality of life and efficiency of urban operations. The smartness

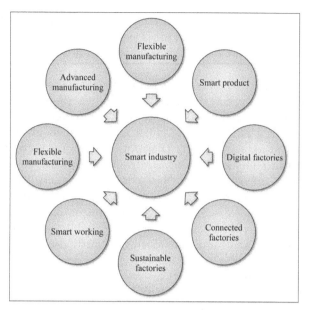

FIGURE 2.2
Transformation because of smart industry.

of the city is the ability to effectively use all its resources and to operate automatically with maximum efficiency. The smart city provides many services
including transportation, waste management, environmental monitoring, and
traffic management, to name a few. (Refer Fig. 2.3.) The key features required
by smart cities, i.e., interconnection, intelligence, and instrumentation are all
supported by IoT [111]. Therefore, it is true to say that the backbone of smart
cities is IoT. The communication devices for these applications are designed
specifically to perform low power operation but can be used for large areas that
demand longer communication range. LoRa technology is efficiently used in
smart city applications. Infrastructure building, transportation, energy, governance, education, citizens are the key components of smart cities whereas
sustainability, quality of life, urbanization, and smartness are the various attributes of smart cities [147]. The sustainability defines city infrastructure,
climate change, social issues, waste management, water management governance, etc. The quality of service is calculated from the emotional and financial
well-being of the citizens. The urbanization includes aspects, such as- infrastructure, technology, and economics. The smartness includes, aspects such as-
smart living, smart economy, smart mobility, etc. Design cost, reliable communication, operational efficiency, disaster resilience, system failure, public
safety, and carbon emission are the few challenges for building smart cities.

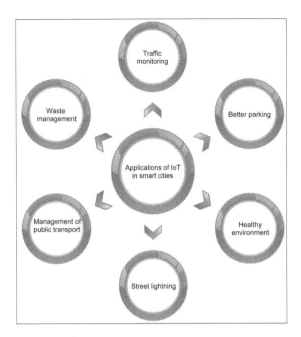

FIGURE 2.3
Applications of IoT in smart cities.

In context of users, the applications of IoT are grouped into four categories:

- Personal IoT: These applications are used by an individual person. For example, users of a smart watch.

- Group IoT: These applications are used by a small group of people. For example in terms of a smart home, connected cars, smart education, etc.

- Community IoT: These applications are used by a larger group of people. For example, smart cities and smart parks, etc.

- Industrial IoT: These application refers to industrial subset of IoT application. For example, smart factories, smart agriculture, etc.

Activity

Multiple Choice Questions

1. What are the components of a smart grid?

    A. Electric vehicles

    B. Vehicle-to-grid

    C. Solar plant

    D. All of the above

2. What is acronym for IoE?

    A. Internet of Energy

    B. Internet of Electricity

    C. Internet of Evolution

    D. Internet of Engine

3. Which of the following is not an IoT health application?

    A. Blood pressure monitoring

    B. Wheelchair management

    C. Remote surgery

    D. Electricity bill generation

4. What are the components of smart farming?

    A. Aerial drones

    B. GPS

    C. Temperature sensors

    D. Electric vehicles

5. Which is not an applications of IoT-based agriculture?

    A. Precision farming

    B. Melanoma detection

    C. Weed pressure mapping

    D. Smart green house

6. What is the another name for smart industry?

    A. industry 4.0

    B. industry 5.0

C. industry 6.0

D. industry 7.0

7. Which of the following category of users finds rise in applications targeting health from a smartwatch?

A. Personal IoT

B. Group IoT

C. Community IoT

D. Industrial IoT

8. Which of the following category of users is used by citizens to contribute to a smart city?

A. Personal IoT

B. Group IoT

C. Community IoT

D. Industrial IoT

9. Which of the following category of users is used in the applications of connected cars?

A. Personal IoT

B. Group IoT

C. Community IoT

D. Industrial IoT

1. d   2. a   3. d   4. a, b, c   5. b   6. a   7. a   8. c   9. c

3

IoT challenges

Despite having many benefits, IoT faces many challenges to be adopted worldwide. Fig. 3.1 (b) shows top issues faced by IoT network. This chapter summarizes the challenges faced in the world of IoT.

3.1 Security

For a secure IoT paradigm, parameters, such as data privacy, confidentiality, integrity, authentication, authorization, and availability are important to achieve. Notably, IoT components are unattended mostly, so it is easy to compromise them. Also, adopting weak passwords and using default passwords are common loopholes for authentication attacks [186]. Moreover, device connection via web interface opens up chances for attacks, such as- Structured Query Language (SQL) injection and cross-site scripting. Similarly, in order to provide remote services, IoT devices use telnet services to which attacks, such as Distributed Denial of Service (DDoS), eavesdropping and TCP SYN can be launched easily [219]. For example, the Mirai botnet attack on Oct. 21, 2016 infected multiple IoT devices. Next, these attacked IoT devices were used to flood Domain Name System (DNS) service provider "Dyn" by launching DDoS attack. As a result, this botnet brings down various social network sites. Similarly, attacks such as- Sybil and spoofing attacks can be launched on IoT devices to lower down network performance and to destroy data privacy. Fig. 3.1 (a) shows security spending worldwide on IoT for the year 2016-2021. Hence, it is important to build IoT devices with high security control.

Notably, providing security to IoT paradigm is complex over the traditional network due to the presence of heterogeneous data generated from variety of sensors. Also, security is a prominent challenge due to openness of system which has inter-connection to the Internet via a wireless communication medium. Additionally, conventional security solutions including firewall, and anti-virus are not convenient for IoT because of limited space and energy [33]. Hence, designing optimal energy consumption based security solution is one of the important issues in IoT that needs special attention [188]. Literature supports various cryptographic protocols including Rivest–Shamir–Adleman (RSA), Elliptic-curve cryptography (ECC), Diffie

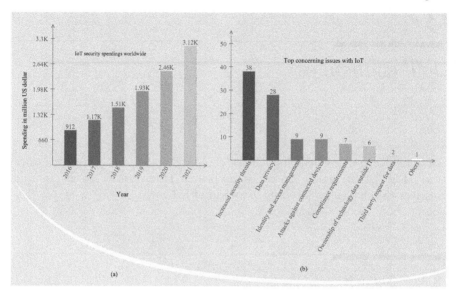

FIGURE 3.1
(a) IoT security spendings worldwide (b) Top issues with IoT.

Hellman (DH) key exchange, etc. to handle these security problems. Security solutions that use encryption are also not suitable for IoT as these constrained devices are not capable of implementing complex encryption and decryption. Additionally, all these security protocols rely on a pair of cryptographic keys and for generation, management of these key pairs, IoT manufacturers are dependent on a centralized, trusted third-party. Over and above, digital certificate checking, maintenance, and revocation are also dependent on a centralized party called "Registration authority". Notably, having a centralized party can become a single point of failure and also a reason for privacy attacks on data. Furthermore, it is problematic to issue a digital certificate to each and every object as strength of IoT objects in quite large. Hence, key requirements including authorization, authentication, availability, non-repudiation, and trust need to be addressed for future IoT networks.

3.2   Data Management

IoT devices generate huge amounts of data that needs to be processed and analyzed in real-time. The current framework of the data center is not efficient to deal with the heterogeneous nature of data. A lot of research is going in both academic and industrial areas to handle data management issues in IoT.

As per a report from the international Data Corporation the data generated by IoT devices is expected to grow to 79.24 ZB by the year 2025 from 33 ZB in the year 2018 [7].

One of the major concerns for data management is data storage. There are basically three types of IoT data storage, i.e., local, distributed, and centralized. The local type signifies that data generated by IoT sensors will be stored on the IoT device itself. The distributed processing signifies that data will be stored at the edge and processed via distributed technologies whereas the centralized type means that collected data is stored at a data center. As mentioned, IoT devices lack power and have limited storage, so data storage on IoT devices is not possible. Also, data centers employed to store data generated by IoT devices should have enough energy and power resources in order to process queries when required. However, in future, the forecasted data generated by IoT devices can overload cloud infrastructure. Moreover, storing data at a distant and centralized location can lead to high response time while processing any query. Therefore, IoT data should be stored at a distributed location that is closer to the data-generation point.

3.3 Privacy

IoT system compromises multiple devices that generate and exchange heterogeneous data having privacy-sensitive information. For example, smart health wearables and equipment generate a large amount of IoT data that contains the user's location, health conditions, sleeping patterns, etc. Notably, this data is stored on third-party cloud providers. Additionally, the user's behavior from its browsing Internet interest is collected by third-party in order to enrich the user's experience. Hence, providing privacy is often required in such scenarios including healthcare, electricity data, military applications, etc. [207]. Privacy is the ability of the devices to have a check on when and with whom personal information of the devices is to be shared [217]. Also, the personal data being collected should be accessed by authorized service providers. Traditional privacy-preserving methods are expensive for IoT due to high energy consumption and processing overhead. Notably, by relying on a centralized cloud server (third-party auditor), users are not aware of how much personal information is being shared with other parties. Additionally, most of the state-of-the-art privacy framework is based on centralized structure and hence not suitable for IoT because of scalability issues and single point of failure. Hence, the IoT system requires a lightweight, scalable, and distributed privacy safeguard.

3.4   Heterogeneity

IoT connects different IoT entities with different complexities and different vendors. Recently, researchers have developed multiple hardware and software platforms for IoT. Instead of involving one particular type of hardware device or software, interactions in IoT depend on a sea of different types of smart and connected devices. The date release, version, technical interfaces, and bitrates of IoT devices may be different. Moreover, the IoT system depicts heterogeneity in terms of communication protocol, data format, and infrastructure. As many heterogeneous things are connected to the Internet, a specified architecture that supports for easy connectivity, control, and communication is required. Over and above, to support automation, different devices should have synchronized clocks. Also, the environment for IoT is dynamic, i.e., a device might have a connection to an entirely different set of devices than at another time. Due to high heterogeneity of devices, IoT lacks scalability, interoperability, reliability, availability, and security in the network. Therefore, interoperability must be deployed among all network technologies taking into account their mode, network providers, and vendors.

3.5   Latency

Latency is a major challenge that is to be considered in the evolution of IoT. Delay in network operation degrades IoT system performance and quality-of-service (QoS) [169]. Generally, IoT data has to be sent to the cloud for computational processing because of limited computational capabilities of these devices. However, IoT users request for accessing this data from different parts of the globe. So, to handle such multiple requests is a difficult task for a centralized cloud server. Moreover, due to the presence of cloud server at a distant location, latency in accessing services is obvious. Besides, there are some delay-sensitive applications (military, health, transportation) that demand immediate processing of queries. Hence, it is important to design a computing infrastructure that supports low latency and fast response time. Along with high delays, communicating directly with the cloud creates network bandwidth overload. Nevertheless, with the recent advancements including fog/edge computing the problem of latency is mitigated with a little investment on computing and storage resources [126], [189]. Hence, some information should be processed near to devices in order to implement IoT with fewer challenges. It can be noticed from Fig. 3.2, that cloud framework had a greater delay as compared to edge/fog computing technologies. Therefore, it is preferable to use fog/edge computing for latency sensitive services [184]. Fog/edge computing supports an intelligent layer between cloud and

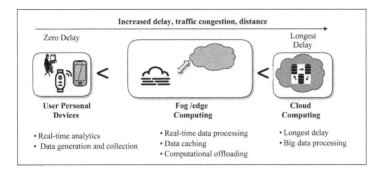

FIGURE 3.2
Comparison of data processing at different computing locations.

IoT devices that enables low latency, location awareness, and geographical distribution for IoT [128], [206]. Clearly, cloud computing supports centralization whereas fog computing gives rise to decentralization. Moreover, a recent technology named Tactile Internet has been used as a latest Internet network that achieves ultra low latency along with high availability, reliability, and security [57], [100], [56], [115].

3.6 Communication Challenge in IoT

IoT devices communicate between themselves and with the outside environment via the Internet. IoT communication is the base for remote monitoring, data analytics, and information exchange. To fully connect IoT devices, a reliable and bidirectional signaling is required for collection and transferring data between devices. In this context, IoT supports divergent wireless network. Also, the latest technology in wireless communication is more concerned with delivering sensitive information to destination including energy, latency, reliability, and security [191]. However, IoT network is prone to security attack due to wireless nature of sensor network, attack such as- spoofing, sink hole attack, Sybil attack, worm hole attack, and DDoS. Therefore, to utilize the full potential of IoT, some challenges faced by IoT communication must be addressed.

Over and above, network mobility and coverage remain an open research challenges for IoT that needs to be considered for effective development of IoT use cases as most IoT services are meant to be delivered to mobile users [175]. This is an important assertion of IoT to make sure that IoT nodes are connected anywhere and anytime. Smart mobile phones sometimes experience interruption due to device mobility. Therefore, an effective mobility system is required to manage the growth of connected devices in IoT. The existing cellular network needs to deploy some more base stations to efficiently connect all devices of the network together.

Apart from this, network congestion is another major challenge to be addressed in the implementation of IoT as smart devices are contributing to drive up signaling load in the network as compared to conventional human-to-human (H2H) traffic. With high network congestion, IoT performance and Quality-of-Service (QoS) of the network degrades. Therefore, the TCP/IP protocol has to deal effectively with the network congestion problem [204]. However, the current TCP implementation is not applicable for IoT application scenarios as the traffic pattern of IoT networks is totally different from the traditional network.

The connection of millions of connected devices takes power and CPU consumption. To deal with this problem, communication technology should enforce minimal battery drain and minimum power consumption. Along with this, bandwidth consumption is another issue for IoT connectivity. Moreover, optimal energy utilization is one of the important issues in IoT that needs attention [188], [200]. Therefore, a lightweight network is required to seamlessly transfer data among devices and server.

Conclusion

It can be concluded from the above discussion that a centralized cloud/third-party has several limitations. In particular, the data stored on cloud face privacy issues as the third-party may alter the user's data without consent. Also, centralized servers are more vulnerable to DDoS attack. Moreover, in case of heavy load, centralized server may not generate quick response for user's queries. Most importantly, centralized server may lead to a single point of failure.

Activity

Multiple Choice Questions

1. IoT devices and nodes are naturally vulnerable to _____threats?

   A. Sensors

   B. Security

   C. Connectivity

   D. Heterogeneity

2. IoT involves an architecture that involves ubiquitous presence in the environment.

   A. True

   B. False

3. What are risks and challenges associated with IoT?

   A. Scalability

   B. Privacy and security

   C. Energy consumption

   D. All of the above

4. What in IoT is one of the key characteristics, where devices have different hardware platforms and networks?

   A. Heterogeneity

   B. Sensors

   C. Connectivity

   D. Security

5. Which challenge comes when zombie armies are deployed to send a spam attack on IoT devices?

   A. Heterogeneity

   B. Sensors

   C. Connectivity

   D. Security

6. Storing IoT data in a remote location can create high response time for query processing.

   A. True

B. False

7. Delay in network operation of IoT affects?

   A. System performance
   B. Security
   C. Privacy
   D. QoS

8. Cloud framework has lesser delay over fog computing.

   A True
   B False

9. What are the limitations of centralized third party for data management?

   A. Vulnerable to DoS attack
   B. Single point of failure
   C. Privacy issues
   D. All of the above

10. Which of the following has minimum delay?

    A. Cloud devices
    B. User personal devices
    C. Fog devices
    D. Mist devices

1. b	2. a	3. d	4. a	5. d	6. a
7. a, d	8. b	9. d	10. b		

Part II

Blockchain Overview

4

Python Basics

4.1 Introduction

Python is a high-level programming language used for general-purpose programming, developed by Guido Van Rossum in 1991. Python is specially designed to be highly readable as it uses frequent English keywords. Python is frequently used to create software and web applications on a server. Some of the important features of Python are described as follows:

- It supports concepts of object-oriented programming.

- It can be easily integrated with some other programming languages including C, C++, Java, Common Object Request Broker Architecture (CORBA), etc.

- Python is scalable as it better supports large programs than shell scripting.

- Python relies highly on indentation, here whitespace is used to define scope. Due to its strong structuring constructs, it supports clear writing and logical application.

- Python can be easily connected to all major commercial databases.

- Python is portable as it runs on a wide variety of hardware platforms.

- Python supports interactive mode which enables interactive testing and debugging of code.

- Python supports high-level dynamic data types and dynamic type checking.

- Python is a scripting language as it is suitable for embedding and for writing small unstructured scripts.

- Python programs are much shorter in length than equivalent C, C++ programs for the following reasons:

  - The complex operations can be expressed in a single statement with the support of high level data type in Python.

- Use of indentation rather than using beginning and ending brackets.
- Declaration of variables and arguments is not important.

> **Note:** Python is a compiled and interpreted programming language. The source code first gets compiled to a bytecode then that bytecode is interpreted as machine language on Python virtual machine to give actual output. The concept of bytecode achieves portability. However, to execute Python code, each time Python programs code is required.

After writing the program, save the program with .py in a text editor. Further, execute that file in Python interpreter. Nevertheless, typing commands in Python interpreter is a good way to play with Python features but it is not suggested for solving more complex problems.

The rest of this chapter discusses various important features of Python language with examples starting with simple statements, expressions, data types to concepts of classes, objects, functions, file handling, etc. Let's start Python programming.

4.2 Comments

Comments in Python are represented with a "#". Everything written after "#" in a line is ignored. Notably, comments are not interpreted by Python language.

Listing 4.1
Comments in Python

```
a=5
print(a) #print value of variable a
```

Output: 5

4.3 Multi-line Statement

To denote that line should continue, (multi-line statement) Python allows the use of line continuation character, i.e., \. For example:

Listing 4.2

Multiline statements in Python

```
grand\_total= day1+day2+\
             day3+day4+\
             day5
```

4.4 Blocks and Indentation

Python depicts blocks and nested blocks structure with indentation not by using beginning and end brackets. Advantages of using indentation include reducing need for coding standard, reducing inconsistency, and reducing work. The number of count spaces in indentation is variable but within a block each and every statement must be indented the equal amount. For example:

Listing 4.3

Understanding indentation in Python

```
if true:
    print('True')
if false:
    print('False')
```

The following code will generate an error:

Listing 4.4

Understanding indentation in Python

```
if true:
print('True')
if false:
print('False')
```

4.5 Creating Variables and Assigning Values

Variables are used to store values at a reserved memory location. After creating a variable, a space in memory is reserved. Unlike other programming languages, there is no need to declare variables explicitly. After assigning a value to a variable, use that variable in place of value. The equal sign is used to assign value to a variable. Python strings are expressed in single quotes or double quotes with same results. Print statement is used to display the value of a variable. For example, the statements

Listing 4.5
Creating variables

```
a=100
var='hello'
print(a) #print value of a
print(var)
print(var[0])
```

Output: 100
hello
h

Variables can have a variable length and they can be arbitrarily long. A variable can have both letters and numbers, however, they can't start with a number.

4.6 Data Types

Variables can store data in different types. Numbers, strings, lists, tuple, dictionaries are the standard data types. Python number data types store numeric value. For example:
a=1, b=2.
Python includes three different numeric types, i.e., int, float, complex. In contrast, a string is made of a sequence of characters. However, strings in Python are immutable, which implies it can't be changed. Strings are declared with single or double character. For example: a="abc". Rest of the data types are discussed further in this chapter. type() function is used to get the data type of any variable.

Listing 4.6
type() function in Python

```
type('hello')
type(7)
type(1.25)
type([1,2,3])
```

Output: str
int
float
list

4.7 Operators

Similar to other programming languages, Python supports the following operator groups:

- Arithmetic operator

- Comparison operator

- Assignment operator

- Logical operator

- Bitwise operator

- Membership operator

- Identity operator

4.7.1 Arithmetic operator

This category includes mathematical operations, such as- addition(+), subtraction(-), division(/), modulus(%), and power(**). For example:

Listing 4.7
Arithmatic operators in Python

```
# Examples of Arithmetic Operators
a = 10
b = 4

# Addition of numbers
addition = a + b

# Subtraction of numbers
substraction = a - b

# Multiplication of numbers
multiplication = a * b

# Division (float) of numbers
divlsion = a / b

# Modulo of both numbers
modulus = a % b

# Power
pow = a ** b

# print results
print(addition)
```

```
print(substraction)
print(multiplication)
print(division)

print(modulus)
print(pow)
```

14
6
40
2.5
2
10000

4.7.2 Comparison operator

This operator is used to compare values and returns either true or false as per the condition. This category includes greater than(>), less than(<), equal to(==), not equal to(!=), greater than equal to($\geq$), and less than equal to($\leq$). For example:

Listing 4.8
Comparison operators in Python

```
a = 20
b = 5

if ( a == b ):
        print ('a is equal to b')
else:
        print ('a is not equal to b')

if ( a != b ):
        print ('a is not equal to b')
else:
        print('a is equal to b')

if ( a < b ):
        print ('a is less than  b')
else:
        print ('a is not less than b')

if ( a > b ):
        print ('a is greater than b')
else:
        print('a is not greater than b')

if ( a <= b ):
        print ('a is either less than or equal to  b')
else:
        print    ('a is neither less than nor equal to  b')
```

```
if ( b >= a ):
      print ('b is either greater than  or equal to b')
else:
      print ('b is neither greater than  nor equal to b')
```

Output:
a is not equal to b
a is not equal to b
a is not less than b
a is greater than b
a is neither less than nor equal to b
b is neither greater than nor equal to b

4.7.3   Logical operator

This category performs logical AND (and), logical OR(or), and logical NOT (not). For example:

Listing 4.9
Logical operators in Python

```
a=True
b=False
print (a and b)
print(a or b)
print (not a)
```

Output:
False
True
False

4.7.4   Python Bitwise operator

It performs bit-by-bit operation. Bitwise operator includes Bitwise AND($\&$), Bitwise OR($\vee$), Bitwise NOT($\neg$), Bitwise XOR($\oplus$), Bitwise right shift($\gg$), and Bitwise left shift ($\ll$).

Listing 4.10
Logical operators in Python

```
# Examples of Bitwise operators
a = 10
b = 4

# Print bitwise AND operation
print(a & b)

# Print bitwise OR operation
print(a v b)
```

```
# Print bitwise NOT operation
print(¬a)

# print bitwise XOR operation
print(a ⊕ b)

# print bitwise right shift operation
print(a ≫ 2)

# print bitwise left shift operation
print(a ≪ 2)
```

Output:
0
14
-11
14
2
40

4.7.5   Assignment operator

This operator is used to assign values to a variables. The available assignment operators are:

=: Assigns values from right side of operands to left side of operand

+=: Adds the right operand with the left operand and assigns result to the left operand

-=: Subtracts the right operand from left operand and then assigns to the left operand

*=: Multiplies the right operand with the left operand and assigns to the left operand

\=: Divides the left operand with right operand and then assigns the result to the left operand

%=: Takes modulus using left and right operands and assigns the result to the left operand

**=: Performs exponential calculation on operators and assigns the value to the left operand

Listing 4.11
Assignment operators in Python

```
# Examples of Bitwise operators
var1 = 21
var2 = 10
var3 = 0

var3 = var1 + var2
print('Value of var3 is ',var3)
```

```
var3 += var1
print('Value of var3 is ',var3)

var3 *= var1
print('Value of var3 is ',var3)

var3 /= var1
print('Value of var3 is ',var3)

var3 = 2
var3 %= var1
print('Value of var3 is ',var3)

var3 **= var1
print('Value of var3 is ',var3)
```

Output:

Value of var3 is 31

Value of var3 is 52

Value of var3 is 1092

Value of var3 is 52

Value of var3 is 2

Value of var3 is 2097152

4.7.6 Membership operator

This operator is used to check for membership of an element in a sequence. There are two membership operators discussed below:

in: Results to true if element is present in the sequence otherwise false

not in: Results to true if element is not a member of the sequence, otherwise false

For example:

Listing 4.12

Membership operator in Python

```
a = 10
b = 20
list = [1, 2, 3, 4, 5 ];

if ( a in list ):
    print ('a is present in the given list')
else:
    print ('a is not presentin the given list')

if ( b not in list ):
    print ( 'b is not present in the given list')
else:
    print ('b is present in the given list')
```

Output:

a is not present in the given list
b is not present in the given list

4.7.7   Identity Operators

These operators are used to compare two memory locations, i.e., to check whether two values are located in same part of memory. There are two identical operators in Python.

is: Returns true if operands are identical

is not: Returns true if operands are not identical

Listing 4.13
Identity operator in Python

```
a = 50
b = 50

if ( a is b ):
     print ('a and b have same identity')
else:
     print ('a and b do not have same identity')
```

Output:
a and b have same identity

4.8   Input and Output in Python

The built-in input() function is used to take user input from the keyboard. The parameters inside parentheses prompt for the keyboard input. The input function automatically identifies whether it is a string, number, or list that is entered by the user. However when an input is entered, first it is converted to a string. Even an integer value is converted integer using typecasting.

Listing 4.14
input() function in Python

```
name=input('Enter your name: ')
print('Hello', name)
```

Suppose the user has entered abc as name.
Output: Hello abc

The way to produce output is by using print() function by passing no or more expression separated by a comma. Print with no parameters ,i.e., print() is to advance to next line. By default, Python print() function ends with a new line, i.e., print() function will go to next line automatically.

Listing 4.15

print() function in Python

```
print ( 'one ')
print ( 'two ')
```

Output:

one

two

4.9 List

Lists are a powerful feature of Python. They are the same as arrays. The list is a data type used to declare a sequence. Lists are declared with comma separated items in a square brackets. To access list items, index number is used. Notably, list might have items of different types. A list can have strings, integers, as well as objects. Also, lists can be altered even after declaration.

Listing 4.16

Python list

```
List A =[ 'Apple', 'Banana', 'Mango']
print ( List A [1])
%print ( List A )
```

Output: Banana

Listing 4.17

Python list

```
List B =[22, 'Banana', 5]
List B . append (6)
print ( List B )
List B . pop ()
print ( List B )
print ( List B [1])
```

Output:

22, 'Banana', 5, 6

22,'Banana', 5

5

Note: Tuple is same as list with a difference that tuples are immutable, i.e., after declaration they can't be changed.

4.10   Dictionary

Python dictionaries has keys and values and is written with curly brackets. However, keys should be unique within a dictionary while values can be same. To access any item, use keys name inside square brackets.

Listing 4.18
Python dictionary

```
dictionary={'Name': 'A', 'Age':10, 'Contact':12345}
print(dictionary['Age'])
```

Output: 10

4.11   Python Conditions and if-else

Python if-else statements are used with logical conditions, such as- equal, not equal, less than equal to, greater than equal to, greater than, and less than. If statement is specified using the if keyword.

Listing 4.19
Python if-else statement

```
a=5
b=10
if (b>a):
    print( 'value of b is greater than a')
```

Output: value of b is greater than a

> **Key point** Python uses indentation to define scope

Further, elif keyword is used to check if previous condition is not true then try with this condition and else executes if any of the preceding conditions get false. greater than equal to, greater than, and less than. Elif statement is specified using elif keyword.

Listing 4.20
Python if-else statement

```
a=5
b=10
if b>a:
    print( 'value of b is greater than a')
elif a==b:
    print('value of a is equal to b')
else
```

```
    print('value of ais greater than b')
```

Output: value of b is greater than a

4.12   Loops

Generally, statements of any programming language are executed sequentially. However, there may be a situation when there is need to execute different paths. A block of loop allows to execute one or more than one statement multiple times. Python supports two loop commands:

- While loop

- For loop

While loop: While loop is used to execute a statement or a block of statement until given conditions are satisfied. After the statements get false, the very first statement after while gets executed.

Listing 4.21
Python while loop

```
count=0
while count <5:
    print(count)
    count=count+1
print('Goodbye')
```

Output:
0
1
2
3
4
Goodbye
While can be used with else statement as well

Listing 4.22
Python while loop

```
count=0
while count <5:
    print(count)
    count=count+1
else:
    print('Count is greater than or equalto 5')
```

Output:

0
1
2
3
4
Goodbye

    For loop: In Python the for loop is used for sequential traversal, e.g., a list or an array.

Listing 4.23
Python for loop

```
fruits =['apple', 'mango', 'banana']
for x in fruits:
    print(x)
```

Output:
apple
mango
banana

Listing 4.24
Python for loop

```
for i in range(0,5):
    print(i)
```

Output:
0,1,2,3,4

4.13   Functions in Python

A function is a block of statements that take some input, perform some computation, and produces output. Basically, functions are used to ease repeatedly done tasks together. Functions are executed when called. There are some build-in functions in Python such as- print() and also one can create functions using def keyword. To call a function, use the name of that function followed by a parenthesis.

Listing 4.25
Python functions

```
def fun(): #defining a function
    print('Hello')
fun() #calling a function
```

Listing 4.26

Python functions

```
def evenorodd( x ):
    if (x % 2 == 0):
        print (even)
    else:
        print (odd)


evenorodd(5)
evenorodd(6)
```

Output:
Odd
Even

4.14   Classes and Objects in Python

As previously discussed, Python is an object-oriented language. A class is similar to an object constructor or like a blueprint for creating objects while object is a copy of class with actual values. Classes ease bundling of data and functionality together. Each class holds its own data members and member function which can be accessed using objects. Nevertheless, a class can have many objects. Attributes of a class are always public and are accessed using the dot (.) operator. To create a class keyword class is used.

Listing 4.27

Class and object in Python

```
class class1: #class named class1 is created
    x=10
o1= class1(o1.x) #object named o1is created
```

output: 5

Listing 4.28

Class and object in Python

```
Class Dog:

# A simple class
# attribute
attribute1 = "animal"
attribute2 = "dog"

# A sample method
def fun1(self):
        print("I am a", self.attribute1)
```

```
        print("I am a", self.attribute2)


# Object instantiation
Charlie = Dog()

# Accessing class attributes
# and method through objects
print(Charlie.attribute1)
Charlie.fun1()
```

Output:
animal
I am a animal
I am a dog
To create real-life applications, we need to understand a special function called init() which is an initialization method to create a new instance of the class. In particular, the init() method is used to assign values to object properties when the object is created.

Listing 4.29
Class and object in Python

```
class Person:
def __init__(self, name, age):
self.name = name
self.age = age

p1 = Person("John", 36)

print(p1.name)
print(p1.age)
```

output:
John
36

4.15   File Handling in Python

A file has a location on disk with some stored information. Like Java and C++, Python also supports file handling and enables users to handle files by reading and writing them. Each line of code in the file includes a sequence of characters. Also, each line ends with a special terminator called end of line (EOL) which tells the interpreter that a new line has begun. Most of the file manipulations are done using a file object.

4.15.1   open() function

Clearly before reading or writing a file, one must open it first. To open a file in order to read or write, open() function is used. The open() function creates a file object and takes two arguments, i.e., file name and mode. Syntax:
open(filename, mode)
mode field tells how the file can be opened. For example:
r: Opens a file for reading only
rb: Opens a file for read-only purpose in binary format
w: opens a file for writing only
r+: Opens a file for both reading and writing in binary format
wb: Opens a file for write only purpose in binary format
a: Opens file for append
a+: Opens a file for both appending and reading

If the file with specified name does not exist, it will throw an error of FileNotFoundError.

4.15.2   close() function

close() method closes the file object and refrains any further action on that file.
Syntax:
fileObject.close()

Listing 4.30
File handling in Python

```
#Open a file
fo = open("foo.txt", "wb")
print ("Name of the file: ", fo.name)

# Close opened file
fo.close()
```

output:
Name of the file: foo.txt

4.15.3   read() function

This function reads a string from an open file.
Syntax:
fileObject.read([count])
The count parameter specifies the number of bytes to be read from the specified file. If the count parameter is missing, the file is read until the end of the file.

Listing 4.31
File handling in Python

```
abc = open("foo.txt", "r+")
string = abc.read(10);
print ("Read String is : ", string)

foo.close()
```

output:
The first 10 characters from the file named foo.txt.

4.16   write() function

This function allows user to write strings to an open file. Notably, write function does not add implicitly a newline character, i.e., \n to end of string.
Syntax:
fileObject.write(string)

Listing 4.32
File handling in Python

```
# Open a file
abc = open("foo.txt", "wb")
abc.write( "Python \: is a high level language. \n

        Python follows OOPS concepts")

# Close opend file
abc.close()
```

output:
Python is a high level language
Python follows OOPS concepts

Activity

Multiple Choice Questions

1. How do you insert comments in Python code?

   A. *This is a comment* \
   B. #This is a comment
   C. "This is a comment"
   D. None of these

2. Which one is NOT a legal variable name?

   A abc
   B 10abc
   C _abc
   D abc_abc

3. What is the value of the following Python Expression?

   A. 9.0
   B. 9
   C. 4.0
   D. 4

4. What is the output of the following code?
   ```
   x = 100
   y = 50
   print(x and y)
   ```

   A. True
   B. False
   C. 100
   D. 50

5. What is a correct syntax to output "hello world" in Python?

   A. print("hello world")
   B. echo("hello word")
   C. put("hello word")
   D. None of these

6. What is the correct file extension for Python files?

(a) .py

(b) .python

(c) .pyt

(d) None of these

7. What will be the output of the following code ?
print type(type(int))

   A. type 'int'

   B. type 'type'

   C. error

   D. 0

8. Suppose listA is [31, 41, 5, 20, 5, 125, 1, 3], what is list1 after listA.pop(1)?

   A. 31, 41, 5, 20, 5, 125, 1, 3

   B. 31, 41, 5, 20, 5, 125, 1

   C. 31, 41, 5, 20, 5, 125, 1, 3, 3

   D. None of these

9. What is the output of the following program?
```
j = 0
while i ≤ 5:
        print j
        j++
        print j+1
```

   A. 0 2 1 3 2 4

   B. Error

   C. 5 4 3 2 1

   D. None of these

10. What does ¬¬¬¬¬¬5 evaluate to?

   A. +5

   B. -5

   C. 10

   D. 11

1. b   2. b   3. a   4. d   5. d   6. a   7. b
8. b   9. b (there is no ++ operator in Python)   10. a

5

Cryptography Primitives

5.1 Introduction

Confidentiality, integrity, availability also referred to as CIA triad, is the model developed to define policies for achieving information security (Refer Fig. 5.1). Along with this non-repudiation and authentication are the other security attributes to be achieved by a Peer-to-peer (P2P) network.

- Confidentiality: Confidentiality signifies that information, data, and resources are protected from any unauthorized parties. Data encryption, and passwords are the common method of ensuring confidentiality.

> **Key Points** Confidentiality is similar to the word privacy; however, they are not interchangeable. In fact, confidentiality is an extension of privacy that pertains to identifiable data.

- Integrity: This attribute signifies the protection of information from unauthorized alteration. Integrity ensures accuracy and completeness of data. Access control mechanism, checksum, and hashing are some measures to ensure the integrity of data.

- Availability: This attribute ensures access to information when needed by authorized parties. If a server/system remains available preventing service disruption and uninterrupted access, this signifies high availability. Disruption of service even for a short time can cause loss of revenue, customer disappointment, and organization repudiation damage. Among all availability attacks, DoS is the most frequently used by hackers. Proxy servers, firewalls, and routers are the countermeasures to ensure the availability of data.

- Non-repudiation: This attribute ensures that the sender of the data can't later deny having sent the data and recipients can't deny having received the data. In legal terms, repudiation signifies denial of something that is true. Digital signatures, timestamps, hash functions are some of the ways to obtain non-repudiation.

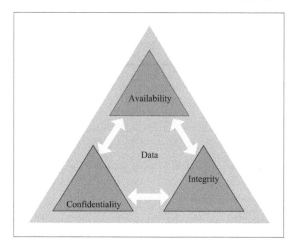

FIGURE 5.1
CIA triad of information security.

- Authentication: It is an act of identifying an individual. However, authentication does not claim about the access rights of the individual. In particular, authentication confirms the user's identity.

Notably, cryptography plays a very important role in ensuring the attainment of these above-mentioned security attributes. Next, we will discuss the basic cryptographic primitives. We will start by discussing the details of cryptographic hash functions followed by discussing the concept of digital signatures.

5.2   Encryption/Decryption Process

5.2.1   Encryption

Encryption is the process of transforming original data into an unrecognisable form. Data is usually encrypted to save it from stealing. Encryption is performed by the sender.

5.2.2   Decryption

In contrast to encryption, decryption is the process of converting cipher text back to plain text. Decryption is done at the receiving side.

5.2.3 Symmetric key encryption

This type of encryption uses the same cryptographic key for both encrypting plaintext and decrypting ciphertext.

5.2.4 Asymmetric key encryption

This encryption process involves 2 pairs of keys. Here, both sender and receiver have a pair of public and private keys. The public key is used to encrypt plaintext whereas the private key is used for decryption purpose. To accomplish many cryptographic tasks public and private keys are used.

5.2.5 Public key

The public key is published for all other users to see. Public keys are generated using typical asymmetric algorithm to match them against the associated private key. The most popular algorithm used for creating public key are: RSA, ECC, and digital signature application (DSA). These mentioned algorithms are based on a heavy computation method to create random numeric combinations of different lengths to prevent them against brute force attack. The length of the key depicts strength of protection. The large key size assures more cryptographic security to prevent hackers from preventing them.

5.2.6 Private key

In contrast to public key, private key is a secret key that is only known to the owner of the key. Private keys are created using same algorithms that create public key.

> **Key point** The private key is used for decryption, digitally signing, and authentication whereas a public key is used for encryption, verification of digital signatures, and authentication.

5.3 Cryptographic Hash Functions

A cryptographic hash function (H) takes an variable length input or message (M) and produces a fixed size output called hash values or message digest (h), i.e. as represented in Fig. 5.2

$$h = H(M) \tag{5.1}$$

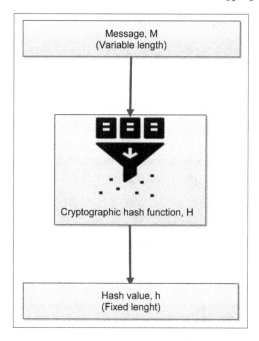

FIGURE 5.2
Block diagram of cryptographic hash function.

Generally, the size of message digest is smaller than the actual input data. Therefore, the hash function is sometimes referred to as compression function.

Key Points

- A hash function follows the many-to-one property and thus faces collision.

- In blockchain, the size of message digest is 256 bits.

- Hash functions are efficiently computable as this calculations as these calculation does not need a significant amount of resources.

- A good hash function produces evenly distributed output.

- Even a single bit change in M will change the complete hash code.

5.3.1 Typical properties of a hash function

- It should be completely difficult to reverse a hash function, i.e., for a given hash value h_1, it should be hard process to find input M_1 that exactly hashes to h_1. This property is called irreversibility or pre-image resistance. Also, this type of hash function is called one-way function.

- For a given input and its corresponding hash, it should be computationally difficult to find a different input having same hash, i.e., for a input M_1 having hash value h_1, it should be hard to find any other input M_2 such that $H(M_1) = H(M_2)$. This property of hash functions is called second-image resistance.

- Another important property of hash functions is known as collision free property which states that if two messages are different, then there message digest will also be different , i.e., if two messages M_1, M_2 are not equal $(M_1 \neq M_2)$, then $H(M_1) \neq H(M_2)$.

- Given two messages M_1, M_2, and a hash function h, it is difficult to find a value k such that $M_2 = h(M_1 \parallel k)$. This property of hash functions is called puzzle friendliness.

5.3.2 Requirements of hash function:

- **One way:** Once hash is calculated it can't be used to restore the original document. For example, like a human being fingerprint, one can't retrieve the looks of a person from human fingerprint.

- **Deterministic:** It states that if two similar documents are passed through a hash algorithm, it should always generate the same hash.

- **Avalanche effect:** It states that even changing one bit in the document, hash of the changed document should be significantly different from hash of the original document.

- **Must withstand collision:** It implies that the hash function should have collision resistance property.

5.3.3 Applications of cryptographic hash functions

- Password storage: Whenever a user creates an account with user name, ID, and password, the ID provider does not store the password. Instead, the provider pass the password from a hashing algorithm and only stores hash of the password. Every time user attempts to log-in, the provider hashes the password entered by the user and compares it against the saved hash. The provider has a password file that has table of pairs in form [User ID_1 $h(P_1)$] for a given user id (ID_1) and password (P_1). If the two hashes

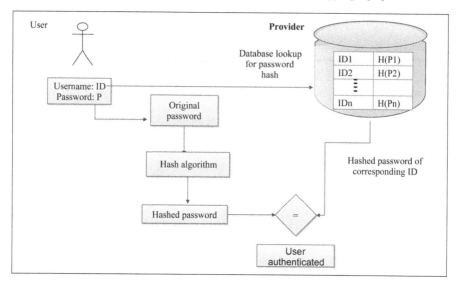

FIGURE 5.3
Password storage using hash functions.

match, only then authorization is provided to the account otherwise not. The whole process has been depicted in Fig. 5.3.

- Data integrity check: One of the very popular applications of hash function is data integrity check. This way, hash functions can assure correctness of the data, i.e., user can detect any modifications, insertions, and deletions made to the original file.
Case 1:
The message (M) along with computed hash value of M is encrypted with symmetric encryption. Encryption ensures confidentiality of the message. To check integrity of the message, First, the decryption is applied to the received encrypted block and the message from the block is then extracted. Next, apply the same hash algorithm to the message M and the computed hash value is matched against the received hash value. The whole process has been shown in Fig. 5.4.
Case 2:
In some cases, only the hash code is encrypted in order to reduce the burden for applications that don't demand confidentiality. To check the integrity of the message, decrypt the hash received with secret key and compute hash digest from the message and compare it with the received hash digest from the source. The whole process has been shown in Fig. 5.5.

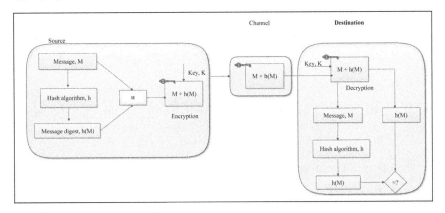

FIGURE 5.4
Data integrity check with message encryption.

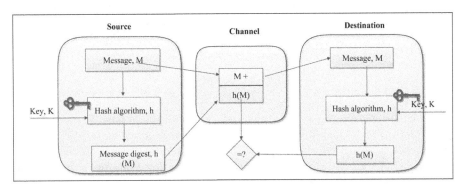

FIGURE 5.5
Data integrity check without message encryption.

5.3.4 MD5 message-digest algorithm

Message-Digest algorithm 5 (MD5) is an extension of Message-Digest algorithm 4 (MD4) and is developed by Ron Rivest in 1991. However, MD5 is a little slower than MD4 but assures better security over MD4. In particular, it is used to verify the integrity of the data. Also, it is used as DSA by compressing a large file in a secure way before encrypting the file with private key. This hashing algorithm takes input of arbitrary length and produces a 128-bit fingerprint as output.

The fundamentals of MD5 are based on Merkle Damgard schema. This algorithm process data in 512-bit block and each block is broken into 16 blocks, each of 32 bit. The stepwise working of MD5 to produce 128-bit output is defined as follows:

- **Append padding bits:** Padding implies adding some extra bits to original message. Here, message is padded such that total bit length is 64 less than exact multiple of 512. In order to pad the first bit is 1 and rest bits are 0. For example, for a message of 1000 bits, 472 bits are padded (1000 + 472 = 1472 which is 64 bit less than multiple of 512.)

- **Append length:** After padding, insert 64 bit at the end by calculating length of original message mod 2^{64}. Hence, the resulting message is multiple of 512 bits.

- **Dividing the message:** Divide the resulting message in 512 bit block.

- **Initialize MD buffer:** A four word buffer is initialized next. The four buffer namely (A, B, C, D) are 32-bit registers and its values are predefined. Notably, the final output in these buffer only.

- **Process message in 16 word block:** Each block of 512 bit is processed in 4 rounds and for each round four functions F, G, H, I are used. Further, each round consists of 16 steps using some constants. Hence, a total of 64 operations are performed for each 512 bit and the output from this block is fed to the next block as value of A, B, C, D.

5.3.5 SHA-256

Blockchain bitcoin mining makes use of a special type of hash function called SHA-256 and this hash function generates 256-bit message digest. SHA stands for secure hashing algorithm. SHA-256 also operates similar to MD4, MD5 as SHA-1. Computation of hash function begins by first preprocessing the message. For preprocessing:

- First, the message is padded so that total message size becomes multiple of 512 bits. For this follow:

    - Lets assume that message has length l in bits and $l \bmod 512 \neq 0$.
    - Append a bit with value 1 at the end of the message.
    - Next, append k zero bits such that $l+1+k \equiv 448 \bmod 512$.
    - After this append a 64-bit block having value l written in binary. This length is appended in order to avoid trivial collisions. To extract original message read last 64 bit (for calculating the length of message) and next start fetching bits from left to right till observed length.
    - The resultant length of the message after padding should be multiple of 512 bits.

  For example, the given message is 'abc'.

    - It has length 24 (8*3).

- First it is padded with a one at the end of message.
- Next, 448-(24+1) zeros are appended, i.e., 423 zeros.
- Finally, 64 bit block having 24 written in binary is appended which results in:
  01100010110001001100111 $\underbrace{00.....0}_{423 \text{ times}}$ $\underbrace{00.....011000}_{64 \text{ bit}}$.
  Now, result has length 512 bits.

- Next, parse the original message M, into N blocks of 512 bit each, i.e., M^1, M^2,.........., M^N.

- After this, each 512-bit block is divided into 16 sub blocks M_0^i, M_1^i,......., M_{15}^i with each having length of 32 bit.

- Each message block is processed one at a time. To process each block initialize with a fixed hash value, h^0 of 256 bit also called the initialization vector (IV).

- Next, sequentially compute:
  $H^i = h^{(i-1)} + C_{M^i}(H^{(i-1)})$
  where, C is compression function and + is addition modulo 2^{32}.

5.4   Digital Signatures

The digital signature is another important fundamental behind secured blockchain architecture. It is a cryptographic method to validate the authenticity and integrity of data. Along with this, digital signatures prevent non-repudiation, i.e., the sender can't deny for the origin of the document. Digital signatures work similar to the physical signatures; however, they are electronic signatures. Nevertheless, the signing authority can only sign the document and anyone having a valid key can verify the signatures. Also, the signatures of one document cannot be transferred from one document to another.

Digital signatures are realized with the concept of asymmetric key cryptography (Public-key cryptography). Asymmetric key cryptography uses two different keys, i.e., a public key and a private key. The public key is known to the user only whereas the private key is known to everyone in the universe. For preserving the confidentiality of data, the data to be transferred is encrypted using the public key of the receiver whereas the private key is used at the destination node to decrypt the message.

5.4.1 Model of digital signature

To generate digital signatures, the message is signed using the private key of the sender and at the destination side, signatures are verified using the public key of the sender. However, by integrating the concept of cryptographic hash with digital signatures, the size of digital signatures can be reduced. So, rather than signing the original message, the message digest is signed. The following steps are taken in generating the digital signatures:

- First, hash the message (M) to obtain message digest $h(M)$. Next, the generated hash is signed using the private key of the sender which results in digital signatures.

- Next, the message and the digital signature are transferred over the channel.

- Receiver after receiving the particular digital signatures, decrypt it using the public key of the sender (This assures the **authenticity** of the sender). After applying the decryption algorithm, the receiver will get the message digest $h(M)$.

- Simultaneously, from the original message received receiver, will compute the hash of it. Let's call this value $h'(M)$.

- If $h(M)=h'(M)$, the **integrity** of the original document is preserved.

- As it is assumed that only signer of the document knows the private key, so no other can generate the signature of the signer. Hence, it ensures **non-repudiation** attribute.

The whole process of generating hash function has been depicted in Fig. 5.6. Therefore, by applying the hash function, the size of the signature can be reduced.

Key points

- A cryptographic key should be prevented from being guessed by others. However, it is assumed that the cryptographic algorithm is known to everyone.

- The key should have sufficient length as a key with long length is difficult to guess as compared to short length key.

- The key should be truly randomly generated with sufficient entropy.

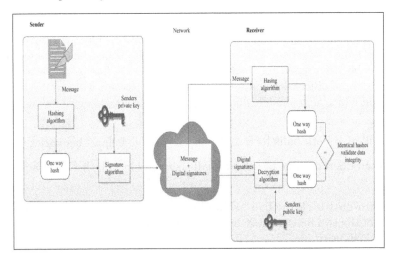

FIGURE 5.6
Digital signatures.

5.5 Zero-Knowledge Proof

Another concept that is associated with blockchain is zero-knowledge proof. It is a cryptographic method to prove to the verifier that prover knows a value without actually revealing any data except revealing the fact that prover knows the value. By simply, generating the final output, the prover is supposed to prove that they can compute something without telling the computational process whereas the verifier only knows the output.

For example, A wants to prove B that he/she knows the key without disclosing secret key to B, and B verifies that A is actually having the key. Hence, they have the capability to revolutionize the way of data handling, collection, and the way data is transacted with. Zero-knowledge proof has 3 important properties:

- Completeness: If the fact is true, the prover should convince the verifier for this fact and zero knowledge proof should return true.

- Soundness: If the fact/statement is false, the prover can't convince the verifier that prover's statement is true.

- Zero-knowledge/Privacy: If the information provided by prover is true, no verifier learns any other information expect the fact that information is true. In other words, the provider information should not reveal anything else to the verifier.

To better understand zero knowledge proof, let's take the popular and classic example of zero knowledge proof that is of **two balls and colour-blind**

friend

Suppose A has two identical balls having different colours (say one red and one green) and your friend B is colour blind which means B can't differentiate between the balls based on their colour. However, A has to prove to B that two balls are of different colours. Nevertheless, A doesn't want to reveal which is red and which is green. This is how proof system for this problem will work:

- A will give both balls to B and puts both balls behind his back.

- B then takes out one of the two balls from behind his/her back and shows it.

- B then puts back the ball behind his/her back again and then reveal just one of the two balls, simply by picking one of the two balls at random with equal chances.

- Next, B asks A "Did I switch the ball?".

Third and fourth steps are repeated till B assures that there are two different colored balls. Obviously, by balls color A can certainly tell whether or not B switched them. Moreover, A could guess right with probability not higher than 50% that whether the ball his switched or not if balls are having same color and therefore indistinguishable. If A and B repeats this process multiple times A will be caught if he/she lies.

Clearly, the above proof system is zero knowledge as B will never learn which is green and which is red ball.

Over and above, zero-knowledge proof has two variants: interactive and non-interactive zero-knowledge proof. In interactive proofs, the prover and the verifier exchange more than one message to prove or verify the information. It demands verifier to constantly ask questions about the knowledge the prover possesses. Unfortunately, the interactive zero knowledge proof has limited transferability. In contrast, non-interactive proof system demands no interaction between prover and verifier except a common reference string between both parties.

Keypoint

Zero knowledge proof application in blockchain: Both of the popular blockchain use cases, i.e., Bitcoin and Ethereum are based on public addresses to depict the true identity of the user which maintains anonymity in the network. Notably, due to the distributed nature of the blockchain, interactive zero knowledge proof is not an efficient solution. Moreover, a real world use case of zero knowledge proof is Zcash that enables native transactions to be fully encrypted while being verified by network consensus rule and Zcash is a non-interactive zero knowledge proof system.

5.6 Hash Tables

It is a popular data structure that supports fast insertion and search operation irrespective of the size of the data. It is basically a method to identify a specific object from a group of similar objects. In particular, hash tables (also called hash map) store data in a format of array and each data value is associated with a unique index value. Hash tables make use of hash function to generate an index, i.e., location where a data element is to be inserted. The information in data structure has two main components, i.e., a unique key and a value. For instance, a key could be unique ID (key doesn't have to be an integer every time) and value is the phone number. The hash function will decide where to map the key and where to store corresponding value with it. The efficiency of mapping is dependent on the efficiency of hash function. Basically, the set from which we use input element is much larger than capacity of the hash table, so that collision can be avoided. Clearly, if the number of items in the table grows, collision rises as well. To measure how full the hash table is, the concept of load factor (α) is used which is defined as the fraction of number of used keys (n) and the total capacity of the table (m).

$$\alpha = \frac{n}{m} \tag{5.2}$$

Notably, n can't exceed the total capacity of the table. If α approaches to maximum value, the chances of collision rises significantly.

In a linked list insertion operation is efficient whereas lookups still consume linear time. Additionally, in a sorted array lookup are efficient but insertions are insufficient. Notably, for n elements, linked list can search in $O(n)$ whereas binary search takes $O(log_2 n)$ and array consumes $O(n)$ time for searching. In contrast to this, hash table allows insertion, deletion and searching very fast, i.e., $O(1)$ time in average case (Refer to table 5.1). Lets take an example of hash

TABLE 5.1

Average and worst case complexity for hash tables.

	Average complexity	Worst case complexity
Space	$O(n)$	$O(n)$
Insertion	$O(1)$	$O(1)$
Deletion	$O(1)$	$O(n)$

table data structure as shown in Fig. 5.7 with hash function: $h(x) = x \, mod \, 10$ where x is the key. Suppose items are in (key, value) format and items are (1,999), (2, 9876), (45, 5434), (90, 9877). Therefore, the hash table organizes data so that any data can be looked up quickly for a given key. Nevertheless,

Index	Key	Value
0	1	9999
1	2	9876
2		
3		
4		
5	45	5434
6		
7		
8		
9	90	9877

FIGURE 5.7
Example of hash table.

there may be a case hen two or more data items collide and hashes to the same index. This is called the problem of collisions. For example, if we have to insert an item (55, 7767), this insertion will result in collision as at index 5 already there is an item. A function is referred to as good hash function that avoids collision. Collision resolution techniques are divided into two main parts, i.e., closed addressing and open addressing. In order to avoid the collision, closed addressing uses additional data structures whereas open addressing hashing stores all data inside the table. More formally, in case of collision resolution with open addressing, cells $h_0(x)$, $h_1(x)$,........, $h_{m-1}(x)$ are attempted in succession for the eq.,

$$h_i(x) = (h(x) + f(i)) mod m \tag{5.3}$$

where, $f(0)=0$ the function f is called collision resolution strategy, $h(x)=$ primary hash function, x is the key and m is the table size. Next, we will discuss the popular collision resolution techniques. The categorization of collision resolution techniques has been represented in Fig. 5.8

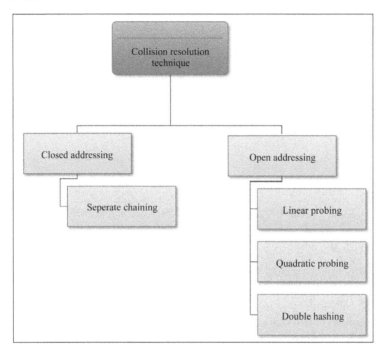

FIGURE 5.8
Categorization of collision resolution techniques.

5.6.1 Separate chaining

One possible way to avoid collision is simply to store data with same index into a linked list at the corresponding index of the array. This method is referred to as separate chaining. Here, each array slot holds a pointer to linked list having values for all keys that hashes to same hash index as shown in Fig. 5.9. **Lookup:** Of course, this solution will end up in linear time, i.e., $O(n)$ for lookup in worst case. As in worst case, all the keys might have same index of the hash table so, in order to perform sequential search, time requirement is $O(n)$. Also, cache performance for this method is not good. Although with this method is easy to implement and hash table never gets fills.
Deletion: To delete, first keys need to be searched and then deleted. As worst case time complexity for searching is $O(n)$, so for deletion time taken is $O(n)$.

5.6.2 Linear probing

Linear probing is a popular method to handle collision. Probing simply implies finding the next empty cell where the key is to be placed in case of collision. This method comes under collision resolution with open addressing. To insert

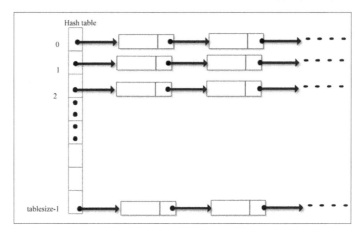

FIGURE 5.9
Each array slot containing pointer to linked list.

in case of collisions, the immediate next cells are tried until an empty cell is found. Therefore, the size of table should be equal to or greater than the total number of keys. Formally, for linear probing, f is a linear function and mostly it is $f(i) = i$ in the equation 5.3, i.e., $h_i(x) = (h(x) + i) mod m$ Clearly, the worst case complexity for searching is $O(m)$.

However, linear probing faces the problem of clustering, i.e., if multiple consecutive items form a group then it will take a lot of time to find an empty slot for insertion or in case of searching an item. Let's understand linear probing with an example, Say 3, 17, 14, 6, 21, 13, 7, 22 are the keys to be inserted in series and $h(x) = (2x + 3) mod 10$ is the hash function for key x. Refer Fig. 5.10 Hash for each key is given by:

$h(3)=9$
$h(17)=7$
$h(9)=1$
$h(6)=5$
$h(21)=5$
$h(13)=9$
$h(7)=7$
$h(22)=7$

Insert 3,17,14,6: Insertion of these 4 elements doest not face any collision. So, they are inserted at their hash indexes calculated according to given hash function.

Insert 21: As $h(21)=5$ and this location is already occupied by key 6. So, lets try linear probing with the equation: $h_i(x) = (h(x) + i) mod m$ where i=0 to m-1

i=0: $h_0(x) = (h(x)+0) mod m \implies h_0(x) = (5) mod 10 = 5$ which is occupied.
Next, **i=1**: $h_1(x) = (h(x)+1) mod m \implies h_1(x) = (5+1) mod 10 = 6$ and this

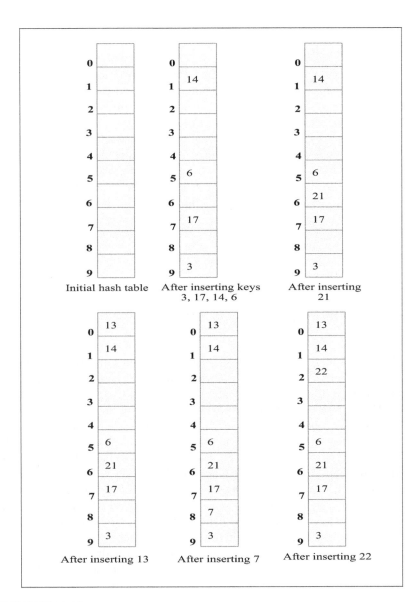

FIGURE 5.10
Example of linear probing.

location is free. So, 21 is inserted at location 6.

Similarly, 13, 7 and 22 are inserted.

This example of insertion is presented in Fig. 5.10.

5.6.3   Quadratic probing

This is another open addressing scheme to resolve collision in hash table. It works by taking hash value of the key and adding successive values of the quadratic polynomial. More formally, for quadratic probing, $f(i) = i^2$, i.e., $h_i(x) = (h(x) + i^2) mod m$ where i=0 to m-1.

This scheme has good memory caching as it preserves the locality of reference. Also, it avoids clustering problem as compared to linear probing. Let's understand quadratic probing with an example. Refer Fig. 5.11. Again consider 3, 17, 14, 6, 21, 13, 7, 22 are the keys to be inserted in series and $h(x) = (2x + 3) mod 10$ is the hash function for key x. Hash for each key is given by:

h(3)=9

h(17)=7

h(9)=1

h(6)=5

h(21)=5

h(13)=9

h(7)=7

h(22)=7

Insert 3,17,14,6: Insertion of these 4 elements doest not face any collision. So, they are inserted at their hash indexes calculated according to the given hash function.

Insert 21: *h(21)* is 5 which is occupied by the key 6. So, lets try quadratic probing with the equation: $h_i(x) = (h(x) + i^2) mod m$ where i=0 to m-1

i=0: $h_0(x)=(h(x)+0) mod m \implies h_0(x)=(5) mod 10 =5$ which is occupied. Next, **i=1:** $h_1(x)=(h(x)+1^2) mod m \implies h_1(x)=(5+1) mod 10= 6$ and this location is free. So, 21 is inserted at location 6.

Insert 13: $h(13)=9$ which is already occupied. So, lets try quadratic probing **i=0:** $h_0(x)=(h(x)+0) mod m \implies h_0(x)=(9) mod 10 =9$ which is occupied. **i=1:** $h_1(x)=(h(x)+1^2) mod m \implies h_1(x)=(9+1) mod 10= 0$ and this location is free. So, 13 is inserted at location 0.

Insert 7: As $h(7)=7$ is already occupied, so lets try quadratic probing. **i=0:** $h_0(x)=(h(x)+0) mod m \implies h_0(x)=(7) mod 10 =7$ which is occupied. **i=1:** $h_1(x)=(h(x)+1^2) mod m \implies h_1(x)=(7+1) mod 10= 8$ and this location is free. So, 7 is inserted at location 8.

Insert 22: $h(22)=7$ which is already occupied. So, lets try quadratic probing **i=0:** $h_0(x)=(h(x)+0) mod m \implies h_0(x)=(7) mod 10 =7$ which is occupied. **i=1:** $h_1(x)=(h(x)+1^2) mod m \implies h_1(x)=(7+1) mod 10= 8$ and this location is also not free.

i=2: $h_2(x)=(h(x)+2^2) mod m \implies h_2(x)=(7+4) mod 10= 1$ and this location

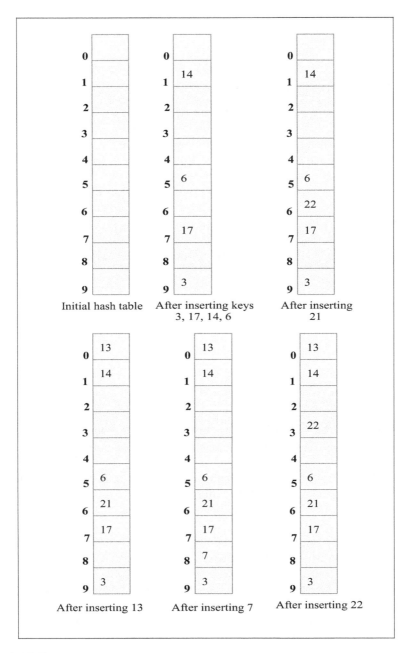

FIGURE 5.11

Example of quadratic probing.

is also not free.

i=3: $h_3(x) = (h(x) + 2^2) \bmod m \implies h_3(x) = (7+9) \bmod 10 = 6$ and this location is free. So, 22 is inserted at location 6.

5.6.4   Double hashing

This technique applies a second hash function to the given key in case of collision, i.e., $f(i) = i * h_2(x)$ and $i = 0 \, to \, m-1$ where, $h_2(x)$ is another hash function. The second hash function provides an offset value to resolve collision. This technique also comes under a double hashing technique. Notably, a good second hash function makes sure that all cells are equally probed. Unfortunately, the computational cost of double hashing is high as compared to other probing schemes. Let's understand quadratic probing with an example as represented in Fig. 5.12. Again consider 3, 17, 14, 6, 21, 13, 7, 22 are the keys to be inserted in series and $h(x) = (2x+3) \bmod 10$ is the hash function for key x. Assume other hash function $h'(x) = (3k+1) \bmod 10$ Hash for each key is given by:

h(3)=9
h(17)=7
h(9)=1
h(6)=5
h(21)=5
h(13)=9
h(7)=7
h(22)=7

Insert 3,17,14,6: Insertion of these 4 element doest not face any collision. So, they are inserted at their hash indexes calculated according to given hash function.

Insert 21: $h(21)$ is 5 which is occupied by the key 6. So, lets apply double hashing with the equation: $h_i(x) = (h(x) + i * h'(x)) \bmod m$ where i=0 to m-1.
i=0: $h_0(x) = (h(x) + 0 * h'(x)) \bmod m \implies h_0(x) = (5+0) \bmod 10 = 5$ which is occupied.
i=1: $h_1(x) = (h(x) + 1 * h'(x)) \bmod m \implies h_1(x) = (5 + 1 * 4) \bmod 10 = 9 \bmod 10 = 9$ and which is also not free $[h'(21) = (3*21+1) \bmod 10 = 4]$
i=2: $h_2(x) = (h(x) + 2 * h'(x)) \bmod m \implies h_1(x) = (5 + 2 * 4) \bmod 10 = 13 \bmod 10 = 3$ and which is free. So, key 21 is inserted at location 3.

Insert 13: $h(13)$ is 9 which is occupied by the key 3. So, lets apply double hashing with the equation: $h_i(x) = (h(x) + i * h'(x)) \bmod m$ where i=0 to m-1.
i=0: $h_0(x) = (h(x) + 0 * h'(x)) \bmod m \implies h_0(x) = (9+0) \bmod 10 = 9$ which is occupied.
i=1: $h_1(x) = (h(x) + 1 * h'(x)) \bmod m$. Notably, $[h'(13) = (13*3+1) \bmod 10 = 0]$. So, this will always result in hash index 9 which is not free. This signifies choice of second hash function is not goo. So, we can't insert 13 in this hash table.

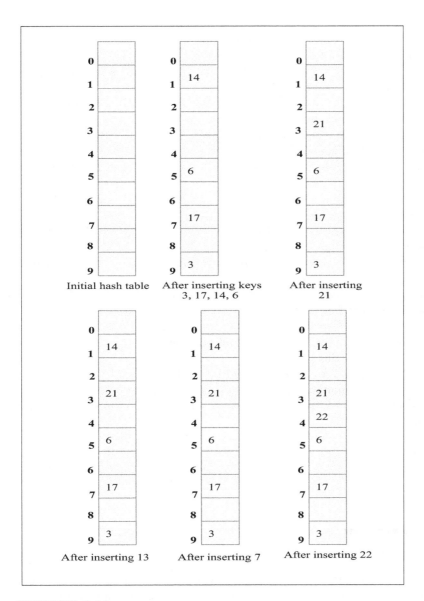

FIGURE 5.12
Example of double hashing.

Insert 7: $h(7)$ is 7 which is occupied by the key 17. So, lets apply double hashing with the equation: $h_i(x) = (h(x) + i * h'(x) mod m$ where i=0 to m-1.
i=0: $h_0(x) = (h(x) + 0 * h'(x)) mod m \implies h_0(x) = (7 + 2 * 0) mod 10 = 7$ which is occupied.
i=1: $h_1(x) = (h(x) + 1 * h'(x)) mod m \implies h_1(x) = (7 + 2 * 1) mod 10 = 9 mod 10 = 9$ which is also not free. Notably, $[h'(7) = (7 * 3 + 1) mod 10 = 2]$.
i=2: $h_2(x) = (h(x) + 2 * h'(x)) mod m \implies h_2(x) = (7 + 2 * 2) mod 10 = 11 mod 10 = 1$ which is also not free.
i=3: $h_3(x) = (h(x) + 3 * h'(x)) mod m \implies h_3(x) = (7 + 2 * 3) mod 10 = 13 mod 10 = 3$ which is also not free.
i=4: $h_4(x) = (h(x) + 4 * h'(x)) mod m \implies h_4(x) = (7 + 2 * 4) mod 10 = 15 mod 10 = 5$ which is also not free.
i=5: $h_5(x) = (h(x) + 5 * h'(x)) mod m \implies h_5(x) = (7 + 2 * 5) mod 10 = 17 mod 10 = 7$ which is also not free.
i=6: $h_6(x) = (h(x) + 6 * h'(x)) mod m \implies h_6(x) = (7 + 2 * 6) mod 10 = 19 mod 10 = 9$ which is also not free.
i=7: $h_7(x) = (h(x) + 7 * h'(x)) mod m \implies h_7(x) = (7 + 2*7) mod 10 = 21 mod 10 = 1$ which is also not free.
i=8: $h_8(x) = (h(x) + 8 * h'(x)) mod m \implies h_8(x) = (7 + 2 * 8) mod 10 = 23 mod 10 = 3$ which is also not free.
i=9: $h_9(x) = (h(x) + 9 * h'(x)) mod m \implies h_9(x) = (7 + 2*9) mod 10 = 25 mod 10 = 5$ which is also not free.
Now, we cant increase value of i to 1 as i could range from 0 to 9. So, value of i can't go beyond 9. We have checked all possible value of i from 0 to 9. So, we can't insert 7 in this hash table.
Insert 22: $h(22)$ is 7 which is occupied by the key 17. So, lets apply double hashing with the equation: $h_i(x) = (h(x) + i * h'(x)) mod m$ where i=0 to m-1.
i=0: $h_0(x) = (h(x) + 0 * h'(x)) mod m \implies h_0(x) = (7 + 7 * 0) mod 10 = 7$ which is occupied.
i=1: $h_1(x) = (h(x) + 1 * h'(x)) mod m \implies h_1(x) = (7 + 7 * 1) mod 10 = 14 mod 10 = 4$ which is free. Notably, $[h'(7) = (22 * 3 + 1) mod 10 = 7]$.

5.7   RSA

Introduced in 1978, RSA (Rivest, Shamir, Adleman) is the first widely adopted cryptosystems. RSA follows the idea of public-key encryption which is based on two components, i.e., public key, and private key. Everyone on the network has its own public and private key pair. The public key is known to everybody on the network and it is used to encrypt the message and also to verify signatures. In contrast, a private key is only known to the receiver and is used to decrypt the sent message and also to create signatures. Applications of RSA include both digital signatures and public key encryption. In RSA, the public key of the receiver is used to encrypt the message whereas the private key of the receiver is used to decrypt the message as shown in Fig. 5.13 . Encryption is a process of transforming the original message into an unrecognizable form called ciphertext whereas decryption is a process of converting encrypted message back to the original message. The process of RSA involves 3 steps, i.e., key generation, encryption, and decryption.

5.7.1 Steps for key generation:

- Select the variables p and q where both p and q both are large prime numbers and p≠q. The whole security of RSA is dependent on the difficulty of factoring large prime numbers. A poor choice of p and q can make RSA less secure and vulnerable to different attacks.

- Compute $n = p * q$, n is a part of the public key and should be large so that it is difficult to extract p and q from it.

- Compute ϕ(n)=(p-1)(q-1). ϕ(n) is called as Euler's totient function.

- Next, public key e is generated such that gcd(ϕ(n), e)=1 or e should be co-prime to ϕ(n); 1¡e¡ϕ(n).

- Finally, create the private key d such that d≡e^{-1}modϕ(n).

Both (n, e) are part of RSA public key and is publically available and private key consist of (n, d).

5.7.2 Encryption

Lets assume a sender has to sent a plaintext message M to a receiver having public key (n, e). To encrypt message use:
Cipher text= $M^e modn$.

5.7.3 Decryption

To decrypt, receiver uses its private key as:
Plaintext= $C^d modn$

5.7.4 RSA example

Key generation

- Assume p=17, q=11.

- Compute n; n= 17*11=187.

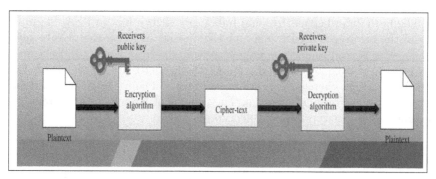

FIGURE 5.13
RSA algorithm structure.

- Compute $\phi(n)$; $\phi(n)=(17-1)*(11-1)=160$.

- Choose e such that $\gcd(\phi(n), e)=1$; choose $e=7$.

- Compute d such that $d \equiv e^{-1} \bmod \phi(n)$; $d*e \equiv 1 \bmod 160$ and $d < 160 \implies d=23$ as $23*7=10*160+1$.

Therefore, public key=(7, 187)
private key= (23, 187).

> **Key point** Public key cryptosystem follows asymmetric property as the person who encrypts message or verifies the signature on the message can't decrypt or sign signatures on the message.

5.8   Elliptic Curve Cryptography

Another way to perform public key cryptography is with elliptic curves. ECC is one of the most powerful concepts of cryptography. ECC is used for authentication, while secure web browsing over SSL/TLS. Popular cryptocurrency such as- Bitcoin and Etherem use the concept of elliptic curve. ECC is applicable for key generation, digital signatures and encryption/decryption services. Notably, ECC requires smaller key sizes as compared to RSA to provide equivalent security. Clearly, smaller key size are easy to manage and work with. A 256 bit ECC is equivalent to 3072-bit key size RSA algorithm. As ECC achieves equivalent security to RSA, with lower computing power and battery usage ECC has been popularly used for mobile applications. The key generation algorithm of the ECC uses the properties of elliptic curve equation which is discussed as follows:

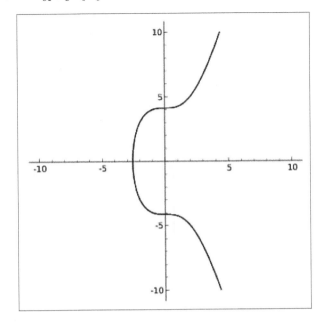

FIGURE 5.14
An illustration of elliptic curve.

An elliptic curve is defined as a set of points that satisfies a cubic mathematical equation (Refer Fig. 5.14), i.e.,

$$y^2 = x^3 + ax + b \qquad (5.4)$$

where $4a^3 + 27b^2 \neq 0$
To plot such a curve we need to compute $y = \pm\sqrt{x^3 + ax + b}$ for combination of every a and b.

Properties of elliptic curve

- Depending on values of a and b, elliptic curve takes different shapes on the plane

- All elliptic curves are symmetric around x-axis. For example, if we take $a = 27$ and $b = 2$, then for $x = 2$, $y = \pm 8$, i.e., $(2, -8)$ and $(2, 8)$ are the resulting points.

- Any non vertical line intersects the curve in atmost three points.

- The points on an elliptic curve form a group. The group operation applicable for points on elliptic curve is called addition law. To add a point P the on curve with another point Q, use the rule:

  – First, join P and Q with a straight line.

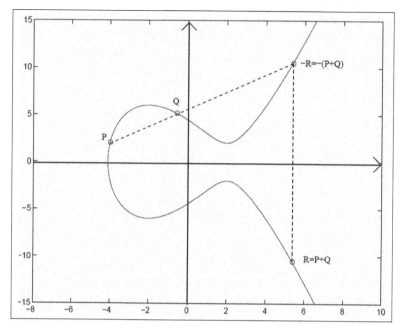

FIGURE 5.15
Addition of points on elliptic curve.

- Call this point -R where this straight line intersects with the curve.
- The mirror image of this point with respect to x-coordinate defines the addition of points P and Q and is denoted by R in Fig. 5.15.

Key point
A trapdoor function f is defined as a function that is easy to calculate but whose inverse f^{-1} is difficult to compute.

Activity

Multiple Choice Questions

1. Which encryption/decryption key is only known to parties exchanging secret messages?

   A Public key

   B Private key

   C Security token

   D e-signatures

2. Which is not a function of private key?

   A Encrypting text

   B Authentication

   C Decrypting text

   D None of these

3. What is cipher?

   A Algorithm for encryption

   B Decrypted message

   C Encrypted message

   D Secret key

4. Cryptographic hash function converts a arbitrary block into a ....?

   A Variable size string

   B Fixed size string

   C Both fixed and variable size string

   D Can't say

5. Which among the following is the component of CIA triad?

   A Confidentiality

   B Integrity

   C Authentication

   D Availability

6. What are thr requirements of a hash function?

   A One-way

B Avalanche effect

C Deterministic

D All of the above

7. Cryptanalysis is ......

A To decrease the speed of encryption

B To increase the speed of encryption

C To generate ciphertext

D To find insecurities in cryptographic algorithm

8. Digital signature is based on .....?

A Public key encryption

B Private key encryption

C Blockchain technology

D None of the above

9. What are the properties of zero knowledge proof?

(a) Completeness

(b) Soundness

(c) Zero knowledge

(d) None of the above

10. Which among of the following is collision rsolution technique?

A Quadratic probing

B ECC

C DSA

D All of the above

1. b   2. a   3. c   4. b   5. c   6. d   7. d
8. a   9. a, b, c   10 a

6

Blockchain Technology and Technical Foundations

6.1 Fundamentals of Blockchain

Blockchain is a growing list of blocks that combines cryptography with distributed computing in order to provide decentralized, transparent, and strong consistency support. In particular, blockchain technology is replacing the existing transaction management system [112]. Notably, the traditional way of writing something in a shared document is that user1 will send the document to user2 and user2, after receiving the document update the document with its own content and send it back to user1. However, this method does not allow both parties to write on the document simultaneously. As a solution, with Google Docs provided by Microsoft Word both of user1 and user2 can write simultaneously. Nevertheless, this Google doc platform is centralized and involves a third party. Mostly, the traditional distributed databases are centralized, have high complexity, and they rely on trusted database company.

Centralized architecture has a central co-ordination system and every node on the network is connected to this system. Any information sharing in the network has to involve this central coordination system. Nevertheless, there are some disadvantages with a centralized system.

- Single point of failure: What if the system or the server crashes. Unfortunately, in case of a crash of this central system, all nodes on the network get disconnected to the network and all operations get terminated. This situation may lead to the loss of entire information. Therefore, complete dependency on a single server is not efficient.

- Bottleneck: Bottlenecks are common in case of increased traffic.

- Single point of attack: As there is a single central authority, there are chances of a single point of attack. Therefore, this type of architecture can easily suffer a denial-of-service attack.

- Delay: As a centralized server is mostly located at a far location from users, so time to access data increases.

- Higher privacy risk: As centralized architectures involve a trusted third party, so the user is unaware of how the information of users is secured with the third party. The trusted third party may share the private information of users with other parties.

Over and above, there are other architectures to support information sharing, i.e., distributed and decentralized architectures:

In a decentralized architecture, rather than having a single co-coordinator, multiple co-coordinators are present and nodes of the network are connected to any of these coordinators. So, in case of one co-ordinator node failure, nodes of the network can connect to any other co-ordinator to share information. Decentralization supports fault tolerance as decentralized systems are less likely to crash accidentally. Moreover, due to the presence of multiple co-ordinators, there is no chance of a single point of attack. On the other hand, in a distributed architecture, all nodes of the network participate in the computations and there is no single authority in charge. All nodes of the network co-ordinator with each other and collectively involves in the information sharing process. A decentralized system is actually part of the distributed system. In a decentralized and distributed network, both user1 and user2 has their own local copy of the document and both of the users can simultaneously write on the document.

Blockchain is a platform that provides support for decentralized and distributed architecture where nodes of the network can share information among themselves. In contrast to a client-server model, blockchain implements a digital P2P network. In a blockchain network, there are multiple nodes connected via the Internet and each node maintains a local copy of global sheet. However, these local copies should be updated always as per the global information. In particular, this local copy of data is called a public ledger. A popular example of the public ledger is the banking transactions and the first popular use case of blockchain is the Bitcoin network. Blockchain bitcoin is referred to as decentralized system for exchanging cryptocurrency and it also shares distributed ledger. Many other blockchain cryptocurrency platforms were introduced including Ethereum leveraging the same public model as Bitcoin, whereas platforms such as- Hyperledger, Ripple are some permissioned blockchain. Although the distributed applications of blockchain are used in many other sectors including healthcare, IoT, smart grid, etc. Blockchain provides a decentralized common platform for multiple parties who don't trust each other and are involved in information sharing or rational decision-making process. This technology provides an effective way of storing transactions in a secure, transparent, and highly resistant way. The blockchain network makes sure regarding ensuring consistency and maintaining synchronization of the document. Anything stored on the blockchain has transparent nature and anyone modifying it is accountable for their actions. Moreover, the decentralized nature of this network ensures that a single node on the network can't append invalid blocks to the chain. Before a transaction is added to the blockchain network, it is validated by all the participants on the blockchain network.

Before adding a new block to the blockchain network, it is always linked to the previous block with cryptographic hash of the immediately previous block. Therefore, cryptographic linking ensures the integrity of the network. As every block is cryptographically linked to the previous block hash that is why the name blockchain is defendable. If any block is altered, attackers need to modify all subsequent blocks which are quite difficult.

According to Wikipedia, A blockchain is a continuously growing list of records called blocks, which are linked using cryptography [8].

Blockchain technology is primarily based on the fundamentals of cryptography and distributed ledger technology. In particular, blockchain uses the concept of hash functions, ECC, digital signatures and Elliptic Curve Digital Signature Algorithm (ECDSA) to maintain integrity, confidentiality, and non-repudiation of the system. A distributed ledger is a kind of database that is shared and synchronized among nodes of the decentralized network. Moreover, each record in distributed ledger is timestamped in order to achieve the integrity of the document. However, a consensus mechanism is used by network participants to achieve mutual agreements on a single state of the network in a distributed environment. Clearly, the consensus mechanism minimizes the risk of fraudulent transactions.

Blockchain mining is a process of validating transactions before it is added to the network and miners are the entity that is responsible for validating and generating a new block in the network. Some special nodes with some special characteristics (different for every blockchain network) are only regarded as a miner. Further, the mined block is broadcasted in the network to be verified by other nodes before final inclusion in the network. Whenever a new Bitcoin transaction is made it is first placed in a transaction pool. Rather than validating a single transaction, miners collect a certain number of transactions from the transaction pool to form a candidate block. Hence, a candidate block is referred to as a block that has been created by a miner but it is not added to the network. It may so happen that multiple miners can mine a block with exactly same or some different transactions simultaneously or in a near identical time. However, when two blocks get mined simultaneously, there is a possibility that only one miner's blocks get more number of blocks on top of it. If multiple valid blocks to the existing chain appear, in that case, only the longest subbranch is accepted and continued further; and the blocks that are not accepted are called orphaned blocks and that path is called forks. In other words, orphan blocks are those blocks which do not have any link to main branch due to missing predecessor. Additionally, if there are two different chains of the same length then accept the chain which has been broadcasted by more number of miners. Transactions from these blocks which are not validated are sent back to the transaction pool. In such cases, efforts of miners go useless as mined blocked becomes unrecorded.

6.1.1　Characteristics of blockchain technology

- Decentralization: Blockchain technology does not depend on a centralized system or any governing authority to perform all transactions. Instead, the network is controlled by nodes of the network making it decentralized. Every node on the network has its copy of shared ledger which is updated. Moreover, it solves the problem of a single point of failure.

- Better security: Cybersecurity is defined as a capability to prevent and recover from cyber-attacks. Blockchain technology provides better security as there is not any chance of system failure. The use of a cryptography system by blockchain provides protection for users. Another reason for the popularity of blockchain technology is basically its capability to deal with the threat of an individual's privacy. All transactions are verified and it is quite hard to modify these transactions.

- Immutability: Immutable ledger is the main advantage of the blockchain system. Immutability implies data on the network can't be changed or altered. Blockchain stores permanent records of transactions. After a block is verified and added to the network, it can't be modified or deleted. Moreover, the lack of centralization promotes scalability and robustness. Centralized architecture can be tampered and requires trust in a third party to maintain integrity.

- Anonymity: Blockchain provides anonymity as nodes are known by their public keys on the network. Therefore, the identities of the nodes are kept private.

- Transparency: Any node on the network can audit transactions and every node has access to same universal ledger. Every state of data and every updating state is visible to node of the network.

- Redundancy: As copy of distributed ledger is stored with every full node on the network, hence redundancy is inherent for blockchain.

- Efficiency: All transactions are automatically executed via pre set procedures. Hence, blockchain technology reduces cost of labor along with improving efficiency.

6.1.2　What constitutes a block of blockchain?

The first block in a blockchain is called genesis block and this block doesn't have ant previous block. All network participants should have the same genesis block in order to attain the correctness of the blockchain network. The previous hash value for a genesis block is zero. The structure of blockchain comprises of strings of blocks, each holding transactions of data and metadata. Data inside a block contains transactions generated by participants of the network and blocks hold the transaction in a secure way so that they can't be tampered. A transaction is an atomic event or the smallest building block allowed by a particular protocol. For instance, in Bitcoin blockchain transactions are user's payments. On the other hand, the metadata contains information regarding block including parent block hash, timestamp, etc. This informative metadata is used by miners or the other nodes of the network to verify a block or to append a block to the blockchain. The structure of chained block is represented by Fig. 6.1. Metadata of the block is stored in block header ad consists of the following field:

- Version: The version number is used to track protocol upgrades used by blockchain nodes.

- Timestamp: It specifies the creation time of the block.

- Nonce: It is a random number used to solve the Proof-of-Work (PoW) cryptographic puzzle as shown in Eq. 6.1.

$$SHA - 256(SHA - 256(Previous block hash||Tx_1$$
$$||Tx_2||.......||Tx_n||nonce)) < Difficulty$$
$$(6.1)$$

- Difficulty/Target: This is used by PoW algorithm to solve mining process. For a block to be added in the blockchain network, it has to generate a valid hash and difficulty value is used in achieving this task.

- Previous block hash: As mentioned earlier, every n^{nt} block of blockchain stores hash of previous block, i.e., $(n-1)^{nt}$ block. In order to compute hash of $(n-1)^{th}$ block, all header field of $(n-1)^{nt}$ block are collectively hashed twice.

- Merkle tree: It contains the value of root of merkle tree which is explained in detail later in next chapter. It is basically a tree structure where the nodes at leaf level contain the hash of the document and every intermediate node contains the hash of left and a right child. As it is presented in Fig. 8.3, there are 8 transactions, i.e., t_1, t_2,.............,t_8. Leaf nodes of the Merkle tree contain the direct hash of these transactions and then level 1 has intermediate nodes with hash value of its left and right child (,i.e., obtained hashes are again paired to calculate the hash for next level). This hash will be recursively calculated until a single root hash is obtained.

> **Key point** Mandatory fields are transactions, Merkle root hash, and hash of the previous block which are used by every blockchain network, rest other are specific to particular blockchain application.

In addition to this, Merkle hash tree is used in membership verification. Notably, to verify membership of any given transaction, the verifier does not need to possess a complete Merle tree, rather only (log n) piece of data is

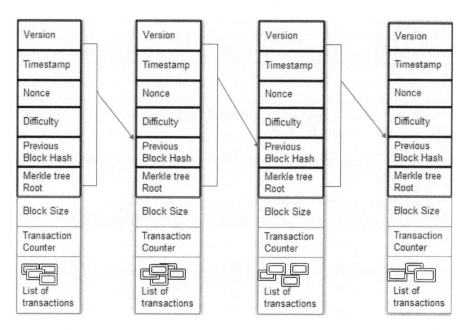

FIGURE 6.1
Structure of chained blocks.

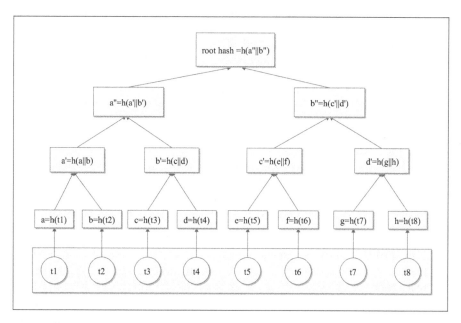

FIGURE 6.2
Structure of Merkle Tree.

enough where n is the total number of nodes in the tree. As every node has access to block header, so the root value of Merle hash tree can be downloaded from there. Suppose, user A has root node of Merkle tree for a block and user B wants to prove user A that transaction t_4 is in the block. (Refer to Fig. 8.3. To accomplish this, user 2 has to provide user 1 some siblings of the nodes in the tree path from t_4 to the root, so that user A can recompute root hash of the tree and match it against the one downloaded from the block. For example, To verify the presence of transaction t_4 in the block user 2 has to actually provide user1 c, a' and b" along with hash of transaction t_4. With knowing c and a, b' can be computed and b' when combined with a' can compute a" and finally root hash can be computed with a" and b". Infact, user 2 can actually prove the presence of t_4 in the block without even revealing its content by just proving hash of t_4.

Therefore, even in the presence of a large number of blocks in Merkle tree, membership of any element can be proved in relatively short time. With having only hash values of top level nodes, it is easy to traverse down to any leaf node in order to check whether it is tampered or not.

> **Key point** With merkle tree membership of any transaction can be verified in O(log n) time and space complexity.

6.1.3   Bitcoin basics

Bitcoin is regarded as the first fully functional digital currency. It completely executes a P2P banking system without any central financial organization [160]. The bitcoin blockchain network is a network where users can send or receive cryptocurrency among themselves. It comes under the public blockchain and anyone in the world can be a part of the Bitcoin network. Here, transaction is a transfer of cryptocurrency from one node of the network to another network. Every registered node on the blockchain network has a pair of public and private keys held in the Bitcoin wallet of that person. Over and above, the Bitcoin wallet address never carries the name or identity of the person. Basically, a wallet address is the mathematical correspondence of the public key used by the user. Therefore, using the Bitcoin address maintains the anonymity of the network. Notably, the user can have more than one address. Suppose, user A wants to transfer some Bitcoins to user B. Anyone having user B walled address can transfer Bitcoin to his account however, to release money only public key of user B is required. To accomplish this, user A will create a transaction specifying the amount of money user A wants to transfer and user B address. Next, the user will sign the transaction and broadcast this transaction in the network. To create digital signatures, take the hash of the transaction and apply encryption using senders private key. Anyone in the network or specifically a miner can validate this transaction's integrity, authentication, and non-repudiation using user A public key. Notably, when a

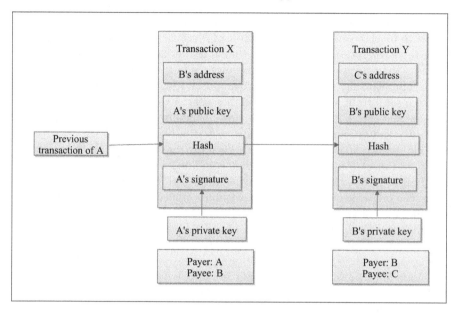

FIGURE 6.3
Illustration of Bitcoin transaction.

user sends Bitcoin to another address, wallet of that user creates a transaction output having an address of another user to whom money is being transferred and this transaction is recorded on blockchain network with Bitcoin address of the sender as the transaction input. In another way, an input is a reference to the output of a previous transaction. In the case of multiple transactions, all the total coin value is added up and it can be used by the output of the new transactions. For example, in Fig. 6.3, Payer B creates a transaction Y by signing its own coins received from transaction 1 using his/her private key and adding its own public key and address of payee C. Anybody on the network can use B's public key to validate the transaction and to ensure B is spending the right coins. However, for any transaction to be accepted by the rest of the network, transaction blocks need to be validated and miners validating the nodes must include PoW in the block. Here, miners are special nodes with good computational power and resources. Notably, the block size in a Bitcoin network can't exceed 1 MB to achieve fast propagation.

PoW is a cryptographic difficult hash generated by miners. Particularly, it is a Bitcoin consensus algorithm. The concept of PoW and mining makes a transaction computationally impractical to modify. In PoW, basically, miners have to find a nonce value so that the hash of the block has a certain hash value. The first miner to solve the puzzle gets a reward in the form of incentives from the network. All the other nodes in the network validate the blocks mined by miners. For a block to be added in the Bitcoin network, more than 51% of the network nodes should approve the blocks. Hence the only way to attack the blockchain network is when 51% of the hash power is with attackers. This detailing of this algorithm is explained in the coming section.

Another reason for the popularity of Bitcoin is its ability to solve the problem of double-spending. Double spending is a problem when the same Bitcoins are used for more than one transaction. For example, user A has 100 Bitcoins and user A tries to send the same amount of 100 Bitcoins to both user B and user C simultaneously. The property of timestamping and distributed ledger ensures double-spending of Bitcoins.

> **Key point** Bitcoin addresses are random numbers and it may be possible that two different users end up in creating same address and it results in a collision. In such a situation, both original and colliding owner of address could spend Bitcoins sent to that address.

Multi-signature transactions: It is a type of transaction that is signed by multiple users and it transfers funds from a multi-signature address. This kind of transaction is used if more than one person is appointed to look after possession of Bitcoins. In order to append such Bitcoins, each one of the persons or majority of them has to sign the transactions. It implies that more than one private key is used to create digital signatures.

6.2 Types of Blockchain

The foremost application of blockchain is to execute secure transactions. However, depending on user's requirement there are multiple ways in which blockchain network is implemented:

- Public blockchain: A public blockchain network is a permissionless system where any node with access to the Internet can participate to be a part of the network. Here any user of the network can access records, verify, validate transactions, and perform mining tasks. The more the number of participants in the public blockchain network, the more it will be secure as the blocks are then verified and validated by more participants of the network. Bitcoin, Ethereum, Litcoin, Steller, dash are examples of the public blockchain.

- Private blockchain: In contrast, a private blockchain is owned by an organization or enterprises where participants are restricted and only authenticated users are allowed. Actually, private blockchains are the restrictive version of public blockchain. Private blockchains are used with the private organization for storing sensitive information. A new user can't join the network without having an invitation from the network. The invitation procedure involves use of conditions to be satisfied before a new user can join. Private blockchain is fast than public blockchain. Notably, private blockchain possesses centralization as compared to public blockchain. Hyperledger, multichain, Corda are the popular examples of private blockchain. High customizability, better access controls, better scalability are some of the advantages of the private blockchain [47].

- Consortium blockchain: This types of blockchain is regarded as semi-private systems. Clearly, it is not a public network but a permissioned network. However, rather a single organization governing, multiple organization governs the network. This type is beneficial for cases where multiple organization operates in the same industry. Here, only a few selected nodes have the right to oversee consensus mechanisms and to authorize transactions. Compared to a public blockchain, consortium blockchain provides faster speed. Also, this blockchain type does not face scalability problems. Quorum is a popular example under this category.

The difference in above discussed blockchain type in tabular form is discussed in Table 6.1.

TABLE 6.1

Differences in blockchain type.

Blockchain type			
Characteristic	Public	Private	Consortium
Permissionless	Yes	No	No
Read rights	Anyone	Invited users only	Depends
Write rights	Anyone	Approved participants	Approved participants
Ownership	Nobody	Single entity	Multiple entities
Transaction speed	Slow	Fast	Fast
Centralized	No	Yes	Partially

6.3   Blockchain Applications

Due to its distributed, immutable, and trustworthy nature for all transactions, blockchain technology has various applications. Not only the financial sector, but blockchain technology also has the potential to revolutionize commerce, industry, education sector, etc. Authors of [182], suggested that the growth of blockchain applications can be divided into three phases, i.e., blockchain 1.0, blockchain 2.0, and blockchain 3.0. Blockchain 1.0 covers the usage of cryptocurrency as a P2P payment system. Blockchain 2.0 includes smart contracts, smart property, and decentralized applications with simple cash transactions. Blockchain 3.0 covers applications beyond finance and cryptocurrency, such as- healthcare, governance, agriculture, and smart grid, etc.[49].

- Education: One of the worth mentioning application of blockchain is in the education sector. Similar to financial, educational sector has leveraged blockchain to keep student's data safe for the coming years. As blockchain keeps track of information efficiently, library information services in colleges and schools can implement blockchain. Some universities and institutes have used blockchain to support degree management and evaluations for course learning outcomes. Another use is to reward students for their success and achievements based on transparent records stored on the blockchain network. For example, the University of Nicosia is the first place where blockchain is used to manage certificates of students from massive open online course (MOOC) platform [170]. In addition to this, blockchain technology helps in reducing student's fraud degrees. With blockchain, all degrees and certificates are stored digitally on the blockchain network without requiring any intermediary to verify them. Also, ride sharing applications can use to organize carpooling services. This will surely reduce the burden on public transport.

- Healthcare: Mostly, existing healthcare systems are maintained by a central authority. Therefore, all the data generated by patients can be accessed by these third parties without the patient's consent which leads to privacy concerns. To address this problem, recently blockchain technology has been extensively used in healthcare networks for various applications, such as- data management, data sharing, data storing, data analyzing, and access management systems. The foremost use case in health sector is for improved and secured medical record management [208]. With blockchain, the information measured by IoT sensors, such as- temperature, blood pressure, heart care, and pulse rate is shared securely and transparently over the blockchain network. The patient can now control and check what and how much information is to be shared with the doctor or any other healthcare officer. Another use case is to verify the claimed transaction for health care financing task. Literature supports many work that integrates blockchain with healthcare system, such as [102], [97].

- Voting system: In a democratic country, maintain security in an election system is a matter of national security. Nowadays, electronic voting machines are used by the government to achieve the voting mechanism successfully. Notably, these e-voting systems are based on a centralized network where everything is handled by a trusted third-party. However, such kind of system is a concern of physical security, privacy, and lack of transparency. Importantly, one of the main concerns for such systems is the prevention of database manipulation. By leveraging the fundamentals of blockchain and smart contract a secure e-voting system for transparent democracy can be created. The usage of SHA-256 hash function and linkage to the previous block with the help of cryptography prevents any kind of modifications to the database. Moreover, the digital signature usage ensures reliability to the system. Additionally, the concept of anonymity supported by blockchain ensures that voters can submit their votes without any fear of identity leakage.

- Smart grid: To design a smart infrastructure for IoT based smart cities an intelligent and automated electricity distribution system is required. In this context, the smart grid has revolutionized the energy sector in many ways. A smart grid aims to construct an automated power infrastructure that can minimize energy waste. Although in the existing literature smart grid utilities are served by a central third party who balances users' electricity load and payments. This central authority stores all the information related to electricity generation, consumption, and transfer. Nevertheless, because of more time consumption, single point of failure, and the increasing number of distributed resources, centralized management is not effective. With blockchain, different electric utilities exchange energy and make payments without a third party. All involved transactions are stored on publically distributed ledger after verification by all network participants. All records and energy transactions are stored by every network participant which ensures trust and transparency on the network. Simultaneously, because of resistance to a single point of failure, DDoS attacks are minimized by integrating blockchain with smart grid [124]. Moreover, the elimination of third-party reduces transaction costs. Over and above the interconnection among network participants realizes P2P information sharing that achieves automatic scheduling. Also, automatic delivery of electricity bills can be implemented with blockchain. Hence, blockchain enables self participation, secure payments, transparency in allocation and generation of electricity, flexible demand response management, P2P energy trading, and real-time pricing data [125].

- Intelligent transport system: Another potential use case of blockchain technology is in developing an intelligent transport system (ITS) or autonomous driving cars. With the rapid growth in automobile industry, computing techniques, and devices, there is popularity in the growth of ITS. However, information collected by different sensing units, Roadside unit (RSU's) and Base station (BS's) of ITS is generally stored on cloud-based platforms and thus faces security and privacy risks due to centralization. ITS needs to secure and authenticate data to make real-time decisions. Blockchain provides trustworthy data as the entire network contributes to data verification and validation. With its decentralized properties, blockchain can promote trusted communication among vehicles and RSU's in autonomous transportation systems. Also, the distributed data verification mechanism ensures an immutable and traceable distributed ledger that heps building a secure financial system in ITS for P2P money transfer. For electric vehicles (EV's) energy trading between EV's and charging stations, blockchain provides secure payment handling and transaction management [155]. Similarly, toll payments can be enabled with blockchain for standardized collection. Also, ride-sharing services can leverage blockchain to make secure payments and to display transparent information [98]. Moreover, insurance contracts can be stored on the blockchain network and smart contracts can be deployed for taking actions to claim money and to detect any kind of contract violation. Additionally, with the smart contract facility, custom clearance can be fast and more effective which reduces processing times at checkpoints [99].

6.4 Smart Contracts

Smart contracts are automatic and irreversible applications implemented in a distributed environment. Nobody except the developer having full access to the code can edit or modify the execution behavior of smart contracts. Smart contracts manage digital documents efficiently as they are self-executing and self-verifying [95]. It is actually a piece of code developed to set up an agreement between more than one party, having conditions to be met before execution. Every party must fulfill their commitment as per their agreement. For example, a smart contract for payment on a specific date and time which implies on the arrival of a specified date and time the predefined condition is satisfied and the payment is transferred to the receivers account automatically. Therefore, eliminating the need for a trusted third party. When placed on a blockchain environment, it leverages properties (such as- irreversibility, tamperproof, transparency, etc.) of blockchain technology. The bytecode of a smart contract is visible to everybody on the blockchain network. It is worth noticing that one smart contract may needs outcome from another smart contract. Not only payment transactions, smart contracts are also used to execute many different processes, such as insurance, supply chain management, mortgage loans, real-estate, voting, etc. With the popularity of IoT technology, smart contracts are used to enable M2M interaction.

Currently, the biggest platform for the smart contract is Ethereum. Solidity is an object-oriented, high-level language specifically designed for implementing smart contracts. Solidity is inspired by common languages such as- C++, Python, and javascript having features including inheritance, libraries, etc. The compiler of solidity converts the code into EVM bytecode. The fundamental steps for executing a smart contract are:

- After the finalization of contractual terms, programming code is developed specifying predefined conditions and outcomes.

- Deploy the smart contract to the blockchain network and replicate it among all participants of the network.

- Once the terms and conditions are satisfied, the contract is executed and the outcome is triggered.

Notably, the Bitcoin network was the first one to use the concept of smart contract for the blockchain in a way that one node can transfer coins to another node following some rules. Additionally, the network participants will only validate transactions if some predefined conditions are met. In contrast, Ethereum replaces Bitcoin's restrictive language with a language that enables developers to write their own code of programs. It implies, with Ethereum developers can write their own program.

6.5   Issues with Blockchain

Blockchain technology has the potential to disrupt a wide range of industries but it faces its own set of challenges as shown in Fig. 6.4. However, over time literature introduces many improvements to eliminate these challenges.

- **Storage**: The foremost problem of blockchain is data storage as every full node on the network has a copy of the distributed ledger. Clearly, this increasing repository of data is difficult to handle. In this context, mechanism such as- sidechains or chilchains should be encouraged in research [32].

- **Scalability**: Another problem is the increasing size of public blockchain network. With the increase in the number of transactions, the size of blockchain becomes large. For example, the current size of Bitcoin blockchain is approximate 269 GB [9]. It is important to store all transactions occurring on the network for validation purposes. Therefore, the problem of scalability prevails in blockchain. Also, consensus protocol effects scalability of the network. Additionally, with the increase in network size more resources will be required, therefore system's capacity scale will be reduced. Due to high scalability transaction execution in blockchain can become slow. Sharding is a new method to improve scalability and to increase transactional throughput. It is a method of partitioning that groups subset of participants into smaller networks who are only responsible for transactions meant for their shards. This way each shard will have its unique set of smart contracts that will be easily executed.

- **High computation**: The majority of blockchain available in market consumes lots of energy as they are based on Bitcoin infrastructure and uses

PoW as a consensus algorithm. This protocol involves complex mathematical puzzles and demands high computation power for verification. However, this computationally intensive task is important to generate new blocks in blockchain. Also, this algorithm involves consumption of high energy resources. Solving mathematical puzzles consume energy equivalent to yearly electricity consumption of Denmark in 2020 [10]. Hence, blockchain can prove costly to the environment. In order to solve energy challenges faced by PoW many other consensus algorithms including Proof-of-stake (PoS), Proof-of-identity (PoI) has been introduced.

- **Lack of standards** : As per a research in [11], one of the reasons blockchain technology is not adopted widely is the lack of trust among users. Lack of standards can create disputes among users. Also, lack of standardization leads to interoperability issues among large number of nodes in blockchain network. There are multiple blockchain projects in the market with having different protocols, privacy measures, consensus algorithm, and coding languages. Additionally, the lack of uniformity caused by these different projects creates consistency issues for security solutions. Moreover, there are many types pf blockchain network including public, private, and consortium each having their own advantages and disadvantages. Therefore, blockchain of different types can't communicate because of interoperability issues. Standardization of blockchain can help in reducing costs and the problem of interoperability. In this context, there is a project in the market named [12] that relies on smart bridge architecture to support universal interoperability.

- **Latency**: Transaction validation is another property of distributed consensus. The total number of transactions in a block and generation time between blocks has a significant effect on confirmation time of transaction. This introduces delay or latency in blockchain network while verification and validation of block because of large data size and increasing network size. Hence, transactions per second are slow for the blockchain network. One solution to solve this problem is to use edge computing for mobile blockchain network, especially with the PoW consensus mechanism. However, this solution faces difficult to distribute the limited edge computing resources among various miners across the different networks. Bitcoin-NG [77], Litecoin [13], Ghost [176] are some of the variants of Bitcoin network designed to improve latency of the network.

- **Privacy leakage**: Another worth mentioning issue of blockchain is privacy leakage. Privacy in blockchain implies that one is able to execute transactions without leakage of identity information. As compared, privacy is not supported in Bitcoin by default as key characteristic of Bitcoin is transparent. All the transactions happening on the network can be checked, tracked, and audited by anybody on the network. It is concluded by the authors of [139], that blockchain does not achieve transaction privacy as the value of transaction against each public key are publically visible. In addition to this, lightweight client has privacy concern as full node has all information about the interested wallet address of lightweight client.

To increase data privacy, data of blockchain network can be encrypted. For example, the model presented [122] stores transaction in an encrypted form. The compiler present in this model translates code written in encrypted form. Similarly, the Enigma project presented in [223] divided data into chunks that are distributed in the network so that no node has access to data. Another solution to provide data privacy is to store private and sensitive data outside the chain, this mechanism is referred to as off-chain solution. Such kind of system is more suitable for highly sensitive data, such as healthcare or military application.

- **Security threats**: Along with privacy concerns, another challenge is security threats faced by blockchain network. There are many security attacks that can be launched in a blockchain system including sybil attack, routing attack, DoS attack, eclipse attack to name a few. Readers can refer to [148], [133] read further in details about these attacks. However, the most popular attack is majority or 51% attack. In the Bitcoin network, any network participants having more than 51% computing power can discover nonce power faster than others which implies that node has power to decide which block is permissible. Mostly the consensus algorithms that are centralized among limited users is prone to majority attack. This attack happens if a BC node controls more than 51% of the hashing(mining) power. To solve security issues in blockchain, data analytics on blockchain data is required with latest machine learning technologies [185], [63], [14].

- **Anonymity concerns**: Anonymity implies non-identifiability of the sender. Nowadays, user authentication with maintaining user anonymity is another requirement among users [39]. By design, blockchain supports anonymity as there is no direct link between wallet address and identity of person. Instead of using true identity, blockchain is pseudonymous and mostly public key is pseudonym for the blockchain network. Unfortunately, this untraceable property motivates people for illegal web purchases. However, using public address protects anonymity to some extent. Once a person transacts with another person, it reveals its public address. As blockchain has the entire history of each wallet, with having public address all previous activity, wallet balance etc. can be checked. Additionally, any party can intercept a transaction to find out IP address of origin. Clearly, this public ledger eases correlating wallet address to identifiable names by simply analyzing the transactions. One way to solve this issue is to use Virtual Private Network (VPN) technology which uses someone else's Internet connection. Also, using a new Bitcoin address for each transaction can also help a little. For example, Monero is another cryptocurrency that uses a different secret address every time for a new transaction. Another trending technique for prevention is onion routing that obscures IP

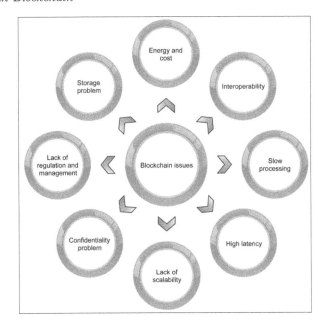

FIGURE 6.4
Issues with blockchain technology.

addresses the node comes online. In this context, Tor [15] is the open-source platform to implement onion routing. This software also helps hiding IP address of the node.

6.5.1 IPFS: A solution to decentralized data stoge problem

As discussed above, storing large files on the blockchain is challenging. In context of storage capacity, it is worth to mention Inter Planetary File System (IPFS) [16]. IPFS network is suitable for sharing big files that demand large bandwidth to upload/download over the Internet. IPFS is a decentralized P2P distributed file system to store shared files. IPFS is an efficient way to store as it eliminates duplication of data. In a P2P connected IPFS, if one node gets collapsed, the rest of other nodes can serve the demanded files. This distributed file system connects all computing devices under same file system. IPFS is basically a replacement of Hypertext Transfer Protocol (HTTP) used to access content on the Internet. In IPFS, the files on the network are hosted on a decentralized server which implies rather than storing the content on a single system, the content is hosted on multiple nodes scattered around the Internet. IPFS saves around 60% of the network bandwidth. Unlike HTTP that downloads a single file from a single machine. IPFS downloads a file in multiple pieces simultaneously from multiple decentralized machines.

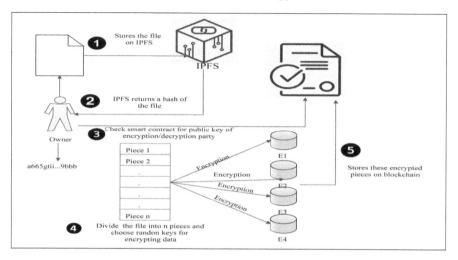

FIGURE 6.5
Data sharing on IPFS.

Rather than referring to files by names as they are stored on IPFS, this system refers to files by their cryptographic hash value. The cryptographic hash of the file is served as an address as well. This hash signifies a root object and all other objects that can be found in the path. In particular, the concept of content addressing is used at HTTP layer which implies rather than referring files by location (the location-based reference model supports centralization), it is addressed by any representation of content itself. To store files, IPFS relies on a distributed hash table (DHT). DHT is dictionary like interface to data that is on nodes that are distributed across the network. Nodes on the network use a mechanism called bitswamp to exchange data between nodes.

When a new file is added to the IPFS network, IPFS generates a multihash address of the file using its content and node ID. To access a particular file, IPFS interrogates network for file having matching hash. After computing the cryptographic hash of the file, ask the peer of the network having content matched to that hash. Next, the content is downloaded directly from the node having the required data. Hence any node on the IPFS network having the hash of the content can look for a specific file via its content ID and node matching that IP will serve it.

The IPFS model can be integrated with blockchain model, such as Bitcoin and Ethereum as both of these systems have similar structures. Rather than storing with actual values on the blockchain, IPFS simply stores hashes of files on blockchain. Further, using these hashes actual location of files can be found.

Fig. 6.5 presents a data sharing mode using IPFS as discussed by authors of [152]. At first, owner of the file uploads it on IPFS including metadata of the file. Secondly, the hash of the file is generated by IPFS and returned back to owner. At third step, owner looks for nodes in the smart contract that provide encryption/decryption services. Next, the owner divides the IPFS hash into k pieces, encrypts them, and finally store them on the blockchain network.

6.6 Python Implementation of Blockchain

We have used the Scientific Python Development Environment (Spyder) included with anaconda to implement blockchain. It enables editing, debugging, and interactive testing. Along with this, we have used Flash and Postman application to successfully create a blockchain network. Flask is a web framework for building a web application and it works with no dependencies to external libraries. To install flask use command: $pipinstallFlask == 0.12.2$ Postman is an HTTP client that is used to test application program interface (API's) by sending requests to web server and then getting a response back. It provides an easy and user-friendly interface and allows anyone to join blockchain network online using servers.

Listing 6.1
Importing libraries

```
#First import libraries
import datetime #To provide timestamp to each block
import hashlib #To compute hash
import json #json is used for storing and exchanging data
#From flask, flask class is imported to create a object which—
#will be a web application
#jsonify is used to exachnge message with postman client while—
# interacting with blockchain
from flask import Flask, jsonify
```

Listing 6.2
Defining a block of blockchain

```
#First we will define a blockchain with all its components
including genesis block,
# function to create block and mining a block
class Blockchain:
#init is used to initaialize object state
        def __init__(self):
#Initialize a empty list that will hold  the blocks of blockchain
            self.chain = []
#It defines a genesis block with previous hash as 0
            self.create_block(proof = 1, previous_hash = '0')

#Defining a block
#proof will be given after mining block based on PoW
#previous_hash links to the previous block
```

```
        def create_block(self, proof, previous_hashvalue):
#Dictionary will define all keys of a block
        block = {'index': len(self.chain) + 1,
                 'timestamp': str(datetime.datetime.now()),
                 'proof': proof,
                 'previous_hash': previous_hash}
#To append just created block
        self.chain.append(block)
        return block
```

Listing 6.3

To get previous block in blockchain

```
#To get previous block in blockchain
    def get_previous_block(self):
#- 1 will give last block index
        return self.chain[-1]
```

Listing 6.4

To compute proof of work

```
#Defining proof of work
        def proof_of_work(self, previous_proof):
#Start with initial value of 1 and increament by 1 in every
iteration
                new_proof = 1
#Use trial and error method
                check_proof = False
                while check_proof is False:
# a non symmetrical function is designed to genrate new proof from
prev proof
#to make more complex develop diff functions
                        hash_operation = hashlib.sha256(str(new_proof**2 -
                        previous_proof**2)
                        .encode()).hexdigest()
#Difficulty has been set to 4, i.e., hash should have fou leading
zeros
                        if hash_operation[:4] == '0000':
#We will check if evry block has four leading zeros in cryptographic
hash
                                check_proof = True
                        else:
                                new_proof += 1 #if not found valid   proof
                                increase new proof by 1
                return new_proof
```

Next, we will make function to check whether a block is valid or not. To check block validity, two main points need to be checked that are

- Every block's proof should have 4 leading zeros in the cryptographic hash.

- Previous hash field should have exactly same value as previous hash of the block.

Listing 6.5
To find hash of a block

```
# To compute hash of the block
    def hash(self, block):
# we will encode our block in right format so that it can be
accepted by
#SHA-256 hash function
#dumps function from json library will convert our block in
dictionary format to string format
            encoded_block = json.dumps(block, sort_keys =
            True).encode()
#Next, we will compute the cryptographic hash of encoded block
            return hashlib.sha256(encoded_block).hexdigest()
```

Listing 6.6
To check whether a blockchain is valid or not

```
# Checking whether a blockchain is valid or not
        def is_chain_valid(self, chain): #check of validity of block
            previous_block = chain[0]
#To start with first block, we will start with first block
            block_index = 1
        while block_index < len(chain):
            block = chain[block_index]
#Check whether the current block's previous hash is not equal to
hash of previous block
            if block['previous_hash'] != self.hash(previous_block):
                return False
#Next, we will check whether whether proof is valid or not
            previous_proof = previous_block['proof']
            proof = block['proof']
            hash_operation = hashlib.sha256(str(proof**2 -
            previous_proof**2).encode()).hexdigest()
#Check whether proof starts with four zeros
            if hash_operation[:4] != '0000':
                return False
            previous_block = block
#To check next block
            block_index += 1
        return True
```

The blockchain class has been created. Also, we will use flask to create a web application to be able to interact with the blockchain.

- First, we will create flask based web application by creating an object of flask class. Actually we will interact with the blockchain through flask.

- Next, we will create an instance of blockchain class.

- Then, we will make a get request to mine a block by solving PoW problem.

- Next, we will again make a get request to get a blockchain.

Listing 6.7

To create a flask based web application

```
# Creating a Flask based Web App
#app is an object of Flask class
app = Flask(__name__)
```

Listing 6.8

To create an instance of blockchain class

```
# Creating a Blockchain
#blockchain is an instance of blockchain class
blockchain = Blockchain()
```

Now, we will mine a new block by making a new request with flask based application. For this, route decorator will be used to inform flask what Uniform Resource Locator (URL) should trigger our function to mine a block. With URL, we have to specify other arguments which is method of request. It could be GET or POST. GET will get some information and POST will create something, for example, transaction.

Listing 6.9

Creating a mine block function

```
# Mining a new block
@app.route('/mine_block', methods = ['GET'])
#Now we will define a mine block function
def mine_block():
#To mine a block, we will first solve PoW problem using previous
proof
#From get previous block, we will get previous proof
    previous_block = blockchain.get_previous_block()
    previous_proof = previous_block['proof']
#With blockchain object, we will call proof_of_work method
    proof = blockchain.proof_of_work(previous_proof)
#We will compute hash of previous block to create a new block
    previous_hash = blockchain.hash(previous_block)
#After finding successful proof, the block is created and appended
to the blockchain
    block = blockchain.create_block(proof, previous_hash)
#Response variable will contain all information of the block
    response = {'message': 'Congratulations, you just mined a block!',
                'index': block['index'],
                'timestamp': block['timestamp'],
                'proof': block['proof'],
                'previous_hash': block['previous_hash']}
#Next, we will return this response displaying in postman
interface in the json format
#Also, http status code for success, i.e., 200 is returned
    return jsonify(response), 200
```

Now, we will create second GET request to display full blockchain in user interface postman application.

Listing 6.10
Getting the full blockchain

```
# To display the full Blockchain
@app.route('/get_chain', methods = ['GET'])
def get_chain():
    response = {'chain': blockchain.chain,
                'length': len(blockchain.chain)}
    return jsonify(response), 200
```

Finally, now we will run the blockchain application from our flask application. We will use postman to make request of mining block and get chain requests to check the actual state of the chain. To achieve this, from app object of flask class, we will call run method which takes two arguments, i.e., host and the port. From flask documentation, we can check this application is running on http://127.0.0.1.5000/. This URL will be entered in postman. Also, it is specified in documentation, that to make server publically available set host=0.0.0.0 and port as 5000.

Listing 6.11
To finally run the app

```
# Running the application
app.run(host = '0.0.0.0', port = 5000)
```

After writing the code, execute the code on the editor. From Fig 6.6 it can be seen that application is successfully running on http:\\0.0.0.0. Now, we will use postman application to make GET request. In postman application, we have to enter the request URL and selecting the type of request as GET as shown in Fig. 6.7. To mine block we have to use mine_block request and to get blockchain state, we have to use get_chain request.

First we will use get_chain request and it can be seen that there is only one block in network, i.e., genesis block as we have not mined any block. Refer to Fig. 6.8. This genesis block has index 1, previous_hash=0 and proof as 1 as coded.

Now, we will mine the first block of the network with index 2 as presented in Fig. 6.9. This block has proof value of 533 which implies that cryptography hash of the encoded string of $533^2 - 1^2$ starts with four leading zeros.

After mining first bock, lets check the status of blockchain with get_chain request. Refer Fig. 6.10.

```
IPython console                                                                                    ⊟
  ☐  Console 1/A ☒                                                                            ■ ⁄ ⌕
      ...:                  'proof': block['proof'],
      ...:                  'previous_hash': block['previous_hash']})
      ...: #Next, we will return this response displaying in postman interface in the json format
      ...: #Also, http status code for success, i.e., 200 is returned
      ...:
      ...:         return jsonify(response), 200
      ...:
      ...: # To display the full Blockchain
      ...: @app.route('/get_chain', methods = ['GET'])
      ...: def get_chain():
      ...:         response = {'chain': blockchain.chain,
      ...:                     'length': len(blockchain.chain)}
      ...:         return jsonify(response), 200
      ...:
      ...:
      ...: # Checking if the Blockchain is valid
      ...: @app.route('/is_valid', methods = ['GET'])
      ...: def is_valid():
      ...:         is_valid = blockchain.is_chain_valid(blockchain.chain)
      ...:         if is_valid:
      ...:             response = {'message': 'All good. The Blockchain is valid.'}
      ...:         else:
      ...:             response = {'message': 'Houston, we have a problem. The Blockchain is not valid.'}
      ...:         return jsonify(response), 200
      ...:
      ...:
      ...: # Running the app
      ...: app.run(host = '0.0.0.0', port = 5000)
    * Running on http://0.0.0.0:5000/ (Press CTRL+C to quit)
```

FIGURE 6.6
Blockchain application.

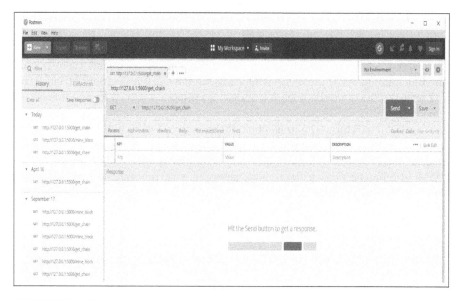

FIGURE 6.7
Blockchain application illustration with postman.

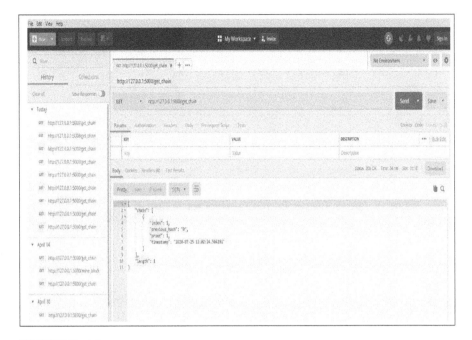

FIGURE 6.8
Blockchain application illustration with postman.

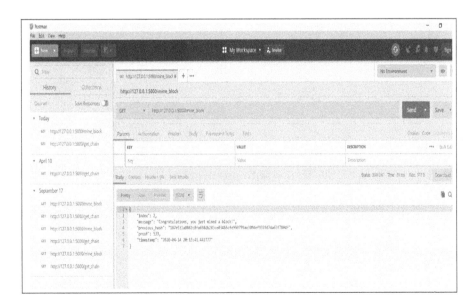

FIGURE 6.9
Blockchain block mining illustration with postman.

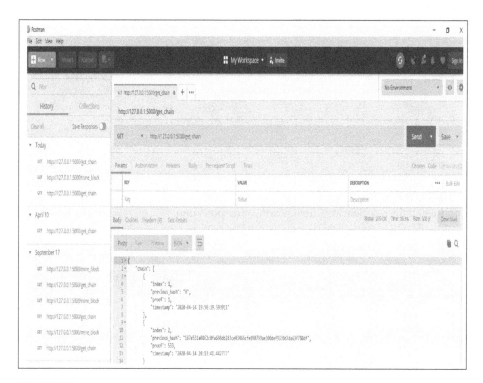

FIGURE 6.10
Blockchain get_chain illustration with postman.

Activity

Multiple Choice Questions

1. What is full form for P2P?

    A. Product-to-product
    B. Peer-to-peer
    C. Pear-to-product
    D. Product-to-peer

2. Which of the following defines a miner?

    A. A type of blockchain
    B. A person who encrypts the text
    C. A computer to store data
    D. A person who validates blockchain transactions and stores them on global ledger

3. Which term is used to define a blockchain split?

    A. Fork
    B. Mining
    C. Nonce
    D. Genesis

4. What is usage of nonce?

    A. To act as hashing function
    B. To prevent double spending
    C. To prevent 51% attack
    D. None of the above

5. What is genesis block?

    A. The very first block of blockchain
    B. The largest size block of blockchain
    C. The smallest size block of blockchain
    D. The block with having maximum number of transaction

6. What empowers Ethereum virtual machine?

    A. Bitcoin

B. CoinDesk

C. Ether

D. Gas

7. What is PoW?

A A transaction verification protocol

B A hashing algorithm

C An encryption algorithm

D A certificate needed to install blockchain

8. Which among the following is used to store Bitcoin?

A Pocket

B Box

C Wallet

D Bank

9. Which of the following constitute a block?

A A hash pointer

B Nonce value

C Transactions

D All of these

10. Where is Bitcoin's central server located?

A India

B Washington

C London

D None of these

11. Which of the following industry can use blockchain technology?

A Healthcare

B Smart grid

C P2P money exchange

D All of these

1. b	2. d	3. a	4. b	5. a	6. d	7. a
8. c	9. d	10. d	11 d			

7

Verification and Validation Methods Used by Blockchain

7.1 Consensus Mechanism

Blockchain operates as a self-regulating system without involving any centralized authority. Due to decentralized and distributed nature, blockchain faces the byzantine general problem [129]. It is a problem of consensus making in a decentralized environment where communication channels cannot be trusted. Therefore, the blockchain network should work with reliability even in the presence of dishonest nodes. Moreover, in the absence of central authority, someone has to ensure validity and verification of blocks. The consensus mechanism is a process to reach a common agreement in a decentralized framework. The consensus mechanism makes sure that all nodes agree on a single state of shared block otherwise network has to face Byzantine general problem [48]. It ensures reliability, correct operation, and fault tolerance even in the presence of faulty nodes. A consensus has to be deterministic, synchronized, and energy sufficient. Fig. 7.1 presents some of the requirements of the efficient consensus algorithm. However, achieving consensus in a distributed and decentralized environment is difficult.

> **Key point** Consensus algorithm for public blockchain has low scalability but it achieves low latency and high throughput whereas private blockchain consensus algorithm has high scalability.

Next, different consensus algorithms are discussed. The tabular comparison between these discussed consensus is discussed in Tables 7.1 and 7.2.

7.1.1 Proof-of-Work

It is the first and most popular consensus algorithm used by blockchain network to achieve Byzantine fault tolerance. Originally, Proof-of-Work (PoW) was designed for public blockchain but in many existing research, PoW has been used by private and consortium networks. The foundation of PoW is a belief that if a node is capable enough to perform difficult cryptography calculations, then it is unlikely that the node will attack the network. The benefit

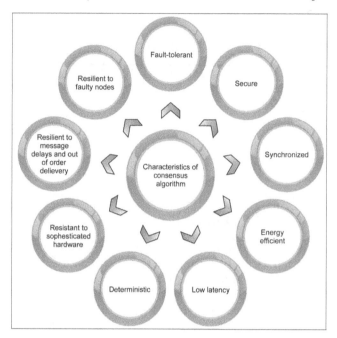

FIGURE 7.1
Characteristics of a consensus algorithm.

of proof related consensus algorithm is that there is no requirement to wait for approval from other network members to mine the block. To add a block to the blockchain network, each miner tries to find a particular nonce value to generate the SHA hash of the block specified in the block header. To solve this kind of cryptographic puzzle, the value of nonce is incremented after every round in order to achieve a hash value equal to or lower than the target value defined for that block. In particular, block hash should have certain zeros at the beginning also called difficulty of the system. After mining, miners will broadcast the block to the network. If majority of the network members will accept the block only then it will be successfully appended to the blockchain. If a miner or group of miners controls 51% of the hashing power then it leads to 51% attack. Clearly, with PoW mechanism, an abundance of energy gets wasted as multiple miners compete to mine a block simultaneously and at last only one block gets accepted by the network.

7.1.2 Proof-of-Stake

Proof-of-Stake (PoS) was specially designed to solve the issue of high energy consumption by PoW. PoS demands less energy over PoW as fewer CPU computations are involved while mining blocks. Rather than relying on external investment like PoW, PoS only uses internal investment (that is cryptocurrency). Although like PoW, PoS is also designed for permissionless blockchain. However, in PoS, miners are referred to as validators and blocks are forged not mined. It is based on the foundation that a node on a network with more participation and cryptocoins is less likely to attack the network. To become validators, nodes have to deposit some cryptocoins as stake. The probability that a stakeholder can append a new block to the chain is proportional to the amount of stake in his/her account. PoS provides security to the network due to the fact that members' stakes are at risk. Unfortunately, with this approach rich gets richer as validators receive incentives for validating a transaction which increases the possibility of the same node getting selected as validator again and again. Moreover, a node only with sufficient amount of stakes can attack the system by investing stakes in comparison to PoW that involves the investment of electricity, CPU computations and timing. Clearly, to launch 51% attack, validators have to control atleast 51% of total digital currency existing in the network which makes the PoS attack more costly. Obviously, not successful attacks would result in large financial losses. The first use case of PoS is PPCoin where participants with oldest and more number of coins posses more possibility to mine the block (this is also called coin age based selection). Here, stake is the number of coins multiplied by holding period [119].

7.1.3 Delegated Proof-of-Stake

This is also an alternative to PoW as PoW demands lots of external resources. In contrast, Delegated Proof-of-Stake (DPoS) demands fewer resources and is more eco-friendly by design. A DPoS is based on a voting system where stakeholders vote for a few delegates (witnesses) who will be responsible for securing the network on their behalf. Here miners are referred to as witnesses and they have the responsibility to successfully create a new block. The voting power of a node is proportional to the number of cryptocoins each user holds. The witnesses are elected based on reputation which is decided by the number of stakes each witness is holding [130]. The top m witnesses with more number of votes participate in the decision making of blockchain network. The value m is chosen such that atleast 50% of the voters deduce that there is enough decentralization [17]. For validating a block, witnesses get some benefits. The elected witnesses validate blocks one by one. In case a witness fails to validate in a fixed time, then the block is assigned to the next witness in the queue and a new witness is selected to replace the careless one. For 51% attack to be launched, the attacker has to control 51% of the selected witnesses. Notably, more participation of stakeholders in selecting witnesses, harder it becomes for an attacker to launch attack.

7.1.4 Practical Byzantine Fault Tolerance

Byzantine fault tolerance is described as the capability of a distributed system to reach an agreement even in the presence of an attacker node in the network sending out misleading information. Practical Byzantine Fault Tolerance (PBFT) was designed to optimize BFT for implementation in blockchain network. Practical Byzantine Fault Tolerance (PBFT) [59] was designed to solve the Byzantine Generals problem [129] for the asynchronous environment. It is based on assumption that less than 30% of total nodes are malicious in network. In other words, a minimum of $3f + 1$ nodes needs to work, where f is the number of faulty replicas. PBFT-based blockchain can tolerate atmost 33% of malicious nodes. The process of PBFT consists of 3 phases which includes.

- Pre-prepare: For each request, a leader node broadcasts pre-prepare message to ask for value that other nodes of the network wants to commit.

- Prepare: Nodes broadcast a prepare message that specifies the value they are about to commit.

- Commit: Leader node confirms the request if $2f + 1$ nodes agree in the previous phase.

However, with an priori list of participants, consensus can be reached with low transaction latency and low network communication overhead in PBFT. Moreover, limited scalability does not make it suitable for IoT applications [107].

7.1.5 Proof-of-Authority

Proof-of-Authority (PoA) [18] is an optimized variant of the PoS model where authorities on the network stake their identities for fair operation of the network. Parity [19] and Geth [20] have implemented PoA. PoA assumes that authorities are honest and trusted. By staking identities, validators do not wish to get associated with a negative reputation. Instead of appointing one authority, a set of authorities is used to reach an agreement about state of the network and the final decision has to be validated by the authorities. The authorities rely on mining rotation approach [36] when a block is created. It is based on the assumption that with N authorities, atleast $\frac{N}{2} + 1$ should be trustworthy nodes. The PoA algorithm is designed for both permissioned and permitionless networks. However, the authors of [68] demonstrated that PoA is not applicable for permissioned blockchain because it faces consistency issues. Unlike PBFT, PoA involves few exchange of messages in the network which improves better performance. However, the usage of a centralized authority limits the usage of PoA in some applications.

7.1.6 Proof-of-Capacity

Unlike PoW, in order to add a new block in Proof-of-Capacity (PoC) storage has to be dedicated instead of computation with CPU's and GPU's [75]. With this consensus, a huge amount of energy can be saved. PoC is also referred to as condensed proof of work because all computations are performed once in advance by the verifier even before the mining begins and the results of this work (plot files) are cached on hard disk. The process of plotting creates a nonce value by using the shabal hashing mechanism. The mining process only needs to read the plot file. If the storage medium contains a quick solution to a recently generated block puzzle, the account of the verifier is incentivized. However, the size of the hard drive determines the time taken to create unique plot files. Unlike PoS, everyone on the network has a fair chance of mining because storage medium is easily available at cheaper prices.

7.1.7 Proof-of-Burn

Proof-of-Burn (PoB) [21] was designed to solve the problem of high energy consumption in PoW and to reduce dependency on hardware resources. In PoB, miners invest coins to an eater address that is a unspendable address (at this address the coins become useless and inaccessible). The eater address does not have any private key assigned to it which implies that only coins can be sent to this address, but coins sent to the eater address can't be used or spent again. By burning or investing coins, a miners represents his/her readiness to bear short-term losses. While burning coins, a transaction is executed for the eater address and with this transaction, a burn hash is calculated. Burn hashes are computed by multiplying a multiplier with a internal hash. If the value of the burn hash is smaller than some predefined value, then the block from PoB is generated. The more a miner burns cryptocurrency, the higher is the probability of mining. After successfully mining a block, miners are rewarded. However, this scheme is costly from an individual miner perspective.

7.1.8 Proof-of-Luck

Proof-of-Luck (PoL) [142]uses a Trusted Execution Environment (TEE) for correct processing of critical operations. The idea behind PoL is that every node on the network requests a random number (luck value) from TEE. The higher the luck value, the higher are the chances to get selected as a miner node. Similar to PoW, nodes on the network receive transaction and miner nodes compete to commit pending transactions in a block having the luck value generated by the TEE. Next, nodes broadcast the generated block to the network and the lucky block gets added to the network. Here, an assumption is made that less than half of nodes are faulty. PoL also requires the installation of a specialized hardware such as- SGX.

7.2   Simplified Payment Verification

Notably, the blockchain network generates the bulk of data which makes it difficult for resource-constrained devices to store all the data on their devices. This problem is specifically faced by mobile devices. The increasing size of the blockchain is clearly a concern for memory-constrained devices IoT devices and Bitcoin mobile users. As reported by [22], the total size of the Bitcoin blockchain is 270.11 GB by the end of March 2020 and clearly, this data will rise in the coming years.

To address this issue, blockchain supports two types of clients in a blockchain network, i.e., lightweight client and full client. A full node is a node of blockchain network which follows all rules of blockchain whereas a lightweight node is the one referencing trusted full nodes. Lightweight clients are also referred to as thin clients. In contrast to a full client, a lightweight client does not need to download the entire blockchain network. Nevertheless, the lightweight client downloads block header of all the blocks. Clearly, it results in less space and bandwidth consumption as no actual transactions are getting downloaded. However, these nodes take part in simple network operation including confirming balance, receiving transaction history, checking the existence of a transaction in a block, verification of block difficulty and downloading block headers, and to perform such operations these clients are dependent on the full client. These clients refer to one or more full client for validation, verification of transactions, and mining tasks. Moreover, these clients do not receive all transactions that are broadcasted in the network. Rather they receive some filtered transactions in which they are interested in from the connected full client. Over and above, a lightweight client can only execute limited verification compared to a full client. If a lightweight node wants to verify the inclusion of a transaction in any block, it will request access to Merkle bunch from the full node. Next, the lightweight node will calculate the Merkle hash value with the received hash value from the full node and compares it with the Merkle hash value that is downloaded from the block header. This whole process of confirming inclusion of a particular transaction to the blockchain without actually downloading the entire blockchain is referred to as Simplified payment verification (SPV). SPV process is however associated with security and privacy issues. Notably, any attacker can cheat lightweight node with fake transactions. Although this problem can be solved by connecting to different full nodes and ensuring that everybody agrees on same chain of blocks.

> **Key point** To solve scalability problem, Satoshi has described the process of reclaiming disk space that mentions eliminating unnecessary old transactions from the blocks. However, before discarding a spend transaction to save disc space, make sure that the transaction in a coin is buried under enough blocks. To achieve this without disturbing block hash, only the Merkle root hash is included in the block.

7.3 Block Validation

Even after the mining process, nodes of the network validates the block before it is added to the main blockchain. The following points should be checked before inclusion of block in a blockchain:

- Syntactic structure: It is a foremost validation that makes sure that block should be in a syntactic structure defined for that blockchain network.

- Timestamp validation: Blocks are considered valid if timestamp value is greater than the median timestamp of immediate previous 11 blocks and less than 2+ network adjusted time where network adjusted time is the median of timestamp values returned by all connected peers to the validator node.

- Transaction: There should be at least one transaction present in that block.

- Merkle hash: Merkle hash is computed from transactions in the received block and is matched against Merkle hash present in the block header. Hashes are actually considered to be the central security element of a blockchain network.

- Previous hash: Verify that the current block should contain the hash of immediate previous block.

- Target: Hash of the bock should have value less than the target hash value.

7.4 Transaction Validation

Transaction broadcasted in the network needs to be validated to ensure that coin is spent by the authorised owner and not by any randomized user. Transaction validation rules are mentioned as follows:

- Empty: This property ensures that neither of the input and output transactions is empty.

- Structure: The defined syntactic structure of the transaction is correct.

- Size: The total size of the transaction should be less than or equal to the maximum block size.

- Range: The output value of each transaction must be in the legal money range.

- Insufficient coins: Transaction should be rejected if the total sum of input values is less than the sum of output values.

- Low transaction fees: Reject the transaction if transaction fees is too low than the defined transaction fees.

- Public key: Verify that public key accepts for each input.

- Double spending: For every input, if there exist referenced output in any transaction in the pool, the transaction will be rejected.

- No output transaction: For every input, if there does not exist any referenced output, reject this transaction.

- Orphan transaction: For every input, probe the main branch and transaction pool to search the referenced output. If output transaction does not exist for any input, that transaction is an orphan transaction.

Activity

Multiple Choice Questions

1. What is the purpose of consensus algorithm?

   A. To make sure all node agree on single state

   B. To solve Byzantine general problem

   C. To ensure fault tolerance in presence of faulty nodes

   D. All of these

2. What is biggest challenge of PoW?

   A. High computational power required

   B. A single miner can't perform mining

   C. A miner can't mine a single block at one time

   D. None of these

3. PoS stands for?

   A Proof-of-Stake

   B Proof-of-Standard

   C Proof-of-source

   D Proof of-secondary

4. PPCoin cryptocurrency uses which consensus algorithm?

   A. PoW

   B. PoA

   C. PoB

   D. PoS

5. How DPoS algorithm selects a miner?

   A. Voting system

   B. The person with more electricity power

   C. The person with more computers

   D. None of these

6. What is the disadvantage of PBFT consensus algorithm?

   A. Limited reliability

   B. Limited scalability

C. High computational power required

D. No fault tolerance

7. In PoB miners invest coins to an ether address.

A. True

B. False

8. Parity uses which consensus algorithm?

A. PoB

B. PoA

C. PoW

D. PoS

1. d   2. a   3. a   4. d   5. a   6. b   7. a   8. b

TABLE 7.1
Comparison of different consensus algorithms.

Consensus algorithm	Characteristics	Strengths	Weaknesses	Miner node selection	Popular applications	Prone to attack	Scalability
PoW [151]	The node with the highest computational power usually mines the block	• Anti-DoS attacks defence • Low impact of stake on mining chances.	• High energy requirements • Wastage of computations and resources • Vulnerable to 51% attack	Proof-based	Bitcoin, Lotecoin, Ethereum, NameCoin, PrimeCoin, DogeCoin, ProjectCoin, Ti-value, DinerCoin, Zest, Savenode,	DDoS, Sybil, Bribe attack, Selfish mining attack	High
PoS [119]	To attack, an attacker needs to own majority of stakes of the network	• Energy efficient • Does not require high computational power • Decentralized	• The rich becomes richer	Combination of random selection and stake, age	Peercoin, blackcoin, and NXT, ShadowCash, Nav Coin	DDoS, Sybil, Bribe attack, Long-range attack, Stake Bleeding attack	High
DPoS [130]	Voting power is used to select delegates	• Faster execution • Does not require sophisticated hardware • Energy efficient	• The rich may get richer • Easier to launch 51% attack • Cartels can be easily organized	Voting-based	Steem, EOS, Lisk, Ark, Bitshare	DDoS, Sybil, Long range attack	High
PBFT [59]	Provides a Byzantine fault tolerance algorithm	• Reduced energy usage • Low latency	• Not scalable	Random selection	Hyperledger fabric, Parity	Sybil attack	Low

TABLE 7.2

Comparison of different consensus algorithms.

PoA [18]	Based on the concept of identity as a stake, reputation based consensus algorithm	• Less computational power requirement • Less transaction latency • High throughput	• Faces consistency issues for permissioned blockchain • Not decentralized • Identities of validators are publically visible	Combination of identity and randomization	Parity, Geth	DDoS, Sybil	High
PoC [75]	Memory has to be dedicated	• Energy efficient • Completely decentralized • No upgradation of resources required	• Could lead to fierce competition • Future monopolies	Precomputed solution on hard disk	BurstCoin, SpaceMint, Chia	–	High
PoB [21]	Requires investment of coins	• Energy efficient • Less resources required	• Expensive from an individual's view point • The rich becomes richer	Burning of coins	SlimCoin, Counterparity	–	High
PoL [142]	Based on random number generation	• Low latency transaction • Energy efficient mining	• Requires specialized hardware	Randomization needed	—	—	High

8

Data Structures for Blockchain

8.1 Data Structures for Blockchain

This section will discuss the important data structures used by blockchain.

- Hash pointers: A pointer in data structures is used to pint address of value stored in memory. The process of fetching the value stored at any memory location is called dereferencing the pointer (Refer Fig. 8.1). Additionally, a hash pointer is a type of pointer that points to address of hash value in order to make it tamper proof. Particularly, rather than just consisting of address of immediate previous block, it also has the hash of data in the previous block. Notably, hash pointers are used to construct a linked list called blockchain. In blockchain, hash pointer points to the hash of data stored in the immediate previous block. Hence, any modification in the chain would be detected with the hash pointers. Suppose an malicious person tampers with a block of blockchain, lets say block 10. With change in content of block 10, hash of this block also got changed (collision free property of hash). To bluff others, he also has to change hash pointers of next block, i.e., block 11. Furthermore hash pointer of block 12 also has to change and so on and so forth. Refer Fig. 8.2 for illustration of hash pointer chain.

> **Key point** Hash pointers can be used in any pointer based data structures that is without any cycles. If cycles are present in data structures then we won't be able to make all the hashes match up. Clearly, in a structure with cycles, there is no end that we can start with and compute back from.

- Linked list: Linked list is one of the most popular data structures. Particularly, it is a sequence of blocks containing some information that is linked to immediate next block through a pointer. The pointer in each block contains the address of next block. The last block has a null pointer which implies it is not pointing to anything. A blockchain is basically a linked list containing data and a hash pointer pointing to previous block.

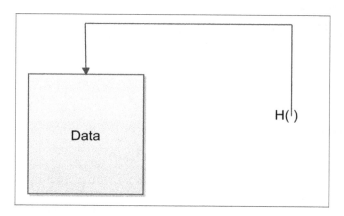

FIGURE 8.1
Illustration of hash pointer.

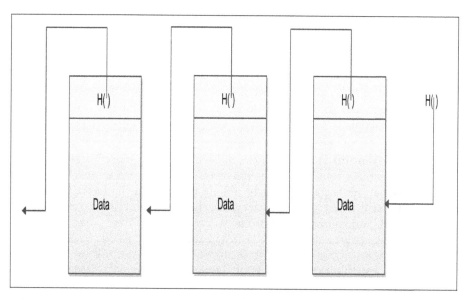

FIGURE 8.2
Illustration of hash pointer chain.

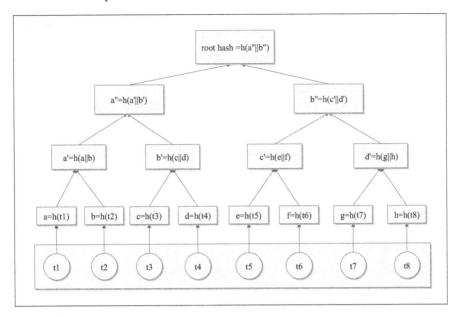

FIGURE 8.3
Structure of Merkle tree.

- Merkle tree: Another important data structure constructed using hash pointer is a binary tree. In particular, this binary tree linked with hash pointer is referred to as Merkle tree. This is the main foundation of blockchain concepts. Merkle tree also called hash tree is named after Ralph Merkle [140]. It is basically a tree structure where the nodes at leaf level contain the hash of the document and every intermediate node contains the hash of left and a right child. As it is presented in Fig. 8.3, there are 8 transactions, i.e., t_1, t_2,............,t_8. Leaf nodes of the Merkle tree contain the direct hash of these transactions and then level 1 has intermediate nodes with hash value of its left and right child (,i.e., obtained hashes are again paired to calculate the hash for next level). This hash will be recursively calculated till a single root hash is obtained. It implies that any change in the transaction will be reflected in the hash value at every level including root hash value including root hash value. So, with a single hash value, i.e., root hash the transactions, the transactions can be collectively stored without fear of alteration in a block. Therefore, the Merkle hash tree makes sure that data stored on the blockchain remains undamaged and unaltered. In other words, Merkle hash preserves the integrity of the document.

Key point To compute Merkle hash, Bitcoin uses SHA-256 hash.

- Tries: Tries is a ordered tree data structure to maintain set of strings. If two strings have a common prefix then they will have same ancestor in trie. Trie is an ideal data structure for storing dictionary. Also, it is used for encoding and decoding. Notably this is not similar to a binary tree whereas it is a N-Ary tree. Infact, tries support better searching than binary search tree and hash tables. Hash tables does not support prefix based search. Moreover, with tries it is easy to print all words in alphabetical order.

  A trie stores key-value pair where key is the path in the tree to reach its corresponding value. With tries, there is no restriction on number of children a node can have. However, all nodes descendants have a common prefix. In particular, each node can have up to 26 children. Each node's children are ordered alphabetically. It can thought of as a node that has a array of 26 size sitting inside. However, a better option is to have a linked list at each node to save space.

  Unfortunately, tries require large memory for storing strings as for each node there are further many pointers. Also, a trie prooves inefficient if there is long key and o other key shares a common prefix. A standard trie take $O(W)$ space, where W is the total size of strings in a set. Insertion, deletion, and search operation of a trie takes $O(l * n)$ where, l is average length of word and n is total number of words whereas the worst case runtime complexity for creating a trie is $O(m * n)$ where, m is the longest word in the string and n is the total number number of words. For example, the trie data structure for set of string S=bear, bell, bid, bull, buy, sell, stock, stop is represented in Fig. 8.4.

- Patricia tree: Patricia stands for practical algorithm to retrieve information coded in alphanumeric. It is also based on fundamental that nodes with same prefix shares the same path (it is also called prefix tree). However, it requires low memory than trie data structure. It is actually a compact representation of a trie in which nodes having single child is merged with its parents. In other words, Patricia tree is similar to radix tree with the value of radix equal to 2. In particular, Ethereum blockchain is based on Merkle-Patricia tree, which is a tree having root node that contains the hash value of whole data structures. Fig. 8.5 represents the patricia tree for string S= bear, bell, bid, bull, buy, sell, stock, stop.

- Merkle Patricia trie: This data structure is a combination of Merkle tree and Patricia tree. Merkle tree is used to maintain data integrity whereas patricia tree in particular enables fast searching of information. These Merkle patricia also shows some form of verification and tamperproofing. Ethereum blockchain cryptocurrency uses Merkle patricia tree to store transaction and world state. Notably, Ethereum is quite different to Bitcoin as it uses smart contracts which keeps on updating everytime. Additionally, Ethereum rather than using one Merkle tree, it uses 3 different

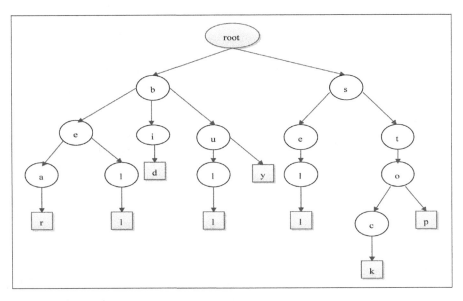

FIGURE 8.4
Illustration of trie data structure.

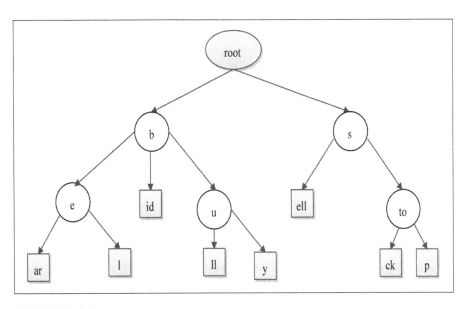

FIGURE 8.5
Illustration of patricia tree data structure.

Merkle tree to attain global state and to impose extra ability to query data within blockchain which are described as:

- stateRoot: which specifies the state of the block.
- transactionRoot: which specifies transaction hash in the block.
- receiptRoot: which specify the amount of gas used in a block.

In Ethereum all information of state is stored in key value pair. Keys are mainly string values that refers to search index. For example, account address is the key and balance is the value corresponding to the key. Merkle Patricia tree introduces 4 types of nodes which are described as follows:

- Empty node: These are simply blank nodes.
- Leaf node: It is the end node that signifies end of path in a tree. Leaf node will not have any further child and it always contains some value corresponding to a key. It is made up of two items, first corresponding to a suffix and second to any value.
- Branch node: It is a node having more than one branch. It is a 17 item structure where first 16 items are hexadecimal value (0—F) and 17 th items corresponds to a terminator node.
- Extension node: It is a type of branch node but with one child. It is an optimized version of the branch node. It is a two item node where first portion signifies key part with size greater than one node and shared by atleast two different keys. Second part corresponds to a pointer to branch node.

Notably, to differentiate between leaf node and extension node, there is a concept of nibble. A nibble is added to the beginning of the key to differentiate both parity (even/odd length key) and terminator status (node is leaf or extension node). The lower significant bit signifies parity while next lowest tells terminator status. Moreover, if key length is even, an extra nibble is added to attain overall evenness. Fig. 8.6 shows illustration of Merkle Patricia tree.

- Binary heap: Binary heap comes under the category of a binary tree. Particularly, binary heap is a complete binary tree which implies each level except possibly the lowest one are completely filled and the lowest level is always filled from the left. Moreover, a binary heap is categorized as either a max-heap or a min heap as per the ordering property. In a max-heap, the key value stored in each node must be greater than equal to the key value in the node's children. In contrast, in a min-heap, the key value stored in each node must be less than or equal to key value in the node's children. Examples of min-heap and max-heap data structure is represented in Figs. 8.7 and 8.8. Ethereum blockchain uses binary heap data structure to solve the block-gas-limit and iteration problem of Ethereum. Ethereum gas is

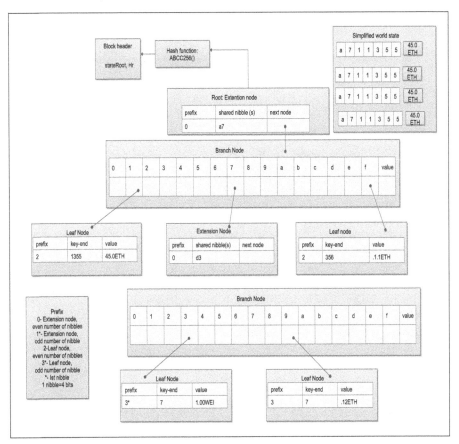

FIGURE 8.6
Illustration of Merkle Patricia tree data structure.

the price for executing certain operations in Ethereum blockchain. For instance, all Ethereum transactions are paid by the sender of the transaction. In such cases, intentionally an attacker can consume more gas by running arbitrary smart contracts for an incoming transaction. Besides, when users of Ethereum network insert data in a smart contract, it can result in too much gas cost to iterate through. In particular, if a developer relies on array data structure, an attacker can fill the array to the mark where iterating via it can result in more gas cost than it should be used for a single transaction to execute. Clearly, a binary heap resolves this issue as this data structure does not demand iteration via all elements of the tree, rather it only iterates through tree's height. Moreover, the self-balancing property of max heap preserves degenerating a tree which leads to $O(log\ n)$ cost even for the worst case (for a total of n elements).

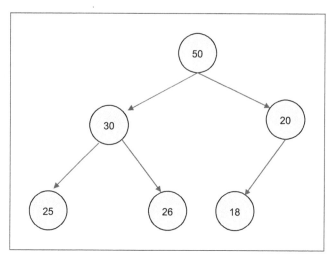

FIGURE 8.7
Example of max-heap.

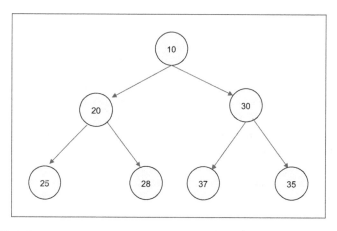

FIGURE 8.8
Example of min-heap.

Activity

Multiple Choice Questions

1. Which of the following data structure is used in blockchain?

   A. Merkle hash tree

   B. Tries

   C. Binary tree

   D. All of the above

2. What is the main purpose of using hash pointers for connectivity in blockchain?

   A. To prevent modifications in block

   B. To encrypt block

   C. To decrypt block

   D. To find nonce value of block

3. Which hashing algorithm is used by Bitcoin to compute Merkle hash?

   A MD4

   B MD5

   C SHA-256

   D All of these

4. What is the total space taken by trie data structure with w as total size of string in a set?

   A. $O(w)$

   B. $O(w^2)$

   C. $O(log\ w)$

   D. None of these

5. What is other name for Patricia tree?

   A. Prefix tree

   B. Suffix tree

   C. Max heap

   D. Binary heap

6. What is the main purpose of using merkle patricia tree?

A. To prevent modifications in block

B. To encrypt block

C. To decrypt block

D. To find nonce value of block

7. Which of the following node is a type of Merkle patricia tree?

   A. Leaf node

   B. Branch node

   C. Extension node

   D. All of these

8. Why does Ethereum uses binary heap data structure?

   A. To solve block gas limit and iteration problem

   B. To solve PoS problem

   C. To authenticate nodes on network

   D. To generate more ethers

9. Hash pointers can be used with any data structures with cycles?

   A True

   B False

10. What is the main purpose of using Merkle hash tree?

    A. To preserve integrity of block

    B. To decrypt a block

    C. To encrypt a block

    D. To find nonce value

1. d   2. a   3. c   4. a   5. a   6. a   7. d
8. a   9. b   10. a

Part III

Probabilistic Data Structures: An Overview

9

Introduction to Probabilistic Data Structures

9.1 Need of Probabilistic Data Structures

There is an exponential increase in the generation of data since last few years. This heavy data growth poses a challenge for industry and academia for storage and query processing. While analyzing logs for huge data sets, it is required to perform different query operations, such as counting unique items, computing frequency of a data item, searching any item in a set, etc. Additionally, we need to probe more complex datasets, such as images, videos, web pages, etc. Clearly, in order to process such query operations on data, it is essential to store data in computer memory. Tapes, hard disk, solid state drives are different types of memory available for a computing system. However, these different types of memory have different characteristics as presented in Fig. 9.1. For example, hard disks are mechanical devices and they are slow to access as compared to main memory integrated on a semiconductor chip which makes querying from database in hard disk time consuming. Hence, for a query, a processor has to every time access the hard disk for the data it requires which clearly would be a slow operation. Also, disk access proves costly as compared to the main memory (that's why a GB of main memory is much costlier than a GB of hard drive).

Besides, a process needs to be in the main memory in order to get executed so, it has to get swapped in from secondary memory to main memory as depicted in Fig. 9.2. Simultaneously, for a developer, main memory is easy to use as creating an array, linked list, or set in main memory is easy as compared to writing files in or out by using a Hadoop database or Apache Solr in secondary storage. These upcoming big data technologies are oftenly used in providing accurate analysis and decision making. These technologies provide distributed data storage and parallel processing. Although the distributed database Hadoop with a heavy processing engine (Spark, MapReduce) is good with batch processing framework where the aim is to improve job throughput rather than handling speed of access issue. Notably, the batch processing of data doesn't impose any time constraints so, it can be stored on disk and queries can be processed in batches. Additionally, the popular approach of using SQL for processing queries on database in secondary storage results

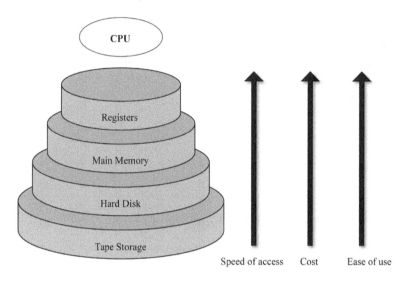

FIGURE 9.1
Computer memory hierarchy.

in high space complexity. For instance, Powerdrill is a column oriented data storage approach that faces the challenge of high memory and computational overhead for large datasets. However, streaming data requires real-time processing with a minimal delay which is possible with improved speed of access. Moreover, streaming data requires processing in a single pass. So, it is always better to work more in main memory for real-time processing of streaming data along with processing data in a single pass. Subsequently, the growing size of databases and applications dataset demands a compact data structure in order to get managed and handled properly.

> The current scenario of data generation has resulted in the release of new applications that need to deal with a huge volume of data. Conventional algorithms assumption of fitting data in main memory fails when dealing with such a huge amount of data. In this context, streaming algorithms (that process data in one or a few passes while consuming a limited amount of storage and time) are getting popular among researchers.

Unfortunately, in order to fix above mentioned issue, deterministic data structures, such as hash tables, array, binary search tree fail to deal with large data sets as it is difficult to accommodate large streaming data into memory at once. The conventional data structures can't go on the further side of linear

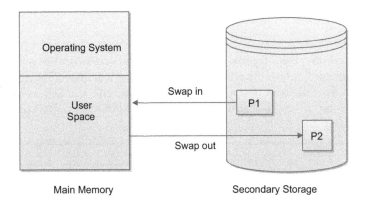

FIGURE 9.2
Memory management via swapping.

processing. Moreover, for large dataset, a polynomial running time complexity served by deterministic data structures is not beneficial. Also, 3 V's (volume, variety, and velocity) of data demands real-time analysis and processing. Additionally, complexity of data and noise in data is not defined. As size of data is not known in prior, one can't predict the memory requirements for storing data. Therefore, there is a need for an effective data structure that can support quick response time and efficient storage space in the main memory. To address these challenges, probabilistic data structures (PDS) are used recently by many researchers and programmers.

PDS allows performing basic query operation on data in the main memory itself. The use case of PDS is to process big data that does not fit inside the main memory. PDS are used for query operations, such as membership check, frequency check, similarity check, and cardinality check. Low memory requirements and good processing speed are the two unique properties of PDS. Nevertheless, the working of PDS is highly dependent on cryptographic hashing functions that enable randomness and flexibility in inserting data. Hash functions when applied on large data sets summarize it in a compact form which dramatically reduces storage requirements and its behavior is hard to predict. Here, also cryptographic hash functions have to satisfy three main requirements:

- Work factor: In order to defend brute force, hash function should be computationally expensive.

- Sticky state: It is impossible to create a state with a plausible input pattern.

- Diffusion: The associated output bit of hash function should be complex function of each input bit.

> Cryptographic hash functions are further categorized into keyed hash functions and unkeyed hash functions. A keyed hash function involves a secret key whereas, for a unkeyed hash function, the key is known to everyone. A keyed hash function is used for message authentication code (MAC).

Notably, PDS's are based on unkeyed hash function. With this insight, the nature of this data structure is randomized because of randomly selected hash functions. Also, in most cases, it is not important to know which item from the set has been matched, sometimes it is necessary to know only whether a match has bee made or not. Hence, only signatures of the items can be stored instead of the value. Over and above, PDS does not result in same structure every time for the same series of operations. Hence, PDS are also known as sketching data structures [116]. Notably, inaccuracy with a specific structure is expected with PDS. However, they have a constant query processing time and can be easily parallelized (as hashes have independent property) to be used for real-time data processing for a quick response. The coming sections will discuss the membership query, cardinality estimation, similarity search, and frequency estimation PDS in detail along with their Python implementation. Refer to Fig. 9.3 for taxonomy of PDS.

> Due to minimized memory requirements PDS are useful for big data and streaming data applications.

9.2 Deterministic Data Structures vs. Probabilistic Data Structures

IT professionals came across different deterministic data structures, for example, Array, hash tables, etc. However, with these in-memory conventional data structures operations such as insert, search, delete are performed with specific key value. These data structures results in deterministic (accurate) results. In contrast to this, results of operation in case of PDS could be probabilistic which implies results are approximate and not always definite. Notably, a conventional data structure can perform all set of operations that a PDS can do but only for small data sets. However, if data set is too large to fit into memory, conventional data structure fails for that case. Additionally, for streaming applications which demands data processing in one go, it is diffi-

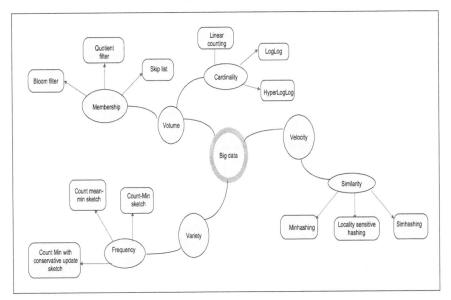

FIGURE 9.3
Taxonomy of PDS.

cult to handle with conventional data structures. Table 9.1 presents difference between deterministic data structures and probabilistic data structures.

9.3   Probabilistic Data Structures Applications

To build effective applications, one practice is an efficient use of data structure. Infact choosing a good data structure is a sign of good programmer. Any application involving large scale business can make use of PDS. Analyzing big data set, statistical analysis, mining huge data set are some use-cases of PDS. For instance, to check whether a particular item on Amazon is available for order or not. However, applications of PDS are not only limited to computer science field but also used in various filed. For example, in classification of DNA sequences into novel or already known genome.

- Duplication of data blocks is defined when more than one file share common data or when same data occurs at more than one place in a given file. Comparing each file with all other files involves heavy processing. PDS helps to solve this problem by storing fingerprint of data blocks rather than storing original data and matching hashes for finding duplicate files [71].

TABLE 9.1
Difference between deterministic and probabilistic data structures.

Deterministic data structures	Probabilistic data structures
No false positives are generated	False positives are generated while query processing
Provides optimal path	Provides good path instead of optimal
Not necessarily make use of hash functions	These data structures strictly uses hash function to process queries
Stores data in actual format	Stores signatures of data instead of actual data
Uses more memory over PDS	Uses much less memory over traditional data structures
Process queries in linear, sublinear, quadratic, factorial etc. time	Only process queries in constant time
Error free results are generated	Error in results are expected. However, errors rates have sppecific structure
Used when complete accuracy is required	Used when speed and low memory is required over exact accuracy
Stores data in inact form	Transform non-uniform distributed data to uniformly distributed data
Example: Array, linked list	Example: Bloom filter, HLL

- DDoS attack is defined when a particular machine is flooded by an attacker so that it may not be accessed by user when required. This demand needs for monitoring network traffic. One solution is to analyze destination IP address of IP packet and if counter value of any IP address exceeds predefined threshold that address is considered as suspicious. PDS can help analyzing these packets with less memory and constant time.

- Similarly, filtering of personal e-mail can be eased with PDS as spam detection system involves a big database having e-mail signatures [216].

- Growth in network traffic demands the need for network monitoring and traffic engineering. To operate efficiently, data centers, and PDS sketches for tasks, such as heavy hitter detection, traffic matrix estimation, traffic pattern detection etc. PDS sketches have proved to minimize the computation cost for information collection in the network [137].

- Cardinality estimation PDS is used to check how many unique IP addresses views an article on any particular site.

- PDS are also used for DNA sequences that involve categorization of sequence as novel or already existing genome. Sequencing implies calculating the right order of base pair in a DNA segment. Also, PDS are used for analyzing co-relation in DNA sequencing [109].

- A worth mentioning application of PDS is to find all elements in data set with a frequency greater than a predefined number. Such a characteristic of PDS is used to detect heavy hitter for a website.

- Likewise, PDS can be used for an application of spell check having 350000 dictionary words in the memory.

9.4   Probabilistic Data Structure Challenges

PDS optimizes algorithm performance by using fixed or sublinear memory and by providing constant execution time. However, the biggest challenge faced by PDS is that they can't provide exact answers and shows some probability of error. However, this error can be controlled with a trade-off with resources of PDS. Hence, for cases where reduced accuracy is unacceptable (such as- bank account, military applications) use of PDS is not recommended. Nevertheless, for cases (such as- recommending a movie, counting unique visitors, preventing DDoS attack) where cost of relatively small mistakes is low, PDS can be recommended.

Activity

Multiple Choice Questions

1. Which of the following memory has slowest speed of access?

    A. Registers

    B. Main memory

    C. Hard disk

    D. Tape storage

2. What are the requirements for a cryptographic hash function?

    A. One-way

    B. Work factor

    C. Diffusion

    D. All of the above

3. In keyed hash function, key is known to everyone.

    A. True

    B. False

4. Which of the following memory has maximum ease of use?

    A. Registers

    B. Main memory

    C. Hard disk

    D. Tape storage

5. Which of following statement about PDS is false?

    • PDS are also known as sketching data structure

    • PDS ae also know as deterministic data structure

    • Results of PDS operations have some error

    • Bloom filter is an example of PDS

6. Which of the following is an example of cardinality estimation PDS?

    A. HyperLogLog

    B. BF

    C. Skiplist

    D. Minhashing

7. Which of the following is an example of membership query PDS?

   A. Cuckoo filter

   B. Minhashing

   C. Simhashing

   D. LogLog

8. Which of the following is an example of frequency query PDS?

   A. Cuckoo filter

   B. CMS

   C. Simhashing

   D. LogLog

9. PDS are useful for big data and streaming data applications

   A. True

   B. False

10. Which of the following is an example of PDS?

    A. Detecting DDoS attack

    B. Spell checker

    C. Monitoring IP traffic

    D. All of the above

1. d	2. d	3. b	4. a	5. b	6. a	7. a
8. b	9. a	10. d				

10

Membership Query Probabilistic Data Structures

10.1 Membership Query Probabilistic Data Structures

Oftentimes while processing streaming IoT data, searching for a particular item is required with minimum latency and space. The aim of membership query probabilistic data structures (MSQ PDS) is to check the presence of an element x in a large set (S) of elements. The membership query operation using a linked list, array or a balanced binary tree requires a memory space linear to the size of set S. Hash table also has a larger size so, the memory it takes will also be larger. On the other hand, MSQ PDS are getting popular for handling queries of big data and streaming applications as these data structures consume less memory. Also, MSQ PDS provides constant query time. In order to provide optimized space efficiency, as opposed to storing the entire set of data, MSQ PDS stores summarized form of data using hashing. Table 10.1 represents a comparison in space and time complexity for membership query operation in different data structures. Insertion and deletion (for some specific MSQ PDS) are the operations that are supported by MSQ PDS.

Nevertheless, a predictable error is expected while using MSQ PDS. However, here errors are managed under a predefined marginal threshold with a trade-off between accuracy and storage requirements. Bloom Filter, quotient filter, and skiplist are popularly used PDS under this category which will be discussed further in this chapter. Moreover, the popularity of Bloom filter resulted in its various variants with some extra capability which is not supported by standard Bloom filter. However, being a part of error prone approach, bloom filter, and quotient filter return results with false positive on membership query whereas skip list doesn't return any error.

False positive implies that even if an element is not present in the set, query result may output true whereas false negative implies that for the presence of an element query results in negative results. The difference between false positive and false negative has been represented in Fig. 10.1. Additionally, the precision and recall value for the model can be computed from Eqs. 10.1 and 10.2 respectively where precision describes how accurate the calculated results are out of total positive predictions and recall depicts the proportion

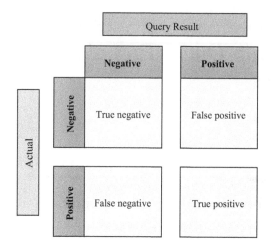

FIGURE 10.1
False positive vs. false negative.

of correctly identified actual positive. The next topic discusses the concept of Bloom filter.

$$Precision = \frac{True\,positive}{True\,positive + False\,positive} \qquad (10.1)$$

$$Recall = \frac{True\,positive}{True\,positive + False\,negative} \qquad (10.2)$$

TABLE 10.1
Space and time complexity for searching in different data structures

	Linear DS	Non-linear DS	Hashing DS	Probabilistic DS
Example:	Array, Linked list	Graph, BST	Hash Tables	BF, QF, Skiplist
Space Complexity	$O(n)$	$O(n)$	$O(n)$	$O(m)$
Search Time	$O(n)$	$O(logn)$	$O(1)$	$O(k)$

n: data size, m: PDS size ($m <\!<n$), k: number of hash function, DS: Data structures, BST: Binary search trees

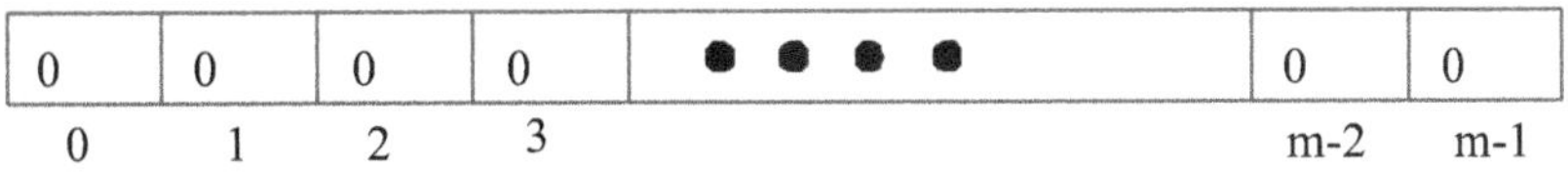

0	0	0	0	● ● ● ●		0	0
0	1	2	3			m-2	m-1

FIGURE 10.2
Representation of Bloom filter.

10.2 Bloom Filter and its Variants

The concept of BF was introduced by Burton H. Bloom back in 1970 [46]. BF resides inside the main memory and with BF its fast to check MSQ. Insertion and lookup are the two operations supported by standard BF. However, lookup operation of standard BF occasionally results in false positive but never in false negative. Apparently, BF should be used in cases where a bit of false positive can be accepted.

10.2.1 Structure of Bloom filter

BF is an array of m bits having index from 0 to m-1 as represented in Fig. 10.2. A single bit is used to represent each entry in the filter, i.e., 0 or 1. Along with this, BF employs k different independent and uniform hash functions. Instead of storing the data itself, BF utilizes hashing to store hashes of the data in a compact form. However, employed hash functions should have fast speed. The number of hash functions can be from 1 to m. The bits of BF are all initialized to zero. It first performs multiple times (k) hashing on each data item and then stores its hash value in the array of size m. Clearly, with an increase in the number of hash functions, the speed of BF gets slow. Notably, searching time complexity with BF is independent of the size of array and stored number of elements. For a fixed error rate, both insertion and lookup operations serve constant time complexity that is proportional to the number of hash functions used. Hence, by encoding information in a bit vector, BF can compactly represent a data and can be transmitted with a low bandwidth requirement. Despite proving quite beneficial, there are some disadvantages of BF which are listed as follows:

- Nevertheless, deletion is not supported by BF as resetting bits to 0 can introduce false negatives (the reseted bit might represent other element entry in the BF). However, the entire BF can be deleted once in a while with reset function. Although, there are various instances of BF which support deletion by keeping a record of variable count in memory, for example, Counting BF [79], Deletable BF [165] etc.

- Poor scaling out of main memory as in secondary memory use of multiple hash functions requires many random access to the disk.

- BF can not be resized dynamically.

- Inability to compute frequency count of each element. It can only check presence of any element.

  Insertion and membership query operations of BF are described as follows:

- To insert an element x, first apply k hash functions to the element x and the position corresponding to $h_i(x)(i = 1, 2, ..., k)$ is set to 1 if already not set.

- To check membership of an element x, pass the element x through k hash functions to get k array positions. If any of the bit corresponding to these positions is zero, then the element is definitely not in the set otherwise, it might be present. Also, it is probable that even if all k corresponding positions are 1, element might not be present into the set (false positive). While designing BF, one of the aims of developers is to design filter with very less false positive rate. However, false negative never happens for BF.

For example, consider a case where BF is 10 bit long with three hash functions (h_1, h_2, h_3) where $h_1 = x mod 6$, $h_2 = (x mod 4) mod 6$ and $h3 = (2 * x) mod 6$. To insert an element 11, pass the key (*11*) through all hash functions which results in 3 indices, i.e, $h_1 = 5, h_2 = 3, h_3 = 4$ and set these three resulting positions to 1. Similarly to insert element 3, positions 0, 3 will be set to 1 as represented in Fig. 10.3. However, membership query for key *5* returns definitely not in the set as positions corresponding to hash function h_2 is zero (See Fig. 10.4). The lookup operation for element 12 will result in false positive as 12 is not present in the set but position corresponding to all three hash functions, (i.e., 0, 0, 0) are set to 1 whereas for element 5, the scenario represents true positive. Simultaneously, Fig. 10.5 represents deletion and it could be observed that deletion of element 3 from the introduces false negative for element 11.

Union and intersection of standard BF

BF also support operation of union and intersection algebraic operations. Suppose *BF(X)* and *BF(Y)* are two BFs that use same size of filter and hash functions. Then, intersection and union operation between *BF(X)* and *BF(Y)* is given by:

$$BF(A \cap B) = BF(A) \cap BF(B) \tag{10.3}$$

$$BF(A \cup B) = BF(A) \cup BF(B) \tag{10.4}$$

Applications of BF

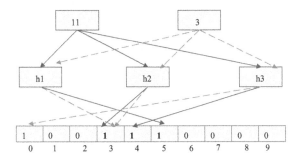

FIGURE 10.3
Insertion in BF.

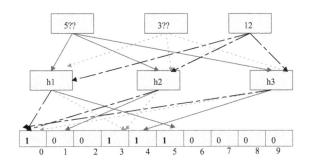

FIGURE 10.4
Lookup in BF.

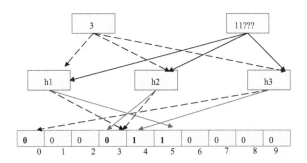

FIGURE 10.5
Deletion in BF.

- Yahoo mail use BF to compactly represent users contact list so that it gets easily fitted in browser cache memory. The use of BF avoids round trip to back end server for checking whether e-mail address of the sender is already present in contact list or not.

- BF is utilized by youtube to assure that recommended videos for a user doesnot match user's watch history.

- URL shortener uses BF to ensure unique URLs are generated.

- Tinder deploys BF to filter out repeats for right swipes.

- Apache HBase, Postgress databases are using BF to check if a particular record exists or not and in case of positive results, records will be fetched from memory.

- Facebook uses BF for one-hit-wonder. One-hit-wonder is used for the sites which get lots of traffic. It basically checks events that happen once and never again. So, BF can be used to probe if a particular web page has been visited before or not. If somebody visits the site only once, not much content and complicated computations will be served. In another case if somebody visits a website more often, more personalized content will be served. To realize this process, a BF is employed and visitors are checked against BF. In case of positive results, site will serve expensive content and for negative results, cached version is served.

- Quora the famous place to ask questions uses BF to filter out stories that users have seen before.

- BF supports spell checkers.

- BF is widely used for forwarding and routing of packets among different nodes.

- Bioinformatics [108].

- Prevention of DDoS attack by inserting BF with entries of malicious IP addresses. [161]

False Positive Probability in BF:
Clearly, the false positive rate is dependent on the number of 1's in the filter and on the count of hash functions.

Probability of a element passed to hash function and setting of a bit is given by $\frac{1}{m}$ and probability of not setting a bit (probability of getting false positive) is given by Eq. 10.5

$$P = 1 - \frac{1}{m} \tag{10.5}$$

As an element is passed through k hash functions. So, probability that an arbitrary bit is not set after mapping an element to k corresponding positions. is given by Eq. 10.6

$$P = \left(1 - \frac{1}{m}\right)^k \tag{10.6}$$

Now, for n insertions, probability that an arbitrary bit is not set after feeding through k hash functions is given by Eq. 10.7

$$P = \left(1 - \frac{1}{m}\right)^{kn} \tag{10.7}$$

Nevertheless, false positive rate (FPR) happens when a bit is falsely set to high. Hence, the probability of an arbitrary bit being set is given by Eq. 10.8

$$P = 1 - \left(1 - \frac{1}{m}\right)^{kn} \tag{10.8}$$

A new element is passed through k hash functions. Therefore, for k hash functions, Eq. 10.8 can be manipulated to give Eq. 10.9

$$P = \left(1 - e^{\frac{-kn}{m}}\right)^k \tag{10.9}$$

It is clear from Eq. 10.9 that FPR is a function of k, m and n. Incrementing the total number of elements and decrementing filter size, lead to increase in the FPR. However, by incrementing k, FPR gets reduced. Unfortunately, the computational complexity of system gets increased by increasing value of k. Also, if value of m is set as ∞, error rate tends to 0 whereas if value of m is 1, in this case error rate tends to 0 which implies 100% chance of getting error. To achieve minimum FPR, for a constant value of m and n for the optimum value of k is computed as depicted in Eq. 10.10. Hence, for a given k, m needs to be linearly increased with n to have a fixed FPR.

$$k_{opt} = ln(2)\frac{m}{n} = 0.7\frac{m}{n} \tag{10.10}$$

Moreover, by fixing a accepted target FPR *(p)* and utilizing optimal value of k, the size of filter m can be computed as:

$$P = \left(1 - e^{\frac{(-ln(2)\frac{m}{n})n}{m}}\right)^{ln(2)\frac{m}{n}} \tag{10.11}$$

which further results in

$$m = -\frac{nln(p)}{(ln(2))^2} \tag{10.12}$$

Thus, from Eq. 10.12, the optimal bits required per elements can be computed as:

$$\frac{m}{n} = -\frac{nln(p)}{ln2} \approx -1.44\log_2 p \tag{10.13}$$

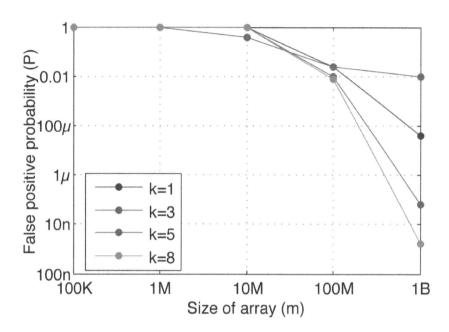

FIGURE 10.6
False positive rate vs. size of array [41].

The graph presented in Fig. 10.6 plots the change in FPR against filter size
for 10M elements [41]. It can be observed that rate of false positive decreases
with an increase in filter size. For a single hash function to achieve p less than
0.01 size of filter needs to be 100 times size of total elements, whereas choosing
$k = 5$ can provide the same in 100M.

10.2.2   Implementation of BF in Python

Listing 10.1
Defining a BF

```
class Bloom_Filter(object):
        def __init__(self, element_count, fpr):
                element_count : int
# Total Number of elements expected to be stored in bloom filter
                fpr : float
# False positive rate in decimal
                self.fpr = fpr
# Size of (m) bit array to use
                self.size = self.get_size(element_count, fpr)
# Total number of hash functions (k) to use
                self.total_hash_function = self.total_hash_function
                (self.size, element_count)
```

```
# Bit array of given size
                  self.bit_array = bitarray(self.size)
# initialize all bits of array to 0
                  self.bit_array.setall(0)
```

Listing 10.2
Inserting an element in a BF

```
def add(self, element):
   digests = []
   for i in range(self.total_hash_function):

# create hash digest for the given element.
# i act as seed to mmh3.hash() function that provides randomization
# With the different seed value, entire different digest is created
                  digest = mmh3.hash(element,i) % self.size
                  digests.append(digest)
# set the corresponding bit True in bit_array
                  self.bit_array[digest] = True
```

Listing 10.3
Lookup operation for an element in a BF

```
   def check(self, element):
           for i in range(self.total_hash_function):
                   digest = mmh3.hash(element,i) % self.size
                   if self.bit_array[digest] == False:

   # if any of the corresponding bit is False then the element is
not present in the BF  else there is probability that
element might exist in the array
                           return False
           return True
```

Listing 10.4
Computing size of array and number of hash functions.

```
def get_size(self,n,p):

# Compute the size of bit array (m)  using following formula
        m = -(n * lg(p)) / (lg(2)^2)
# number of total elements expected to be stored in filter
        n : int
        p : float
#False Positive rate (FPR) probability of BF in decimal
        m = -(n * math.log(p))/(math.log(2)**2)
        return int(m)


def total_hash_function(self, m, n):

# Return the total hash function(k) to be used using following formula
        k = (m/n) * lg(2)
# total size of bit array (m)
```

```
      m : int
#number of total elements expected to be stored in filter
      n : int
      k = (m/n) * math.log(2)
      return int(k)
```

10.2.3   Variants of BF

Some popular variants of BF are discussed as follows and their comparison is presented in Table 10.3.

10.2.3.1   Counting BF

As discussed earlier, deletion in standard BF requires a bit to be reset from 1 to 0 which may lead to the occurrence of false negative as a single arbitrary bit may represent multiple elements. As a solution to this problem, counting BF was designed by authors in [79] for exchanging information related to web cache among various proxies over the Internet.

Notably, the increase in web usage has effected fetch latency in the network. In this context, distributed proxy server improves latency by maintaining a web cache memory of each other proxy server information which allows for access of desired page from neighbor cache nearer to client instead of accessing from original web source. Web cache sharing can be benefited a lot from BF as total message exchange are quadratic in the total number of proxies. The advantage of web caching is to lower down the unnecessary bandwidth consumption because of increasing Internet request. In this process, each proxy server is employed with a compact and summarized information of other proxies cached documents. Web proxy servers periodically construct BF with their current cache entries and broadcast it to the network. For a cache miss, proxy server probes BF for cache hit in other proxies. Queries are then sent to the proxies with positive results. The false positive probabilities are compensated by reduction in bandwidth consumption as BF refrains the transfer of full list of URL cache summaries. The concept of distributed web caching is represented in Fig. 10.7.

Here, in counting BF, rather than using a single bit for representing each entry in the filter, a fixed size counter value is used to track the count of element hashed to that position. In order to avoid counter overflow, poison approximation suggests 4 bits per counter for majority of applications. Instead of just checking the presence of an element, counting BF is used to check the occurrence of elements for θ or more times where θ implies count threshold. For instance, if $\theta=2$ for one hit wonder case it implies one hit or two hits for a particular event. Similar to standard BF, counting BF also generates false positive. However, unlike standard BF, counting BF can lead to false negative if a never inserted element is tried to be removed from the filter. The parameters m, n, k are also defined same as in standard BF. However, counting BF results in wastage of space as reported in [51].

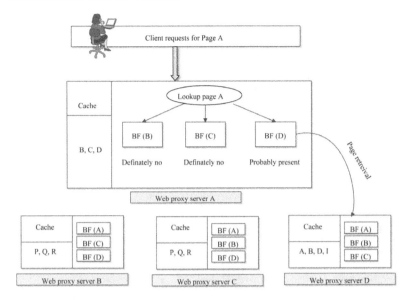

FIGURE 10.7
Distributed web caching.

Initially, all bits in this filter are zero. Operations supported by couting BF are described as follows:

- Insertion: To insert an element, pass it through k hash functions and k counters corresponding to these hash functions are incremented by one. To explain this concept, consider a BF with 3 hash functions, i.e., h_1, h_2, h_3) where $h_1 = x mod 10$, $h_2 = (2x + 3) mod 10$, $h3 = (2 * x) mod 10$, and x represents number to be inserted. The insertion of elements 9, 15, 8 are represented in Fig. 10.8. The hash index corresponding to each element is:
  $h_1(9) = 9, h_2(9) = 1, h_3(9) = 8$
  $h_1(15) = 5, h_2(15) = 3, h_3(15) = 0$
  $h_1(8) = 8, h_2(8) = 9, h_3(9) = 6$

- Lookup: While membership query for an element, feed the element to k hash functions. If any bit mapped to these corresponding locations is zero, it implies that element is definitely not in the set otherwise, it may be present. The membership query for element 9 and 15 results in true positive whereas for element 13 a false positive is reported as represented in Fig. 10.9 ($h_1(13) = 5, h_2(13) = 3, h_3(13) = 4$).

- Deletion: To delete an element simply decrement the counter value of the corresponding location by one as represented in Fig. 10.10 for element 8. In addition to this, Fig. 10.11 represent case where element 13 which is

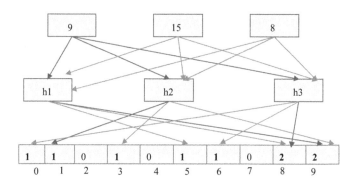

FIGURE 10.8
Insertion in Counting BF.

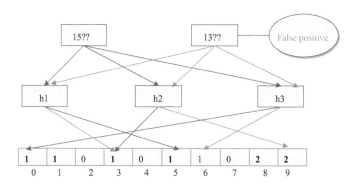

FIGURE 10.9
Lookup in Counting BF.

never added to the filter is deleted and subsequently membership query for element 8 results in a false negative. Nevertheless, counting BF supports deletion but its space cannot be extended on demand [92].

Counting overflow is however an disadvantage of counting BF. If an counter value reaches $2^w - 1$, (where w represents width of the counter), it cannot be incremented after this point. Counting BF also supports the same applications as described for standard BF. Differently, a Counting BF can be incorporated in place of BF to allow deletion of least recently used web information from web cache. A worth application of counting BF is to detect DDoS attacks by setting an approximate count on access of given webpage in a short timespan.

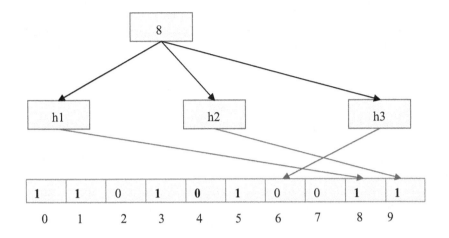

FIGURE 10.10
Deletion in Counting BF.

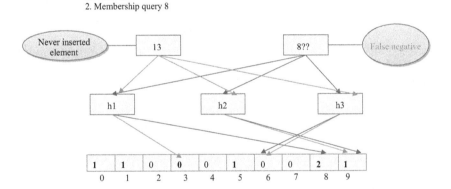

FIGURE 10.11
Understanding false negative for Counting BF.

10.2.3.2 Compressed BF

The intension behind the introduction of compressed BF [146] is to enable BF to be passed as a message among different network nodes. Compression is an effective technique to reduce transmission size and compressing a BF can improve network performance. Arithmetic coding is however recommended by authors for fast compression process. Clearly, here developers are concerned for optimizing transmission size in a network with heavy network traffic. Along with reducing bits to be broadcasted, false positive rate and lookup cost also get reduced. Unfortunately, compression and decompression increase processing costs. Here, hash function is not optimized for m and n rather for transmission size (which is not necessarily m but a compressed array). However, false positive probability is targeted to minimize after compression.

In standard BF, the main concern of the developers is to minimize the probability of false positive by manipulating k for a fixed value of m and n. The standard BF is optimized for $k_{\text{opt}} = ln(2)\frac{m}{n} = 0.7\frac{m}{n}$ when each bit position has $\frac{1}{2}$ probability of being set as 0 or 1. Although, in compressed BF, k is selected so that the probability of each array entry being 1 if $\frac{1}{3}$. Hence, resulting unbalanced filter will contain $\frac{1}{3}$ 1's and $\frac{2}{3}$ 0's so that it is easy to compress. This feature is leveraged to compress m bit array and to suppress its transmission size. To achieve this, reduced number of hash functions are employed for large filter size so that less bits than standard BF are transmitted in the network with low FPR. Specifically, with same number of bits to transfer, compressed BF achieves lower FPR over standard BF. Notably, the FPR is lower down to $0.5^{(z/n)}$, where z is the array size after compression. Here, authors have concluded that with the increase in size of filter it is possible to minimize the use of hash functions. Table 10.2 shows the result when 8 bits per element are used for transmission, i.e., $\frac{z}{n} = 8$ Similar to standard BF, completely random hash functions are used and deletion of elements is not possible. Also, a large value of w can lead to space wastage due to number of unused zeros. Hence, deciding the right value of w is a complex trade-off that depends on type of application and distribution of data. Moreover, other variants of BF such as counting BF can be benefited from this compression. At the receiving node, BF is decompressed. Clearly, this filter still demands larger memory space at the endpoints. Specifically, compressed BF is utilized in P2P sharing among distributed nodes. However, lightweight nodes with few computing powers and memory resources may fail for this complicated algorithm.

TABLE 10.2

Case when 8 bits per elements are used for compression.

Array bits per element	$\frac{m}{n}$	8	14	92
Transmission bits per element	$\frac{z}{n}$	8	7.293	7.293
Hash function	k	6	2	1
False positive rate	P	0.0216	0.0177	0.0108

n: data size, m: BFsize k: number of hash function, z: desired compressed size

10.2.3.3 Spectral BF

Unfortunately, standard BF doesn't support multiset, i.e., it doesn't allow query for multiplicities of an element if an element is repeating more than once in a set. In 2003, spectral BF [65] was designed specifically to support multiset and preferred to be used for streaming data. In fact spectral BF is an optimized extension of counting BF. The term spectral signifies that the multiplicities of element are supported within a requested spectrum. Improved lookup, enhanced accuracy and support of deletion are the reasons for adopting spectral BF over standard BF. Similar to counting BF, a m counter array is used rather than a bit vector. All the counters are initialized to zero. However, the usage of counter instead of single bit increases up the space requirements. Along with insertion and lookup operations, spectral BF supports deletion as well. The time complexity for all these operations is constant, i.e., $O(1)$. Handling ad-hoc iceberg queries, spectral Bloomjoins, providing fast aggressive index are some of the use cases of spectral BF. Ad-hoc iceberg queries perform queries for a threshold specified at query time and return a small portion of data. The facility of spectral Bloomjoins reduces the common rounds for remote databases sites while performing joins in order to minimize complexity and network usage. Moreover, spectral BF is used for scenarios that demands an index on a relation for frequency count queries, for instance, bifocal sampling. Spectral BF employs two scheme for its operations, i.e., minimal increase and recurring minimum. The former is suited for insertion and lookup whereas the later can support deletion as well. For sequence that requires insertions and lookup only, minimal increase shows improved performance over recurring minimum. $O(N) + O(m) + N$ is the total space requirement for this data structure where N is the overall length of array and m is the number of unique elements inserted into array. Now, we will discuss the two spectral BF scheme one by one.

Minimal Increase: This scheme is based on key insight that minimal counter has the most appropriate results for k counter positions corresponding to k hash functions as other items could also be hashed to same locations in large datasets. With this insight, for a increment operation, only minimal valued counter are incremented and rest are kept intact. For a multiset S, say f_x be the frequency of element x in the set.

- Insertion: While inserting an element, positions corresponding to k hash functions are calculated and only minimal valued counter value is incremented by 1. Consider a spectral BF with *10* counter values and *3* hash functions, i.e., $h_1 = x mod 10$, $h_2 = (2x + 3) mod 10$, $h3 = (2*x) mod 10$. Fig. 10.12 represents insertion with minimal increase scheme. Here, element 9, 15, 8, 9, 8, 9 are inserted in series and while insertion only minimal counter value is incremented by 1. For instance, while inserting element 8 for the first time, hash functions returned 8, 9, 6 as array location which has data 1, 1, 0 respectively. So while inserting 8, only value at location

6, i.e., 0 is incremented. However, for second time insertion of element 9, hash functions returned 9, 1, 8 locations which has value 1, 1, 1. As all three places have same counter values, so all get incremented by 1.

- Frequency query: A frequency count query for element x returns f_x. After feeding through k hash function, return the minimum value among the k locations. Fig. 10.13 represents lookup operation with minimal increase scheme. Here, query for element 8 returned 2 as location corresponding to hash functions, i.e., 8, 9, 6 has value 3, 3, 2 respectively and minimum of them which is 2 is returned for frequency query result. Also, query for element 13 returned 1 despite the fact it is not present in the set which is clearly a false positive.

- Deletion: Deletion is not preferable while using minimal increase. As all counter values are not incremented while inserting an element (only minimal counter values are incremented) so, the deletion operation may result in false negative. Fig. 10.14 represents occurrence of false negative while performing deletion in spectral BF. Deletion of element 9 will decrement the counter value of locations 9, 1, 8 by 1 and consequently frequency query for element 8 will return 1 which should be actually 2 as elements as 2 occurrences.

Recurring Minimum: Recurring Minimum employs two different spectral BF's, primary (F_1), secondary (F_2). The key logic for recurring minimum is that elements facing errors while querying have less chances for recurring minima counter values. Here, the items with recurring minima counter values corresponding to k hash functions are maintained in primary spectral BF whereas elements with unique minimum counter values are maintained in secondary spectral BF. Hence, the secondary BF stores elements which faces higher error rates. Nevertheless, hashing twice into BF in case of unique minimum makes recurring minimum a complex method. Operations supported by recurring minimum scheme is discussed as follows.

- Insertion: To insert an item x, increment the corresponding k counters in primary BF. Next, check whether element x has recurring minimum counter value, if so continue the counter value process. Otherwise, if x has single minimum counter value, check for x in secondary BF and increment counter. If not found there, insert x to secondary Spectral BF with a value equal to minimal counter value retrieved from primary BF.

- Frequency query: To query an element, first probe primary BF and check if an element has recurring minimum then return minimum counter value. Otherwise search in secondary BF and the minimum counter value from secondary BF is returned if value is greater than zero, if not minimum counter value from primary BF is returned.

- Deletion: To delete an element, first delete the counter value by 1 in primary SBF. Also, if it has single minimum, decrement its counter value in

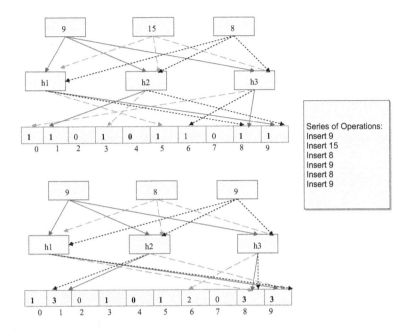

FIGURE 10.12
Insertion in spectral BF following minimal increase scheme.

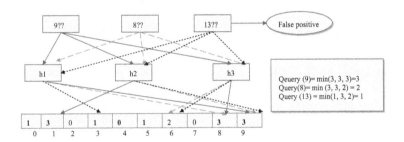

FIGURE 10.13
Lookup operation in spectral BF following minimal increase scheme.

secondary BF as well. Due to the reason that an element is inserted both to primary and secondary BF, false negative can never happen.

10.2.3.4   Deletable Bloom Filter (DBF)

Deletable BF (DBF) [165] was introduced to solve the problem of false negatives that happens while deleting elements in counting BF. However, instead

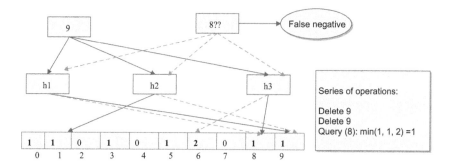

FIGURE 10.14
Deletion operation in spectral BF following minimal increase scheme.

of employing a counter array like counting BF, a bit array of m bits is used. The key insight behind DBF is that it tries to locate the bit region where collision while inserting an element can take place and deletion can only be done in collision free area. Here a bit array of m bits is divided into r region and each region should contain $\frac{m'}{r}$ bits each where $m' = m - r$. At the starting of m bit array, a collision bitmap of size r is kept to code and these r bits are initialized to 0. 1 in collision bitmap is marked for a collision prone area whereas zero represents a collision free region. A key question while designing BF is to choose the value of r as this value decides the capability of a BF to remove elements and FPR. The false positive probability for DBF is calculated as:

$$P = \left[1 - \left(1 - \frac{1}{m-r}\right)^{k*n}\right]^k \tag{10.14}$$

where, n is the total number of elements to be inserted. Operations supported by DBF are described as follows:

- Insertion: To insert an element, the k positions corresponding to k hash functions are set to 1. If any cell among k locations is found to be already 1, it represents case of collision and in response to this collision, the bit corresponding to the region where collision happened in collision bitmap is set to 1. Fig. 10.15 represents insertion in DBF. Here, element 15, 9, 8, 4 are inserted in series with 3 hash functions as: $h_1 = x mod 11$, $h_2 = (2x + 3) mod 11$, $h3 = (2 * x) mod 11$. For element 9, no collision is detected whereas for element 8, collision is detected at 8th location in region 3. So, the corresponding bit in the collision bitmap is set to 1. Similarly, for element 4, collision happens in region 1, 2, and 3 so these same positions in collision bitmap are set to 1.

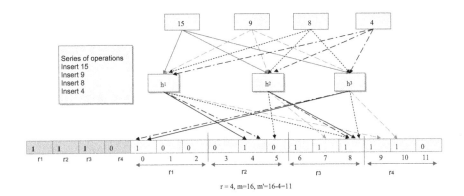

FIGURE 10.15
Insertion operation in deletable BF.

- Lookup query: To query an element, pass the element in question through k hash functions and if any of k location is 0, the element is not in set otherwise it might be present.

- Deletion: To delete, among k computed hashed locations, reset only those bits that lie in collision free zone. If all k bits corresponding to hash functions are located in collision prone area, then the element is non-deletable. Hence, the deletion of an element is only possible if atleast any one bit among k can be reset to 0. This way false negative are avoided but false positives are still possible. Fig. 10.16 represents deletion for DBF. As shown in the figure element 15 cannot be deleted because corresponding hashed locations, i.e., 4, 0, 8 all lies in collision prone area whereas element 9 is successfully deleted as among corresponding hashed locations 9th, 10th location lies in collision free area.

10.2.3.5 Stable BF

Unfortunately, the count of zero in BF decreases with time and there reaches a point when all the queries are answered as probably in the set. The reason behind introduction of SBF is to eliminate duplicates in the streaming data and to evict stale data before error reaches a pre-defined threshold value. Stable BF creates space for more recent items as this data is of more importance than the stale one. Similar to counting BF, an array of d-bit counters is used here and all counters are initialized to 0. So, maximum counter value can reach $2^d - 1$. To deal with stale data, Stable BF evicts stale data to create space for new data. Query processing, URL crawling, monitoring distinct IP addresses, graph processing are some of the applications of Stable BF.

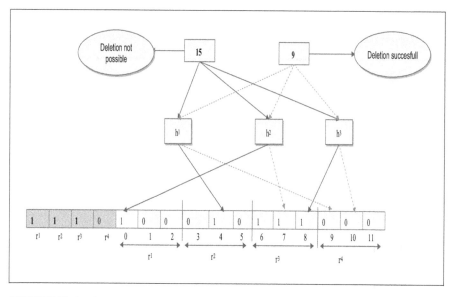

FIGURE 10.16
Deletion operation in DBF.

- Insertion: To insert an item, pass it through k hash functions. After some point when the number of zeros becomes constant, update Stable BF. To update, randomly p counter value is decremented by 1. After this step, all k computed hash locations are set to a maximum value.

- Checking duplicacy: To check duplicate value, query and check whether k hashed cells is hashed to 0 or 1. For a case where any cell returns 0, there is no duplicate item in te set otherwise duplicacy exist. However, randomly setting bits to 0 may result in false negative. Here, false negative is defined as a situation when query for duplicate item is answered as distinct. Also, false negative is dependent on input data distribution. For the elements that don't have predecessor, the chances of false negative are zero.

Moreover, Stable BF guarantees a tight upper bound on FPR while introducing false negative due to randomly eviction of stale information. Setting $p=0$ and $d=1$, Stable BF behaves as SBF. Fig. 10.17 represents a case for $p=2$ and $d=3$.

10.2.3.6   Retouched Bloom Filter (RBF)

One approach to reduce false positive is by increasing the size of bit vector. However, this approach can lead to increased memory usage. Another BF variant to decrease FPR from the filter is introduced by Donnet *et al.* [73] and

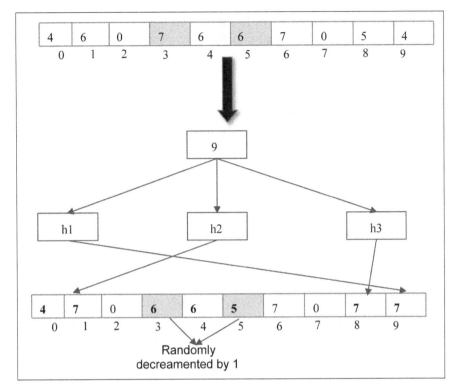

FIGURE 10.17
Understanding Stable BF.

named as RBF. This filter also enhances flexibility of the system. Here, false positives that are more troublesome over others are tried to be removed from the filter. However, this approach introduces random false negatives. False negatives are compensated with the advantage that more concerning false positives are handled. Here the false positives are tried to be identified after the construction of BF but before it has been used. Retouched BF randomly removes some false positive with a trade-off against introducing some false negatives. Notably, false negatives doesn't happen in standard BF.

RBF works by resetting some chosen bits in bit vector to 0 in order to reduce FPR. This process of RBF is named as bit clearing process. Clearly, for an element if any position corresponding to k hash functions are reset to 0 in bit clearing process, it will result in false negative. The bit clearing process can be randomized or selective. The results of RBF are concluded on a metric χ. If the value of this metric is greater than 1, it implies that removed false positive proportion is higher over generated false negative proportion whereas a value lesser than 1 represents that removed false positive proportion is lower than generated false negative.

- Randomized Bit clearing RBF: In random bit clearing process, randomly some bits are reset to 0, despite of the logic whether these bits are reset to 0. For randomized bit clearing process, it is observed that value of χ is calculated as 1 which implies that overall error rate for the system is maintained.

- Selective bit clearing RBF: Unlike randomized bit clearing, only those bits are reset to zero, that contributes to false positive. Selective clearing process has 4 algorithms to proceed which are discussed as follows:

  - Random selection: The first one is random selection that doesn't demand any intelligence for selective clearing process. Here, unlike randomized bit clearing process instead of resetting random bits in bit vector, only a bit among k available can be reset. Here, only one bit is reset that is related with false positive of troublesome keys.

  - Minimum false negative selection: Here, aim is to reduce the probability of occurrence of false negative that are generated with selective clearing process. This is processed by setting locally a counting vector that stores quantity of recorded elements. This algorithm considers possibility of hash collision in the bit vector among the hashed key of the element belonging to a set. The disadvantage with this algorithm is over estimation.

  - Maximum false positive selection: This algorithm aims to remove maximum false positive. For every troublesome key to eliminate that was not previously deleted, among k hashed, chose the position to be reseted that decreaments the number of false positive.

  - Ratio selection: The last algorithm is ratio selection which is a combination of minimum false negative selection and maximum false positive selection algorithm. This also aims to minimizes the generated false negatives and to maximize the removal of false positives.

Selective clearing process decreases the false positive rate at a greater degree than increase in generated false positive numbers. Clearly, RBF incurs extra processing cost of key removal and this cost is a multiple of RBF parameters such as- number of hash functions. For further details and involved mathematics user may refer to [73].

10.2.3.7   Dynamic Bloom Filter

As previously mentioned that BFs are not good for dynamic set, i.e., set whose size changes over time. Static set cannot perform operations of addition and deletion operation with standard BF. BF only works well for sets whose size is known in advance. Moreover, in BF target FPR threshold is computed after knowing the size of total elements. Specifically for applications that does not have any information about upper bound on cardinality of sets, it is difficult to decide BF size. In case, the number of elements exceeds the threshold of set size, SBF becomes quite unsuccessful because of occurrence of too many false positives. Moreover, for the distributed application scenario, all nodes on the network have to adopt similar configuration with an aim to achieve interoperability of standard BF among nodes. To handle such a case, nodes reconstruct their BF if cardinality size of even any one node exceeds the threshold value. For most stand alone applications, that have prior information about upper bound on total number of elements for a dynamic set, a larger space than known upperbound is allocated so that all items can be represented. However, this approach reduces the space efficiency of standard BF.

As a solution to this problem of standard BF, dynamic BF was introduced. For stand alone applications, dynamic BF can insert an item on demand. For distributed applications, dynamic BF handles interoperability issues among nodes as it consumes a suitable memory in order to reduce unnecessary waste and transmission overhead. Also, it controls rate of false match probability at an acceptable level even with an increasing number of elements. Here, in dynamic BF, the false positive probability is referred to as false match probability. Notably, dynamic BF can support static set as well. Here, a BF is called "active" if false probability rate is below a predefined upperbound, otherwise it is referred as full. A dynamic BF comprises of s homogeneous standard BFs. The s is initialized with value 1 and it is in active state. The insertion of elements can only be done in an active BF and a new BF is appended after the previous active BF gets full. Fig. 10.18 represents the data structure of dynamic BF. Let N_R is the count of elements added to BF. Nevertheless, the dynamic BF is initialized with upper bound on false match probability of dynamic BF , max value of s, upper bound on false positive rate of standard BF, filter size m of each standard BF, the capacity C that is maximum number of items to be stored in one standard BF. To create a dynamic BF, initialize one standard BF with the above mentioned parameters. The operations supported by dynamic BF is discussed as follows:

- Insertion: To insert an element, first locate active BF from given dynamic BF. If the current BF is not active, the next BF is employed as new active BF and value of s is incremented by one. Pass the element through k hash functions and insert the element in current active BF. Next increment the value of N_R by 1 for current BF. After multiple insertions, when number of elements exceeds capacity threshold c, i.e., $N_R>c$, a new BF is appended and this newly created BF is referred to as active BF. At a time only one BF is active and rest are inactive. The time complexity for the insertion operation is $O(k)$.

- Lookup query: To search an item, pass the item through k hash functions. If any of the BF stored in dynamic BF returned true, the element might be present into set otherwise if all BFs returned false, element is definitely not present into set. The time complexity for the lookup query is $O(k*s)$.

- Deletion: Deletion in dynamic BF is somehow difficult. To delete, first

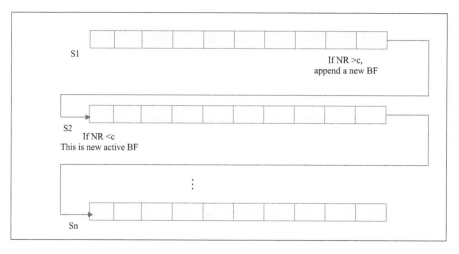

FIGURE 10.18
Data structure of dynamic BF.

check for the presence of an element in dynamic BF using lookup query operation discussed above. If the element is not present, deletion of element will be rejected. If the lookup query results are positive for a single BF, reset the corresponding k bits to 0 otherwise if multiple BFs returned 1, then dynamic BF don't delete the element in order to prevent occurrence of false negatives. The time complexity of the deletion operation is $O(k*s)$.

10.2.3.8 Cuckoo Filter

Similar to BF, cuckoo filter [78] provides fast membership query with great space efficiency. Additionally, cuckoo filter supports deletion, limited counting with same space complexity. Cuckoo filter is based on the concept of cuckoo hashing. Cuckoo hashing is known for its excellence in handling collisions for hashing based data structures. In cuckoo hashing, a cuckoo hash table is employed which comprises an array of buckets and an item is supposed to be inserted Here, two hash functions each for a table is used. Each item is hashed with two different hash functions and each hash function indexes into a bucket. The item is stored in any of the two buckets. The item is first tried to be stored in the first bucket if there is nothing stored there otherwise the item is stored in the second bucket if the corresponding location in the second bucket is empty. In case if the second bucket is not empty, then item stored in the second bucket is evicted and reinserted in alternate hash index. Next, the element is placed in empty location. Clearly, this procedure faces the problem of displacing the older key. If alternate hash location of older key is empty, it is quite easy to relocate otherwise older key has to displace another key. This process is repeated till an empty bucket is found. If this situation leads to a cycle, completely new hash functions are selected and the whole data struc-

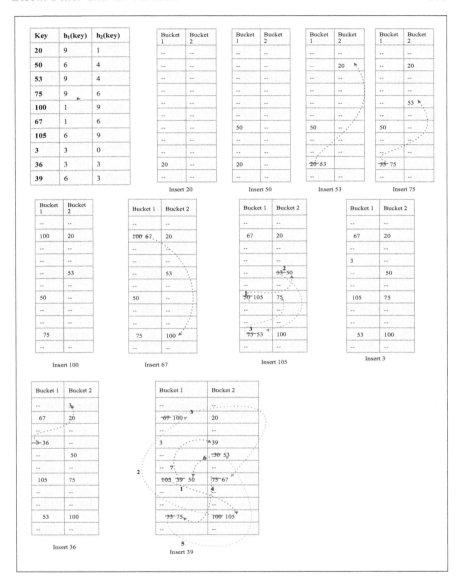

FIGURE 10.19
Insertion in cuckoo hashing.

ture is reconstructed again. Hence, the amortized complexity for insertion is *O(1)*. The query procedure probes both buckets to check item's presence. Fig. 10.19 represents the insertion of element 20, 50, 53, 75, 100, 67, 105, 3, 36, 39 in sequence.

A cuckoo filter is determined by its fingerprint and bucket size. For example, a *(3,5)* filter implies 3 bit length filter and each bucket can store 5 fingerprints. It is concluded that cuckoo filter consumes less space than standard BF if target FPR is less than 3%. The membership query performance of cuckoo filter is better than standard BF even when 95% space of the filter is consumed. However, storing only fingerprint instead of actual item prevents insertion using standard cuckoo hashing. Here, the existing fingerprint has to be relocated to an alternate position instead of actual items. The operations of cuckoo filter are described as follows:

- Insertion: Here, the question is how to restore and rehash the original items for locating to alternate location? To deal with this problem, cuckoo filter employs "partial key cuckoo hashing" to find item's alternate location from its fingerprint. Here, for an item x, the index for two hash buckets is calculated as: $h_1(x) = hash(x)$ and $h_2 = h_1(x) + hash(f(x))$. By using XOR operation it is ensured that $h_1(x)$ can be computed using $h_2(x)$ and fingerprint of x. Thus to relocate a key from either of the location calculated by $h_1(x)$ or $h_2(x)$ the alternate location is computed by $j = i \oplus hash(f[i])$ where, i is the index location of bucket where item is originally stored and j is the index of alternate bucket. With this process, original value of item x is not required. Consider a cuckoo filter with two entries per 10 buckets as shown in Fig. 10.20 . To compute index location for item x use $h_1 = hash(x)$ and $h_2 = i_1 \oplus hash(f)$. Say i_1 and i_2 are the indices computed from these hash functions. This example uses shift fold method to compute fingerprint (f) for item x and hash of x is computed by $x mod 10$. To handle a collision, randomly pick i_1 or i_2 (say i) and displace fingerprint at bucket i to alternate bucket j using the formula $j = i \oplus hash(f(x))$. Following case may exist while inserting:
  Case1: Insert(131)

  (a) Use shift fold method to compute fingerprint f, $f= 13+1 = 14$.

  (b) $i_1(x) = hash(x) = hash(131) = 131 mod 10 = 1$

  (c) $i_2(x) = 1 \oplus (hash(14)) = 1 \oplus (14 mod 10) = 1 \oplus 4 = 5$

  (d) As index 1 is available, insert f at the same location.

  Case 2: Insert(1111)

  (a) $f(1111) = 11 + 11 = 22$

  (b) $i_1(1111) = 1111 mod 10 = 1$

  (c) $i_2(3333) = 1 \oplus (22 mod 10) = 1 \oplus 2 = 3$

  (d) As, both indices 1 and 5 are occupied, this represent collision case.

  (e) Randomly pick i_1 or i_2 and displace the fingerprint from selected location to other bucket. Suppose i_1 is selected, then $j = i_1 \oplus hash(f[i_2]) = 1 \oplus (hash(f[1])) = 1 \oplus (hash(14)) = 1 \oplus 4 = 5$.

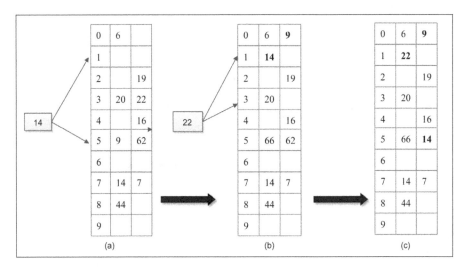

FIGURE 10.20
Insertion in cuckoo filter.

- Lookup: For an item x, first compute fingerprint of x and two indices for the bucket. Next, read the content of these two locations. If there is match then filter returns true otherwise false. This way false negatives are avoided as there are no overflows. False positives can happen if two elements have same fingerprint and also hash indices are same. Clearly, this process has $O(1)$ time complexity. However, FPR becomes high when filter gets full.

- Deletion: To delete an item, first follow the same procedure of lookup query for the element to be deleted. If there is no match, deletion is not possible, otherwise if there is a match, simply delete the copy of that fingerprint from the bucket. To avoid "false deletion", the entry of the element is not cleared. With this insight, false positive nature of the filter is unchanged after deletion. This process takes $O(1)$ time complexity.

However, unlike cuckoo hashing rather than storing original value, only fingerprints are stored in filter. Each element is stored in a f bit fingerprint. The space consumed by cuckoo filter is given by Eq. 10.15 where, ϵ specifies FPR, α is the maximum capacity of filter and B is the number of entries per bucket.

$$\frac{log_2(\frac{1}{\epsilon}) + log_2(2B)}{\alpha} \tag{10.15}$$

10.2.3.9   Hierarchical BF

In network terms, attribution is defined as a process of finding source and destination of some traffic. However, sometimes this process is difficult due to lack of logging mechanism for example, attacker may spoof address by using a

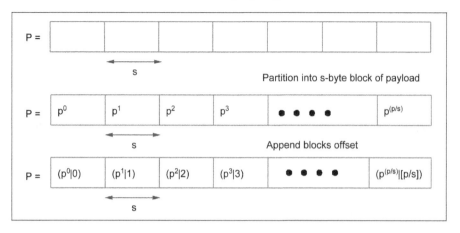

FIGURE 10.21
Hierarchical BF.

zombie machine. Hierarchical BF facilitates the process of payload attribution
where with a given payload, aim is to identify the sender or receiver of the
given payload. This could be beneficial to detect certain security attacks, such
as DDoS, spoofing. Shanmugasundarm et al. [168] basically extended BF in
order to support substring matching. As an advantage, this algorithm even
does not require full packet for attribution, only a significant portion is enough.
Along with this, the algorithm requires low storage requirements and also it
ensures the privacy of data by simply storing hashes of payload rather than
actual payloads.

Here, payload of each packet of length p is first divided into set of q multiple
blocks of size s. Each block is appended with its offset value. Next, each
block with its offset value is hashed and inserted into standard BF. This data
structure is named as block based BF with offset as shown in Fig. 10.21.

10.2.3.10   Stochastic Fair Blue

Although authors do not define this data structure as a variant of BF but it has
a lot in similar to working of BF. Stochastic Fair Blue (SFB) [81] is a technique
that uses counting BF along with blue algorithm. The authors proposed this
scheme in order to solve TCP's congestion control problem. It detects heavy
hitters to enhance the forwarding speed of multicast packets. SFB uses $N*k$
bins, where k is the number of levels with each having N bins along with
k hash functions. Also, each bin associates a dropping/marking probability
p_m. For each incoming packet, apply k hash functions to its connection ID
(source-destination address pair, source-destination port pair, and protocol)
and increments corresponding bin locations. If account of packets hashed to
a bin goes above the maximum size of bin, then increment p_m with a value

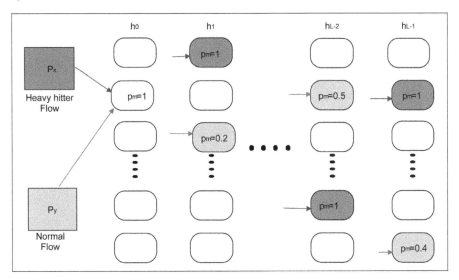

FIGURE 10.22
Stochastic fair blue example.

δ_1 for the bin; otherwise decrement by a value δ_2 in case the link is idle. A packet is placed in heavy hitter list if the value of p_m reaches to 1. In order to reduce FPR, authors have used the idea of conservative update. For a packet, extract p_{min} among corresponding k hash locations. Now, a packet is marked as heavy hitter if $p_{min} = 1$ and is then dropped. So, with BF heavy hitters can easily be detected with less space and less number of operation for each packet.

Fig. 10.22 represents an example of stochastic fair blue. As shown, packet p_x higher up p_m of all bins it is mapped into. However, packet p_y may map in the same bin as heavy hitter flow in a level but in other levels, it maps into normal bin. As p_{min} for packet p_y is 0.2<1, it is identified as normal flow whereas p_x is marked as heavy hitter.

10.3 Quotient Filter

After BF, Quotient Filter (QF) [40] is popular among programmers for checking approximate membership queries (AMQ), i.e., it also checks whether an element belongs to a set or not. QF is a cache friendly scheme based on quotienting technique [120] that even provides scalability outside the main memory.

TABLE 10.3
Comparison between different BF variants.

Year	Filter Name	Characteristics	Applications	Lookup Cost	Insertion Cost	Deletion Cost	Space Requirement	1	2	3	4	5	6
1970	Standard Bloom Filter [46]	• Space Efficient • Constant-time query	Routing and Forwarding, Data deduplication, Query and Search	$O(k)$	$O(k)$	–		×	×	×	×	×	×
1998	Counting BF [79]	• Supports frequency queries • 4 times space overhead compared to SBF	Web Caching, High speed routers, Monitoring and measurement	$O(k)$	$O(k)$	$O(k)$	More	×	~	✓	×	✓	×
2001	Compressed BF [146]	• Compress BF for transmission • Smaller FPR over SBF	P2P information sharing, Resource allocation, IP tracebacking	$O(k)$	$O(k)$	–	More	×	×	×	×	×	×
2003	Spectral BF [65]	• High computation complexity over SBF • Support frequency query	Bifocal Sampling, Ad-hoc iceberg queries, Bloomjoins	$O(k)$	$O(k)$	$O(k)$	More	✓	~	×	×	✓	×
2006	Stable BF [69]	• Evicts stale information to makes space for recent data	URL crawling, Selecting Distinct IP Addresses, Streaming data scenario	$O(k)$	$O(k)$	–	More	×	✓	×	×	✓	×
2006	Retouched BF [73]	• Reduces false positive at cost of false negative	P2P sharing, Resource Routing, Network packet processing	$O(k)$	$O(k)$	$O(k)$	Equal	×	×	×	×	✓	✓
2010	Deletable BF [165]	• False negative free deletion	Packet forwarding	$O(k)$	$O(k)$	$O(k)$	More	×	✓	×	×	×	×
2014	Cuckoo Filter [78]	• Better lookup and insertion performance over SBF • Easier to implement	Fast packet forwarding, Database management	$O(1)^{*}$	$O(1)$	$O(1)$	Less	×	✓	×	×	×	×
2006	Dynamic BF [93]	• High FPR • Partial deletion support	Node replication detection	$O(s * k)$	$O(k)$	$O(s * k)$	More	×	✓	✓	✓	×	×

Supports Multiset(1), Dynamism(2), Scalability(3), Parallelism(4), False negative(5), Bit resetting(6), k: Number of hash functions, *: amortized complexity, ~: Partially

Similar to BF, the membership query result answers "probably in the set" or "definitely not in the set" as QF also generates false positive errors. Increasing filter size can significantly reduce error probability of query whereas inserting more elements into the set can increase the false positive rates. However, no false negatives are generated for any query results. A typical use case of AMQ QF is in database tables stored on disk. Any access to the database stored on disk will first check QF for the particular key. If the filter returns positive results, the disk will be accessed otherwise not.

BF only provides beneficial when it is stored in the main memory. When BF size gets too large its performance significantly reduces. Another option is to store BF on disk but this approach requires too many random access to the disk because of the usage of multiple hash functions. Also, this approach will perform multiple input output operations. Moreover, in-memory buffering technique fails in providing scalability if BF size is much larger than in-memory buffer size. QF on the other hand, stores elements data really close to each other so as to avoid multiple random access. With this insight, QF uses a single hash function and provides ways to tackle high collision probability. However, the size consumed by QF is 20% larger than BF.

The QF is quite fascinated by the concept of hash tables where instead of storing actual elements, hashes of the element along with some meta data bits are stored. The additional meta data bits are used to handle collisions. Insertion, lookup, deletion, merging, resizing are the operations supported by QF. To perform QF operations, first pass the element x through a single hash function that in return generates p bit fingerprint. The fingerprint is further partitioned into two parts: remainder part which has r least significant bits and quotient part which has q most significant bits. The employed hash tables have a total of 2^q slots and the remainder part for any element is stored in location indexed by the quotient. Hard collision happens if different valued elements hash similar fingerprint whereas soft collision happens if two different value fingerprints have same quotient but different remainder.

Suppose a element k generate fingerprint k_f, and after partition lets its remainder be K_R and its quotient be K_Q. If K_R is stored exactly at slot K_Q, the slot is termed as canonical slot. For a soft collision, K_R is stored at next available slot to the right of location K_Q in sorted order. Insertion algorithm makes sure that all fingerprints with same quotient bits are stored contagiously and such a set forms a run. It may also be possible that runs first fingerprint may not get stored in its canonical slot as it may get shifted with already stored remainder of some different quotient. A run having its first fingerprint stored in canonical slot refers to the start of the cluster. A cluster may comprise more than one run which ends at an empty slot or start of some other cluster. Along with elements fingerprint, three additional bits are stored in the slot as shown in Fig. 10.23. These bits are explained as follows:

- *is_occupied*: If this bit is set, it implies that this slot is the canonical slot for some inserted element in the filter. It may be possible that the key is not stored in its canonical slot but stored somewhere else in the filter.

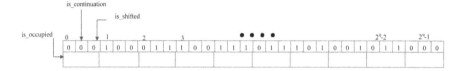

FIGURE 10.23
Structure of QF.

- *is_continuation*: If this bit is set, it implies that slot is occupied with some remainder but definitively not the first remainder of the run.

- *is_shifted*: If this bit is set, it implies that slot is holding a remainder that is not in its canonical slot.

However, with metadata bits, QF consumes 20% more space than BF (but less than counting BF) for the same data size. Also, throughput of lookup operation slows down 3 times. The only way false positive can happen is when there is a hard collision and its probability is given as: $1 - e^{\frac{-\alpha}{2^r}}$, where α is load factor defined as the fraction of total elements and number of slots. When a new element is inserted, its slot is marked occupied and additional bits are updated accordingly. The significance of different combination of additional bits are specified in Table 10.4. Operations of QF are discussed as follows:

Lookup: To query any element k follow the following steps.

- Hash the key to generate its fingerprint k_H.

- Next, partition k_H into quotient k_Q and remainder k_R. Clearly, canonical slot for element k is k_Q. If canonical slot has all metadata bits as false, it implies slot is not occupied. Hence, the element is definitely not present in the set.

- If k_Q is occupied, then locate the run for k. As it is previously mentioned, remainder with same quotient are stored contagiously and it forms a run. The first in a run might not be present in canonical slot, if entire run has been shifted right by some another run in left. So, to locate quotient run, first locate start of the cluster and then find number of run to skip in a cluster to reach run for k_R. For this:

  - Scan left for locating start of the cluster. If *is_shifted* for slots to the left of k_Q is false, it implies start of the cluster.

  - Scan right to keep track of running count that counts number of runs to skip in order to reach quotient run. The slots to the left of k_Q with *is_occupied* set implies another run to be skipped. For each value of *is_occupied* as 1, increment the running count and decrement one if *is_continuation* is clear (implies start of another run) until running

TABLE 10.4

Significance of possible combination of metadata bits.

1	2	3	Interpretation
0	0	0	This Slot is empty
0	0	1	This is start of run and remainder has been shifted from its canonical slot.
0	1	0	This combination is not used.
0	1	1	This remainder is not first remainder in a run and also it has been shifted from its canonical slot
1	0	0	This is first remainder in run that too in canonical slot.
1	0	1	This is holding first remainder in run that has been shifted from its canonical slot. In addition, the run meant for this slot exists that has been shifted right.
1	1	0	This combination is not used
1	1	1	This remainder is not first remainder in a run that has been shifted from its canonical slot. In addition, the run meant for this slot exists that has been shifted right.

1: is_occupied, 2: is_continuation, 3: is_shifted

count reaches zero. When the value of running count becomes zero it implies that quotient run has been reached.

- Next, remainder corresponding to the run with k_R is compared. If matches, the element k is probably present in the set otherwise definitely not in the filter.

Insertion:

- Pass the element k to be inserted through the hash function to compute its fingerprint. First, ensure that the key is not already inserted in filter by using lookup procedure described above. If not inserted already, then follow the next step.

- When the elements are inserted in a run, it is always done in sorted order. The element remainder may have to shift right in any slot even when they belong to same run and update the metadata bits accordingly. However, this shifting does not change the value of *is_occupied* bit.

- If a remainder is inserted at the starting of already existing run, this causes any previous remainder to be shifted to next available slot in right and in response set its *is_continuation* bit. The *is_shifted* also has to be reset in case remainder is shifted.

For understanding QF, consider an example with quotient size 4 and remainder size 28. Let the employed hash function generates a hash of 32 bit. First, element *144, 133, 4033* are added into QF as represented in Fig. 10.24 (a). Insertion for all 3 elements is done in canonical slot as these slots are not occupied.

Next, element 9999 is added. The canonical slot for this element is already occupied. It is observed that *is_shift* and *is_continuation* bit is not set which implies it is beginning of cluster and also runs start. The remainder for element 999 is greater than that of element 144, so it should be stored to the right of element 144, i.e., slot 2 and set its *is_shifted* and *is_continuation* bit. The change in QF after insertion of element 9999 is reflected in Fig. 10.24 (b).

Next, element 14023 is to be added. Since slot 2 is already in use but its *is_occupied* bit is 0. So, element 14023 has to be stored to next available slot to the right, i.e., slot 3 and set *is_shifted* bit for slot 3. Also, set *is_occupied* bit for slot 2 as it is a canonical slot for element 14023. The state of QF after insertion of element 14023 is represented in Fig. 10.24 (c).

Finally, element 55 is added into QF which after passing through hash function generates 0x10000001. Since the canonical slot 1 is not free. The *is_shifted* and *is_continuation* bit value for slot 1 is 0 which implies it is beginning of the cluster and also it is runs start. The remainder for element 55 is smaller than remainder of element 144. So, the existing remainder in slot 1 should be shifted right to slot 2 and accordingly set the *is_continuation* and *is_shifted* bit. The state of the QF after insertion of element 55 is represented in Fig. 10.24 (d).

Now, consider lookup query for element 4045. Say $f(4045) = 733433CD$. As the canonical slot 7 is occupied. The value of *is_occupied, is_continuation* and *is_shifted* infers that it is start of the cluster as well as start of run. See Fig. 10.24 (d). The next slot to the right, i.e., 8 is empty which infers that slot 7 itself is a start and end of a run. Next, the remainder for element 4045 is compared with existing remainder in slot 7. As the match for two values failed, so the element is definitely not present.

Next, consider the case for querying 133 whose fingerprint value is 48921258. It can be observed that slot 4 is already occupied. Also, the value of its *is_shifted* bit is 1 which implies that the element corresponding to the current remainder has been stored in its canonical slot and is shifted. The value 1 for *is_canonical* slot represents that run for which this slot is a canonical slot exists but has been shifted to the right. For locating start of the cluster, scan left from slot 4 and look for *is_shifted* as false, which is found to be slot 1. So, slot 1 indicates start of the cluster. Next, locate quotient run, for this scan to the left from slot 4 and check for *is_occupied*. If the value of *is_occupied* bit is 1 it implies another run to be skipped. There are 3 such slots, i.e., 1, 2 and 4 which indicate that run for element 4033 is third run in the cluster. The

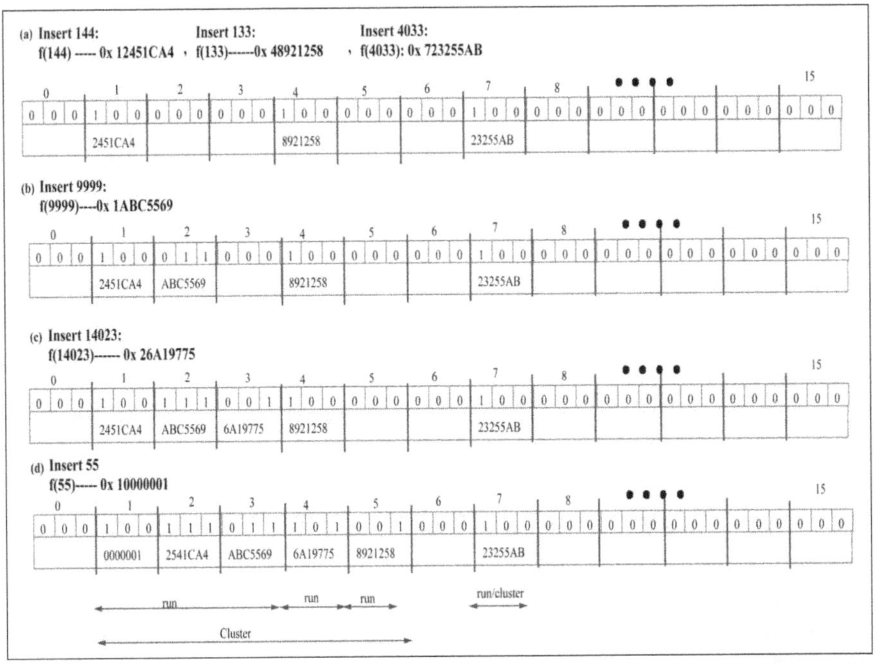
(a) Insert 144:
f(144) ----- 0x 12451CA4
Insert 133:
f(133)------0x 48921258
Insert 4033:
f(4033): 0x 723255AB
2451CA4
8921258
23255AB
(b) Insert 9999:
f(9999)----0x 1ABC5569
2451CA4
ABC5569
8921258
23255AB
(c) Insert 14023:
f(14023)------ 0x 26A19775
2451CA4
ABC5569
6A19775
8921258
23255AB
(d) Insert 55
f(55)----- 0x 10000001
0000001
2541CA4
ABC5569
6A19775
8921258
23255AB
run
run
run
run/cluster
Cluster

FIGURE 10.24
Insertion of elements in QF.

start of current run and end of previous run is detected by *is_continuation* bit being false. The first run is at index 1, second at index 4, and third is at index 5. Hence, index 5 is the quotient run for element 4033. Now, compare the remainder stored in quotient run that starts at index 5 with the remainder of the element in question. However, there is only one slot in that run. So, compare the remainder of the element 4033 with existing remainder at slot 5. As there is a match, so it is concluded that element 4033 is probably in the set.

Algorithm 1 Quotienting technique

Input:Fingerprint f
Output: Quotient f_q and remainder f_r

1: $f_r \leftarrow f \bmod 2^r$
2: return f_q, f_r

Algorithm 2 To find the run

Input: Canonical bucket index f_q

1: $i \leftarrow f_q$
2: **while** QF[i].is_shifted=1 **do**
3: $i \leftarrow i\text{-}1$
4: **end while**
5: $run_{start} \leftarrow i$
6: **while** $i \neq f_q$ **do**
7: **repeat**
8:   $run_{start} \leftarrow run_{start}+1$
9: **until** QF[run_{start}].is_continuation $\neq 1$
10: **repeat**
11:   $i \leftarrow i+1$
12: **until** QF[i].is_occupied=1
13: **end while**
14: $run_{end} \leftarrow run_{start}$
15: **repeat**
16: $run_{end} \leftarrow run_{end}+1$
17: **until** QF[run_{end}].is_continuation $\neq 1$
18: **Return** run_{start}, run_{end}

Algorithm 3 To test element in QF

Input: Element x, hash function h
Output: True for positive and false for negative result

1: $f \leftarrow h(x)$ f_q, $f_r \leftarrow f$
2: **if** QF[f_q.is_occupied$\neq 1$] **then**
3: return False
4: **else**
5: run_{start}, run_{end} $\leftarrow$**Find(f_q)**
6: **for** $i \leftarrow run_{start}$ to run_{end} **do**
7:   **if** QF[i] $=f_r$ **then**
8:    return True
9:   **end if**
10: **end for**
11: Return False
12: **end if**

10.4 Skip List

Skip list follows a linked list alike structure. However, the worst case time complexity for a search operation in linked list in $O(n)$ as the list is linearly traversed while searching whereas for a skip list it is $O(logn)$. For a set S of unique elements, skip list is defined as sequence of linked list S_0, S_1, S_2, ..., S_h. The lower list (base list) has height 0 and this list is supposed to contain all elements of set S in non-decreasing order. Also, each list S_l ($l = 0, 1, 2, ..., h$) contains special items $-\infty$ and $+\infty$. Each successive linked list in a series accommodate subset of elements from immediate previous list and the way subset of elements is chosen defines the type of linked list i.e., deterministic or probabilistic. Any element is inserted into new layer from immediate previous layer with a probability p. For probabilistic (or randomized) skip list, random coin flips are used to construct each higher level of elements whereas in deterministic (or perfect) skip list each higher level consists of $\frac{1}{2}$ of elements from immediate lower list. In probabilistic skiplist, each element is added to the next level with probability of $\frac{1}{2}$. As this chapter is all about PDS, so for the sake of brevity the main focus is on probabilistic type skip list. Unlike other data structures, skip list does not use hashing still, it is considered as probabilistic data structure as it is based on concept of probability to construct subsequent layer above original layer of skip list. The name of data structure skip list is defended as higher level skips some elements from lower list. The operations of skip list are defined as follows:

- Searching: To start searching an item i, start from top lists left most item, i.e., $-\infty$ in every case. At any current position say p, compare item i to be searched with with the item to the immediate right of p and store that element in a new variable say v, i.e., $v \leftarrow (E(r(p)))$ and follow:

  - If $i = v$, return v.
  - Otherwise if $(i > v)$, then move a single step towards right and if $i < v$, move a single step down and compare it to its immediate rightmost item. Repeat the same process until there is no option to go down which concludes that item is not in list.

The search procedure for element 80 is represented in Fig. 10.25. For n elements, the search time complexity for skip list is $O(logn)$ as at each level, number of items are cut down to half.

- Insertion: To insert an item follow the following steps:

  - First follow the search algorithm to locate the position of the element at the bottom level.
  - Next, toss a biased coin more than one time till a tail is encountered. Observe the count of coin showing head before a tail is encountered. Store this number in a variable say x.

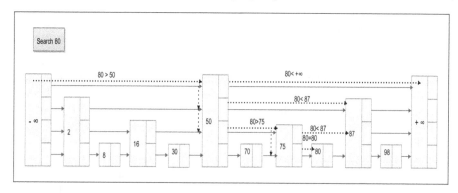

FIGURE 10.25
Searching in skip list.

- If the value of $x=0$, add the item only at the bottom level, i.e., S_0. Otherwise if $x \geq h$, add additional new levels $S_{h+1}, S_{h+2}, ..., S_{x+1}$ at the top of level S_h that only contains two special keys, i.e., $-\infty$, $+\infty$ and element i.

For n elements, the time complexity for inserting an element is $O(logn)$. Insertion of element 85 with value of $x =1$ is presented in Fig. 10.26.

- Deletion: To delete an item i, follow the following steps

  - First search for i, using search algorithm described above and locate the position p_0, p_1,........, p_h for item i.
  - Remove the element from list at levels S_0, S_1,........, S_h corresponding to the positions p_0, p_1,........, p_h.

The time complexity for deletion operation is $O(logn)$ for n elements. The deletion for element 87 is represented in Fig. 10.27.

The skip list provides beneficial in case where data structures need to be accessed concurrently. For example, skip list is used in designing highly scalable concurrent priority queue for heavy scale microprocessors [171]. Similarly, skip list is used to implement lock free dictionaries for a shared object in pre-emptive and concurrent environments in large scale multi-processors [181]. Skip list implement a non-blocking (lock-free) algorithm for shared object which ensures that regardless of contention, atleast one operation will be active.

10.4.1 Skiplist implementation in Python

First, we will define a skip list node where each node is inked by a list of pointers to immediate next node.

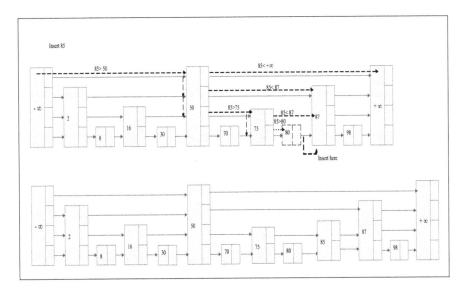

FIGURE 10.26
Insertion in skip list.

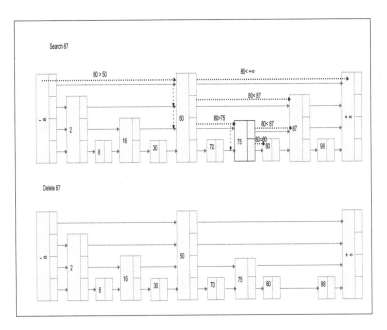

FIGURE 10.27
Deletion in skip list.

Listing 10.5
Defining a skip list node

```
class Skip_node:
  def __init__(self, h= 0, element = None):
    self.element = element
    self.next = [None]*h
```

Next, we will define a skip list

Listing 10.6
Defining a skip list

```
class Skip_list:

  def __init__(self):
    self.head = Skip_node()
      self.length = 0
      self.maximum_height = 0

  def __length__(self):
    return self.length
```

To perform search, insert and delete operation it is important to define a update function that will start searching from top most level and passes the list of any level till an element larger than element in question is found. Then, next level is explored and the process is repeated as discussed above.

Listing 10.7
Update function for skip list

```
def update_List(self, element):
    update = [None]*self.maximum_height
    y = self.head
    for x in reversed(range(self.maximum_height)):
        while y.next[x] != None and y.next[x].element < element:
            y = y.next[x]
        update[x] = y
    return update
```

Listing 10.8
Seraching in skip list

```
def find(self, element, update = None):
    if update == None:

        update = self.update_List(element)
    if length(update) > 0:

        item = update[0].next[0]
        if item != None and item.element == element:
            return item
    return None
```

Listing 10.9

Insertion in skip list

```
def random_Height(self):
        h = 1
        while randint(1, 2) != 1:
            h += 1
        return h

def insert(self, element):

        _node = Node(self.random_Height(), element)

        self.maximum_height = max(self.maximum_height,
        length(_node.next))
        while length(self.head.next) < length(_node.next):
        self.head.next.append(None)

    update = self.updateList(element)
        if self.find(element, update) == None:
                for y in range(length(_node.next)):
                        _node.next[y] = update[y].next[y]
                        update[y].next[y] = _node
                self.length += 1
```

Listing 10.10

Deletion in skip list

```
        update = self.update_List(element)
        x = self.find(element, update)
        if x != None:

                for y in reversed(range(length(x.next))):
                        update[y].next[y] = x.next[y]
                        if self.head.next[y] == None:
                                self.maximum_height -= 1
                self.length -= 1
```

Activity

Multiple Choice Questions

1. Which of the following does not fall in the category of membership query PDS?

   A BF

   B Min Hash

   C QF

   D Skip list

2. In standard bloom filter, what is the search complexity for k hash functions, m filter size and n total elements to be inserted ?

   A. $O(k)$ B. $O(n)$ C. $O(n+k)$ D. $O(m)$

3. Which of the following bloom filter does not support false negative?

   A Counting BF

   B Spectral BF

   C Deletable BF

   D None of the above

4. Which of the following is an advantage of counting BF over standard BF?

   A. Less space requirements

   B. Counting BF never support false positive

   C. Counting BF never support false negative

   D. Counting bloom filter support deletion

5. Which of the following mentioned bloom filter does not support deletion?

   A. Counting BF

   B. Deletable BF

   C. Scalable BF

   D. Dynamic BF

6. What is the time complexity for deletion operation in a skip list having n elements?

   A. $O(logn)$ B. $O(n)$ C. n^2 D. $O(n+n)$

7. Which among the following is not a meta-data bit for QF?

    A. *is_occupied*

    B. *is_continuation*

    C. *is_set*

    D. *is_shifted*

8. QF is preferred over BF because:

    A. QF consumes less space over BF

    B. QF is cache friendly whereas a BF is not

    C. BF provides scalability outside main memory whereas QF does not

    D. None of the above

1. b   2. a   3. c   4. d   5. c   6. a   7. c
8. c

11

Cardinality Estimation Probabilistic Data Structures

11.1 Introduction

The next category of PDS is for cardinality estimation that is popularly used in query processing and data base design. Database models uses algorithms of cardinality estimation to compute selectivity of a predicate. Linear counting, LogLog, HyperLogLog are some of the algorithms that falls under this category. The aim of such a PDS is to count number of unique elements of a set where duplicates are present. For instance, for a set $S = [1, 2, 3, 1, 2, 3, 4]$ the cardinality os the set is 4. An important use case for such PDS is to compute number of unique visitors for a particular website. As per data given by, from May 2019 to Sep 2019, the total visit on Amazon web page is 2.22 B. If we believe that every 10th visitor was unique, the cardinality of such case is 222 million. Notable, with linear space requirements, cardinality estimation is difficult to achieve for any of deterministic data strictures. To compute cardinality estimation, a simple way is to first arrange sets element in ascending order. Next, apply linear scan on set S to eliminate duplicates. If we use merge sort, the cardinality of set S having n elements can be computed in $O(nlogn)$ disc access with $O(1)$ extra space and hence this approach is inefficient. Another way to compute cardinality is by using a hash table data structure where hashes of elements are stored in hash table and cardinality is computed by total number of keys in hash table. Obviously, hashing has advantage of removing duplicates without sorting and hence require a single scan. However, for huge data set, hashing proves bad as it is difficult to fit the large has table in main memory. The time complexity for this approach is $O(n)$ with $O(n)$ extra space. Hence, with the traditional deterministic approaches, the query processing on increasing volume of data can only be processed in linear memory space.

PDS using probabilistic techniques estimates cardinality with low space requirements and linear time. Cardinality estimation PDS are also based on hashing. However, different from simple hashing, these data structure doesn't store values of elements in the hash table. Cardinality estimation using PDS can be done regardless of type of data and it can also be distributed over parallel machines with less communication overhead.

11.2 Linear Counting

As a first attempt to compute cardinality with probabilistic approach, authors in [213] introduced linear counting algorithm. Instead of storing actual element, linear counting simply set a bit corresponding to the element in the hash table. As it may be possible that, two records might collide to same location, so computed count might not be exact. Hence, cardinality is approximated that is computed from occupancy ratio of hash table. For a set having 120 million elements, computing cardinality with linear counting approach requires 1.25 MB of main memory, 1000 disk access, and 1% error rate. Linear counting offers a two step process for computing cardinality which are described as follows:

- Linear counting employs a hash table of size m in main memory along with a hash function. Every entry of hash table is initialized to 0. To each incoming item, a hash function is applied and the corresponding index in hash table is set to 1.

- Next, count of blank entries (,i.e., 0) is noted. Lets call this number x. Then analyze the fraction of empty bits $((V_n))$ by taking fraction of x and m. Final estimated cardinality is computed by putting value in the following equation:

$$\hat{n} \approx -m \ ln \ V_N \tag{11.1}$$

where, n is computed estimated cardinality.

The time complexity of linear counting algorithm is $O(n)$ where, n is the total count of elements in set S. The accuracy in results of linear counting algorithm is dependent on load factor. Here, load factor is defined as fraction of unique elements and hash table size. A higher value of load factor decreases the accuracy of results and lower the value of load factor, higher is the result accuracy. Hence, if the hash table size is very small compared to total number of elements, it can lead to high risk of collisions. Otherwise if hash table size is large enough the risk of collision reduces but it will consume more space, Authors have concluded that for a load factor greater than 1, linear counting produces 1% of error. The expected relative error for estimated cardinality $\hat{n}$ for a given multiset with N unique elements is given by Eq. 11.3. The variable t represents load factor $(\frac{N}{m})$. The relative error signifies, on an average what percentage of estimated cardinality $\hat{n}$ is miscalculated and is given by.

$$\frac{(e^t - t - 1)}{2N} \tag{11.2}$$

The hash table size is also influenced by standard error. The standard error is described as standard deviation of $\frac{(n)}{N}$ and is calculated by following equation.

$$\sqrt{m}\frac{(e^t - t - 1)^{1/2}}{N} \tag{11.3}$$

Although in order to use this method, count of unique items should be known in prior so as to allocate a hash table of appropriate size. Clearly, linear counting approach is faster than traditional approach but it fails to produce accurate results. Hence use case for this data structure is for applications where 100% accuracy is not required. Nevertheless authors in [38] suggested not to use linear counting algorithm for database relations whose cardinality is greater than 20 million because of extremely large table size. that provides more accurate results with less storage requirements. As a better solution, LogLog and HyperLogLog algorithms are also available.

Lets understand linear counting with an example. Suppose $m = 16$ and hash function is based on modular hashing, i.e., $h(k) = (k + 2)mod16$ where k is the key to be inserted. Let set S contains total of 10 elements, i.e., $S = 4, 34, 6, 4, 14, 36, 6, 7, 0, 7$. Notably, cardinality of this set is 7. Pass these elements through hash function and set the corresponding bit to 1. The resulting state of hash table after passing these elements is represented **??** as $h(4) = 6, h(34) = 0, h(6) = 8, h(4) = 6, h(14) = 0, h(36) = 2, h(6) = 8, h(7) = 9, h(0) = 2 and h(7) = 9$. In this case value of x is 11, load factor is $\frac{7}{16}$ and consequently value of $((V_n))$ $\frac{11}{16}$ which is equal to 0.6875. To get final estimated cardinality, put the value of $((V_n))$ in Eq. 11.1 which results in $\hat{n} \approx -16 * ln(0.6875)$ which on solving gives $5.99 \approx 6$. Due to collisions, estimated count is 6 whereas actual cardinality is 7. This whole example is represented in Fig. 11.1

Listing 11.1
Linear counting implementation code

```
class bit_set :
    def __init__(self , size ):
        self.bit = (1 << size)
        self.size = size

    def set(self , position ):
        self.bit |= (1 << position)

    def isset(self , position ):
        return self.bits & (1 << position)

    def zero_count(self ):
        zero = 0
        x = self.bit
            while x > 1:
        zeros += int(not(x & 1))
        x >>= 1
        return zero

    def linear_counting(dataset , mapsize , shift =0):
                bitmap = bit_set(mapsize)
                for element in dataset :
                    bitmap.set((hash(element)+int(random.random()*
                        shift ))%mapsize )
            nzeros = bitmap.zero_count()
            if nzeros == 0:
```

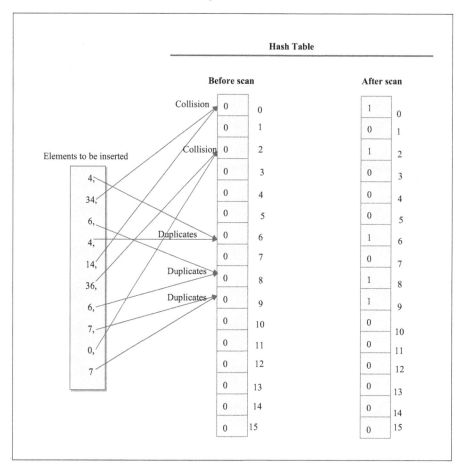

FIGURE 11.1
Example of linear counting algorithm.

11.2.1 Implemtation code of linear counting

The Python implemented code for linear counting is described as follows. Here, first a dataset is defined that takes 300 numbers between 0 and 20. Next, we check number of unique values in dataset using len() function. The depicts that with increase in mapsize, load factor decreases and cardinality estimation generates more accurate results.

```
        linearcounter(dataset, mapsize, shift +10)
            return
# Calculating estimated cardinality
        return (−mapsize*math.log(float(nzeros)
        /float(mapsize)))
```

```
if __name__ == "__main__":
# Generates 300 random numbers between 0 and 20
        dataset = [int(random.random()*20) for i in range(0, 300)]

# To calculate actual the number of unique values in the dataset
        print "no. unique values: ", len((dict([[(p, None)
        for p in dataset])).keys())

# Calculated load factor and its impact o accuracy
                for mapsize in [20, 30, 40, 50, 60, 70,
                80, 100, 120]:
        print "load_factor:", 300/float(mapsize),";
        cardinality estimation of the set:" ,
        linearcounter(dataset, mapsize, 0)
```

11.3   LogLog

Linear counting still consumes O(n) space which is linear space consumption. In this context, LogLog was introduced in [74] which provides solution to cardinality estimation for large datasets. This algorithm uses memory in order of $log_2(log_2(N))$ where, N is upper bound on number of unique items. In order to count, 2^{32} (4 billion) distinct items, this algorithms only requires $log_2(log_2(2^{32})) = 5$ bits of space. To understand the concept of LogLog, take an analogy: Suppose two friends Tom and Jerry went to a conference and there they decided to bet on who interacted with most strangers. So, they started keeping a counter of people they are interacting with. However counting as such can be a tedious task. So for next conference instead of just counting, they started writing their names on paper. This way it is better to count unique people rather than getting confused with total number of conversations. However, roaming around with a pen and a paper is not really easy. So, Tom came up with an alternative, rather than noting down names of persons, hey decided to ask last 6 digits of their contact number and the one with longest sequence of leading zeros in last 6 digits of contact number will be declared as winner. For example, a contact number of a person is 988866336, so longest sequence here is 0 as there are no leading zeros and if contact number is 00639, so longest sequence becomes 2. Clearly if either Tom or Jerry interacts to a few people, probability of getting longest leading zeros is either 0 or 1. As the number of people they interacted becomes large, chances of getting a leading zero sequence increases to being 3 or 4. To get a value 6 for longest zero sequence, either of them had interacted with thousand of people to get someone with 00000 as their last 6 digits of contact number.

Same concept is applied to LogLog algorithm. Here unique elements are counted in large set by hashing each element and then recording longest sequence of zeros for each element. LogLog employs a hash table having m entries or buckets along with a single hash function. Notably, with increase in value of m, average error rate decreases. As output of hash function is of fixed length, insertion of elements has time complexity of $O(1)$. A step by step explanation of estimating cardinality with LogLog is described as follows:

- For each incoming item, compute a fixed length hash of each item.

- Divide the hash obtained from previous step into two parts. First k bits signifies the index to a bucket and from the remaining sequence longest zero sequence is noted and the value of longest zero sequence is stored in that particular bucket. For instance, for a hash table of 16 buckets, a fixed length (10 bit) hash obtained is 1010 001001 and there are total of 16 buckets. So, first 4 bits tells about index of the bucket and from remaining bis longest zero sequence is noted, i.e., 2 is stored at location 10th.

- For each hash obtained, only the largest value of longest string of leading zero so far is stored in each bucket.

- Lets say R_1, R_2,........., R_m denotes entries in the hash table. The final cardinality of the set can be computed by taking arithmetic mean of entries in hash table. To reduce the effect of outliers and to minimize variance, rather than taking average, mean is calculated. Hence, LogLog improves accuracy by storing multiple estimates and then averaging the results. So, final cardinality of the set can be computed as:

$$Estimated \quad cardinality = 0.79402 * m * 2^{\frac{\sum_{j=1}^{m} R_j}{m}} \qquad (11.4)$$

Taking m buckets basically simulates as different m hash functions are taken. The standard error of LogLog algorithm is given out to be $\frac{1.30}{sqrt(M)}$ where, m signifies total bucket entries. Hence for a bucket with 2048 entries and each entry having S bits, an error of 2.5% is expected. The hash table can estimate cardinality till 2^{27}. The clear insight of LogLog is that it is less likely for a number to start with a long string of zeros (probability of a number having 10 leading zeros is less however not rare). Although LogLog algorithm is not suitable for small cardinality and it can only work with sets having large cardinality. Also, it is required to decode a prior upper bound on the total items to be inserted so that hash table can be chosen. Lets take example of LogLog where $m = 16$, index for any bucket takes 4 bits. This example counts unique visitors for a website. Refer to Fig. 11.2 After inserting 4 elements estimated cardinality is $0.79402 * 16 * 2^{\frac{6}{16}} \approx 16.47$. Clearly due to insertion of few elements, results of this algorithm are calculated wrong. However, for large cardinality algorithm will generate more accurate results.

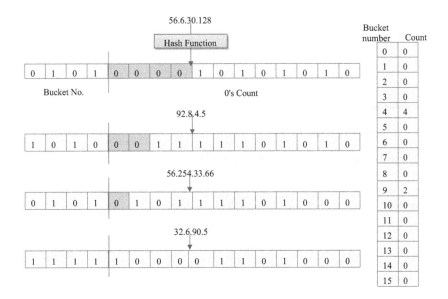

FIGURE 11.2
LogLog example.

11.3.1 Implementation of LogLog in Python

Listing 11.2
LogLog implementation code

```python
def leading_zeroes(number):
# Counts the number of leading 0 bits in hash num
        if number == 0:
                return 32 # Assumes hash output is of 32 bit
        i = 0
        while (number >> i) & 1 == 0:
            i += 1
        return i

def cardinality_estimate(values, k):
# Estimates the count of unique elements in the input set values.
# values: Given elements of set to estimate the cardinality.
"k: The number of bits of output hash to index bucket number;
hence, in total there will be 2**k buckets."

    m = 2 ** k
# Total number of buckets in hash table
    max_zeroes = [0] * m
    for p in values:
        h = hash(p)
        bucket = h & (m - 1) # Take out the k LSB for bucket number
        bucket_hash = h >> k
```

```
max_zeroes[bucket] = max(max_zeroes[bucket], tleading_zeroes
(bucket_hash))
return 2 ** (float(sum(max_zeroes)) / m) * m * 0.79402
```

11.4 HyperLogLog

HyperLogLog (HLL) is most popular probabilistic algorithm that computes distinct items in a multiset. Rather than exact, HLL computes approximates in low storage requirements. HLL [82] is an improved version of LogLog in two ways.

- The insertion of any element in HLL has almost same procedure as discussed for LogLog. Different from LogLog, while combining buckets in step 4th, rather than using arithmetic mean, harmonic mean of the values in the bucket are taken. The sequential implementation of HLL is represented in Fig. 11.3 This is to decrement the effect of uncommon high max-leading zero count in the same bucket. Harmonic mean helps to ignore values that approaches towards infinity. Hence, it reduces the impact of exponentiating a noisy number and improves accuracy of cardinality estimation. HLL further reduces the effect of outliers to improve the accuracy of estimation by removing out the largest value before averaging. The estimated cardinality from HLL is given by:

$$E = \alpha_m.m\frac{m}{\left(\sum_{j=1}^{m} 2^{-R^j}\right)} \quad (11.5)$$

where, α is a constant whose value is chosen as per the number of buckets.

- HLL makes correction for extreme cases, i.e., when all buckets are not occupied and when buckets are almost full and hash collisions causes underestimates. If the calculated estimation E is less than $2.5 * m$ and there are some buckets that has zero value for maximum leading zero, then the final cardinality in this case is replaced with

$$E_{\text{new}} = -m * log(\frac{V}{m}) \quad (11.6)$$

where, V is the count of bucket with zero value for maximum leading zero. Whereas for big cardinalities that approaches the total size of hash table, i.e., for $E > \frac{2^m}{30}$, the final cardinality is computed as:

$$E_{\text{new}} = -2^m log(1 - \frac{E}{2^m}) \quad (11.7)$$

Along with this, HLL supports merge operation that simply applies union of two HLL's and this function returns the maximum value from each pair of buckets, i.e.,

$$HLL_{\text{union}}[j] = max(HLL_1[j], HLL_2[j]) \tag{11.8}$$

where, j varies from 1 to m. One of thee reason that HLL is more popular over LogLog because for the same count of items, HLL results in better accuracy when compared to LogLog. The Standard error rate of HLL is described as $\frac{1.04}{sqrt(m)}$, where m is the number of buckets used. For instance, redis software use 16348 registers by default, so in order to implement HLL, it returns the standard error of 0.81%. Original HLL still returns large error for small cardinality but with little improvements, it can manage very small range cardinality to large range cardinality.

Take an example that counts the number of unique users who visited a website so far. Suppose there are 16 buckets which imply that addressing a bucket requires 4 bits. As shown in Fig. 11.4, for every IP address, first pass it through a HLL hash function that returns 16 bit fixed number. First four bits determine bucket number and from remaining bits count of leading zeros are extracted but only record of maximum number of leading zeros is kept and rest others are ignored. Similarly, for other IP addresses, the same process is repeated. To get the final cardinality, the harmonic mean of count column is taken. After inserting 4 different IP addresses the estimated cardinality can be computed as $\frac{0.673*16*16}{2^{-2}+2^{-4}} \approx 551$ which is obviously not equal to 4 because for small cardinalities the HLL results shows strong bias. However, for large carnalities this algorithm works fine.

11.4.1 Implementation of HLL in Python

Listing 11.3
Defining a HLL sketch class

```
class HyperLogLog(Interface):

    def __init__(self, max_Card, error-rate):

            self.__ALPHA16=0.673
            self.__ALPHA32=0.697
            self.__ALPHA64=0.709

    if not (0 < error-rate < 1):
            raise ValueError("Error_Rate must be between 0 and 1.")
    if not max_Card > 0:
            raise ValueError("maxCardinality must be > 0")

    self.__max_Card = max_Card
    self.__k = int(round(log(pow(1.04/error_rate,2),2)))
    self.__bucket_Number = 1<<self.__k
```

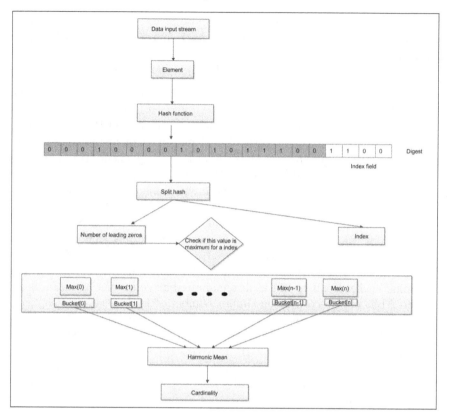

FIGURE 11.3
Sequential implementation of HLL.

```
self._bucket_Size = self._wordSizeCalculator(self._max_Card)
self._bucketList =[0 for _ in xrange(self._bucketNumber)]

self.__name = "HyperLogLog"
self._alpha = self.__getALPHA(self._bucket_Number)
# Function for selecting value of alpha
    def __getALPHA(self,m):
        if m <=16:
    return self.__ALPHA16
elif m<=32:
    return self.__ALPHA32
elif m<=64:
        return self.__ALPHA64
else:
        return 0.7213/(1+1.079/float(m))

    def getName(self):
    return self.__name
```

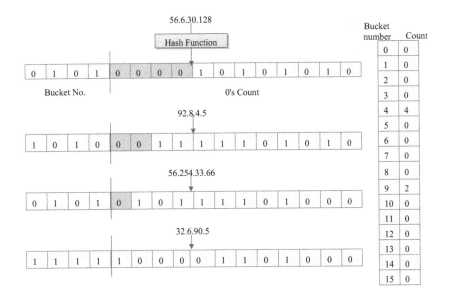

FIGURE 11.4

HLL example.

Listing 11.4
Inserting an element in HLL sketch

```
def add(self, element):

    hash = get_SHA1_bin(element)
    position = int(hash[: self._k], 2)
#Get the location of leftmost 1
    aux = get_index(hash[self._k:], 160 − self._k)
# Fill its own register value to maximum value of zeros seen so far
    self._bucketList[position] =
    max(aux, self._bucketList[position])
```

Listing 11.5
Calculating cardinality estimation of an element in HLL sketch

```
def getCardinalityEstimate(self):

    m = self._bucketNumber
    E = self._alpha*pow(m, 2)/sum([pow(2, −x)
    for x in self._bucketList])
    if E <= 5/2.0*m:
# v is count of bucket with maximum leading zeros
        v = self._bucketList.count(0)
    if v!=0:
        return m*log(float(v)/m, 2)
    else:
```

```
        return E
elif E <= 1/30.0*2**m:
        return E
else:
        return −2**m*log(1−E/2.0**m,2)
```

Activity

Multiple Choice Questions

1. What is the time complexity for linear counting algorithm for n number of total elements

   A. $O(n)$ B. $O(n^2)$ C. $O(logn)$ D. $O(nlogn)$

2. What is the time complexity for insertion operation of LogLog algorithm with a hash table of size m?

   A. $O(m)$ B. $O(1)$ C. $O(m^2)$ D. None of the above

3. For a hash table of size 32. How many bits are reserved for index field and longest zero sequence field ?

   A. $6, 25$ B. $5, 27$ C. $16, 16$ D. $10, 22$

4. HLL stands for?

   A. HydroLogLog B. HyperLogLog C. HyperloglinearD. Hyperlinearlinear

5. What is the space requirement for LogLog data structure with N as upper bound on number of unique elements?

   A. $log_2(log_2(N))$

   B. $log^2(log_2(N))$

   C. $log_2(log^2(N))$

   D. $log^2(log^2(N))$

6. To count, 2^{32} (4 billion) distinct items, LogLog algorithms only requires?

   A. 5 bits

   B. 10 bits

   C. 32 bits

   D. None of these

1. a   2. b   3. c   4. b   5. a   6. a

12

Frequency Count Query Probabilistic Data Structures

12.1 Introduction

This category concerns for estimating the count of a particular items in a set. For example, search engine uses frequency estimators for extracting frequently searched queries and network routers uses them for locating common source and destination addresses. One proposed solution to this randomly extract a sample from the set that shows properties of complete set. However, achieving true randomness is a quite unfavorable task. So, sampling also is not a useful solution to our problem. Also with hash tables, memory requirement becomes high (linear space requirements) as more items are added. Majority algorithm [52] and Misra-Gries [144] algorithms are two popular deterministic algorithms to solve frequency count problem. One of the effective way is to adopt approximation based queries for streaming data. In this context, an trending data structure is "Sketch" which based on summary based approach performs approximation queries. Sketch algorithms based on approximation and randomization are space and time efficient solutions in this context. Sketches refer to a category of algorithm that portrays a large set of data by a compact summary that is much smaller than actual data size [89]. Machine learning, NLP, security are some important area where variants of sketches are being used [203]. Sketches also solves problems faced by sampling technique and supports parallelization in practice. Parallelization in sketches implies that it can be implemented independently on different parts of data and further combines these parts that results in consistent aggregate. In short, parallelization imposes a straightforward divide and conquer approach for problems that faces scalability challenge. Moreover, sketches possess sub-linear asymptotic computational complexity which results in low computational power and storage. The algorithm under this category is characterized by two parameters, i.e., ϵ and δ where ϵ (accuracy parameter)describes the maximum affordable error in frequency estimation results with a maximum probability of δ (confidence parameter). These two parameters can be tuned as per available space. Also, for sketches error could be over-estimation, underestimation or a combination of both while estimating frequency.

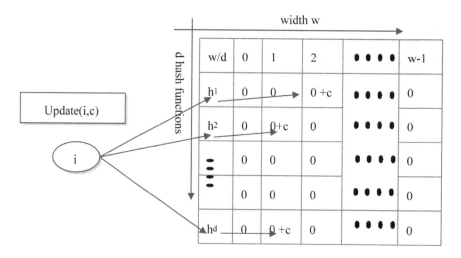

FIGURE 12.1
Structure of CMS.

12.2   Count-Min Sketch

Count-Min Sketch (CMS) [66] is most popularly available sketch data structure for executing frequency count queries. Specifically, this data structure serves efficient query processing on streaming data. CMS uses a compressed represent of data in order to guarantee low storage requirements. Similar to hash table, CMS employs a table with w width and depth d. While designing the sketch, the parameters w and d are fixed. The table is all initialized to zero. Different from hash table, rather than using a single hash function, for each row of table a different hash function is used, i.e., a total of d pairwise independent hash functions are used as shown in Fig. 12.1. Pairwise independence constructs a universal hash family that results in minimum collision [113]. Hash functions from universal families are those classes having less collision probability. The hash functions should be chosen such that they spread out the incoming items so as to attain high accuracy. Each of hash function takes the incoming element and maps it to corresponding column within range of $1, 2, 3, ..., w$. CMS consumes only sub-linear space with an disadvantage of over-counting because of hash collisions. Linear space complexity implies that with increase in data size, memory consumption also increases with a direct relationship between the two. Sub-linear on the other hand does not consumes equal memory to the data. It however consumes less than or half of the memory as compared to data as shown in Fig. 12.2. The operations supported by CMS are described as follows:

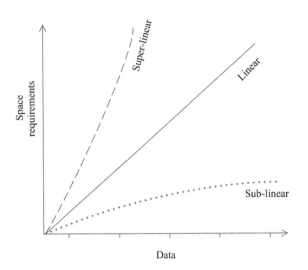

FIGURE 12.2
Understanding sub-linear space requirements.

- Update(i, c): This function updates frequency of any incoming element i by a count c. To each incoming element, all d hash functions are applied and corresponding location between $1 - w$ to each hash function is updated by adding a value c to the existing value.

- Estimate(i): This function computes the frequency of an element i in a set. First locate the locations corresponding to d hash functions. Finally the frequency count for element i is the minimum value out of the d obtained locations. As hash functions are used, there are chances that different element may collide on same cell. Thus by selecting minimum value, closest accurate results are fetched for frequency queries. Clearly, the results from a CMS may overestimate but never underestimate. Notably, CMS performs counting first and then computes minimum, thus named count-min sketch.

- Delete(i, c): To delete element i from the set, simply decrement the d corresponding locations in each row by a count c.

Notably, the frequency estimation of CMS is somewhat similar to counting BF. Like other PDS, CMS use-cases are beneficial for application that does not care about exact frequency count of the element. Database query planning, finding heavy hitters in traffic monitoring, NLP, compressed sensing, joint-size estimations are some of the promising use-cases of frequency query estimation PDS. CMS also supports parallelization as here sub sketches can be merged by taking sum of tables. However, two sketches can only be merged if they are constructed using same value of w and d along with same hash functions. Moreover, CMS enables approximate addition of any summable value that supports a monoid. One of the disadvantage of CMS is that it shows behavior biased estimation of true frequency count of a number. Count-min-log sketch, count-min-mean sketch are some of the most recent improvements over CMS. Clearly, for any item i, actual frequency (f_i) is always less than or equal to estimated frequency $(\hat{f}_i)$. For a sketch of size $w*d$, setting $w = \frac{2}{\epsilon}$ and $d = log(\frac{1}{\delta})$ ensures that estimate operation can exceed actual frequency by atmost ϵN $(\hat{f}_i \leq f_i + \epsilon N)$ with atleast probability $1 - \delta$. Effect of changing values of w and d is represented in Table 12.1. Hence cardinality estimation for size N has atmost of $\frac{2N}{w}$ error with atleast probability of $1 - (\frac{1}{2})^d$. Space consumed by CMS is $O(\frac{1}{\epsilon}log\frac{1}{\delta})$ and time taken by update and estimate is given by : $O(log\frac{1}{\delta}) = O(d)$. CMS also supports deletion by decrementing the corresponding hash location.

One of the major applications of CMS includes monitoring Heavy hitters. Heavy hitters are defined with respect to a threshold ϕ and if count of any item frequency is equal to or greater than ϕ, then that item may be regarded as a heavy hitter. Schechter *et al.* [167] proposed an approach that identifies most popular passwords in order to prevent statistical-guessing attacks. Here, the main contribution of the authors is to deprive an attacker of guessing most popular passwords by not letting any of the passwords to get common. CMS gives better results when combined with BF. Gupta *et al.* [94] presented an Intrusion Detection System model that works on PDS. To check whether a node is suspicious or not from a list of suspicious nodes, all incoming node are passed through a BF, followed by a CMS to count frequency of hits by a particular node if BF returns true.

Lets understand CMS with a example. Consider a 2-D table where value of $w = 6$ and $d = 4$, i.e., 4 hash functions will be used and each row will have 6 buckets. Consider $h1 = imod6$, $h2 = (2*i)mod6$, $h3 = (imod3)mod6$ and $h4 = (2i+3)mod6$. All 24 locations are initialized to zero. Each incoming element is passed through all 4 hash functions and corresponding positions are incremented by their given count. The series of operation update(12,1), update(5,2), update (16,1), update(6,1) is shown in Fig. 12.3. The results of element 12, 5, 16, 6 after passing through given hash function is shown in Table 12.2. The query operation Estimate(6) has been shown in Fig. 12.4 and query operation Estimate(12) has been represented in Fig. 12.5. For element 6, the estimate query return true result whereas for element 12 , it shows an case of over-estimate. Last, the deletion of element 6 by a count 1 is shown in Fig 12.6.

TABLE 12.1
Effects of change in parameters for CMS.

Parameter	Increase	Decrease
w	<ul><li>High Accuracy</li><li>More memory requirement</li></ul>	<ul><li>Relatively more error rate</li></ul>
d	<ul><li>Updates will be processed at low speed</li><li>Less false positive rate</li><li>More memory Requirements</li></ul>	<ul><li>Less time in updating data</li><li>Less memory requirements</li></ul>

TABLE 12.2
Results of elements after passing through hash functions.

Element	h_1	h_2	h_3	h_4
12	0	0	0	5
5	5	4	2	1
16	4	2	1	5
6	0	0	0	3

12.2.1 Implementation of CMS with Python

Listing 12.1
Initializing a CMS

```python
import numpy as np
import mmh3

class Count_Min_Sketch(object):
#Defining a class for CMS
        def __init__(self, w, d, seeds):
# Method to initialize the data structure
```

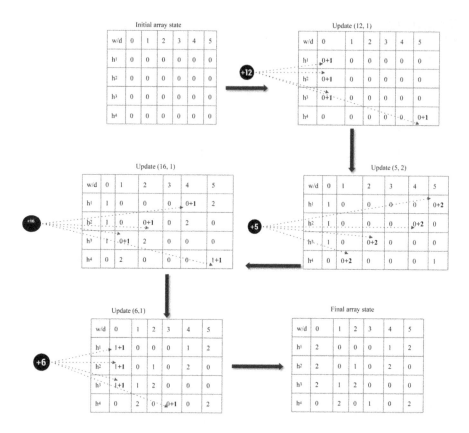

FIGURE 12.3
Update operation in CMS.

```
# w=width of table, d=depth of table and number of hash functions
to use
#seeds: Random seed list
                self.w = w
                self.d = d
 # Initialize table with         all zeros
                self.table = np.zeros([d, w])

        self.seed = seeds # create random seeds
```

Listing 12.2
Updating a element in CMS

```
        def update(self, element):
#Method to insert a elemnt to the CMS
#element: An element to be added to the CMS

            for x in range(0, self.d):
```

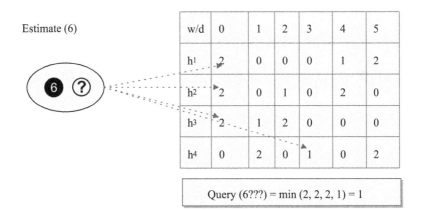

w/d	0	1	2	3	4	5
h1	2	0	0	0	1	2
h2	2	0	1	0	2	0
h3	2	1	2	0	0	0
h4	0	2	0	1	0	2

Estimate (6)

6 ?

Query (6???) = min (2, 2, 2, 1) = 1

FIGURE 12.4
Estimate operation in CMS.

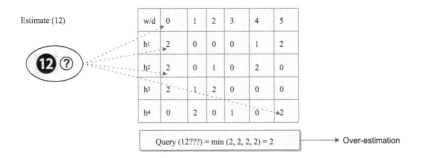

w/d	0	1	2	3	4	5
h1	2	0	0	0	1	2
h2	2	0	1	0	2	0
h3	2	1	2	0	0	0
h4	0	2	0	1	0	2

Estimate (12)

12 ?

Query (12???) = min (2, 2, 2, 2) = 2 ———→ Over-estimation

FIGURE 12.5
Estimate operation in CMS representing over-estimate.

Delete (6,1)

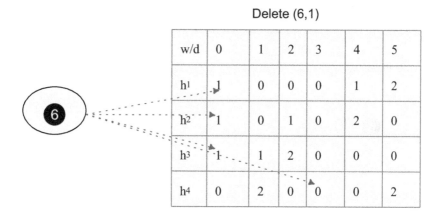

w/d	0	1	2	3	4	5
h¹	0	0	0	0	1	2
h²	1	0	1	0	2	0
h³	1	1	2	0	0	0
h⁴	0	2	0	0	0	2

FIGURE 12.6
Estimate operation in CMS representing over-estimate.

```
index = mmh3.hash(element, self.seed[x])
% self.w
self.table[x, index] = self.table[x, index]
+1
```

Listing 12.3
Updating a element in CMS

```
    def update(self, element):
#Method to insert a elemnt to the CMS
#element: An element to be added to the CMS

        for x in range(0, self.d):
            index = mmh3.hash(elemenr, self.seed[x])
            % self.w
            self.table[x, index] = self.table[x, index]
            +1
```

Listing 12.4
Frequency estimation of an element in CMS

```
    def query(self, x):
#Return an estimation of the amount of times 'x' has ocurred.
#The returned value always overestimates the real value.

        return min(table[i] for table, i in zip(self.tables
        , self._hash(x)))
```

12.2.2　Count-mean-min-sketch

To deal with biasness generated by CMS, authors of [70], introduced a variant of CMS called count-mean-min (CMM). Authors have pointed out that due to property that a counter of CMS is touched by many elements so, an error is expected. Here, the authors characterize this error as noise. Notably, the CMS outputs the least noise counter In CMM, the authors aim to estimate the noise generated by each counter. To estimate noise from counters, note the values of other counters in a row that are not touched by element in question. Here, it is assumed that each element is mapped uniformly and randomly for all rows of the table. The value in each counter that is not touched by element is an independent random variable and follows the same distribution pattern as noise. The structure and updation procedure of CMM is similar to CMS. Here also a 2-D table (w*d) is employed that uses the same hash function $(h_0, h_1, ..., h_{d-1}$. However, the estimation procedure of CMM is different from CMS. Rather than returning the minimum value from d counters, the estimated noise from these d counters is deducted and median of residues is returned. To compute noise in each d counters of a row, take average off all other counters in any row i except for the counters in any row i. Hence, the estimated noise for a counter is given by Eq. :

$$\frac{N - CM[i, h_i(q)]}{w - 1} \tag{12.1}$$

where, N is stream size,
$CM[i, h_i(q)]$ is the counter for element q in row i and $i= 0,1,...., d\text{-}1$,
$w=$ sketch width
$q=$ Element in question
This algorithm may also overestimate and the estimate count is given by median of:

$$CM[i, h_i(q)] - \frac{N - CM[i, h_i(q)]}{w - 1} \tag{12.2}$$

for all i rows.

12.3　Count-sketch

Count-sketch is almost similar to CMS and it provides an estimate of frequency for any individual item. Actually, authors [62] of count-sketch designed it to keep approximate count of highest frequency items in a stream. The difference between CMS and count-sketch two comes in the estimation process and in the nature of guaranteed accuracy for frequency estimate. Authors have proved that proposed algorithm is better than the sampling algorithm. Count sketch also employs a 2-D table of size $w*d$ in size which is interpreted as array of

d hash tables with each having w buckets. Different from CMS, rather than using a single hash function, two hash functions (h *and* g) are being used for each row of count sketch. Each hash functions $h_1, h_2, ..., h_d$ maps from *1,2,....,w* whereas $s_1, s_2, ...,s_d$ maps to -1, +1, i.e., either +1 or -1. The operations supported by count-sketch are discussed as follows:

- Update(q, c): This operation updates an item q with count c to the count-sketch. For each hash table of array, compute the state of updated sketch as:

$$sketch[k, h_i[q]] = sketch[k, h_i[q]] + c * s_i[q] where\ i \in [1, d]\ and\ 1 < k < d.$$
(12.3)

Introducing ± 1 can be helpful in better estimation for element q as it can better handle collision among elements. However, if an element q collides with multiple frequent elements, it wont result in good estimate for element q but in case of collision with infrequent elements impact of ± 1 is positive.

- Estimate(q): This operation find the approximate count of element q in sketch. To execute the operation take median of $sketch[k, h_k[q].s_k[q]]$ where, $i \in [1, d]$ and $1 \leq k \leq d$. Authors have proved in results that the median is comparatively robust over mean. Moreover, mean is sensitive to the outliers.

However, the authors have not mentioned about delete operation anywhere in the base paper of count-sketch. Space consumed by Count-Sketch is $O(\frac{1}{\epsilon^2} log \frac{1}{\delta})$. However, authors have ignored the space requirement of actual storage of elements from stream. Also, etting $w = \frac{2}{\epsilon^2}$ and $d = log(\frac{4}{\delta})$ achieves atmost error of ϵN with atleast probability of $1 - \delta$ where N is stream size. Notably, this algorithm generates overestimates as well as underestimate for a query.

Let's take an example to understand count-sketch more clearly. Consider a table with $w = 6$ and $d = 4$. The value of the hash function for each hash table is $h_1 = imod6$, $h2 = (2 * i)mod6$, $h_3 = (imod3)mod6$ and $h_4 = (2i + 3)mod6$ and $g1, g2$ generate either -1 or $+1$ randomly for any incoming item. The result of elements after passing through hash function h and g is represented in Table 12.3. The operation $update(12, 1)$, $update(5, 2)$, $update(16, 1)$ and $update(6, 1)$ in series has been represented in Figs. 12.7. Similarly, the operations $estimate(5)$ and $estimate(12)$ have been represented in Fig. 12.8 and 12.9 respectively. It is clear from Fig. 12.9 that the query for element 12 results in over-estimation. Notably, the estimation query for count-sketch may result in under-estimation as well.

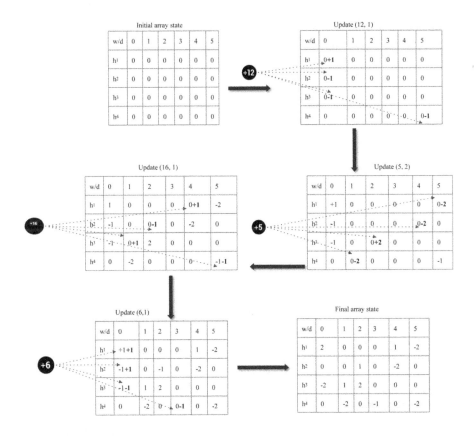

FIGURE 12.7
Update operation in Count-sketch.

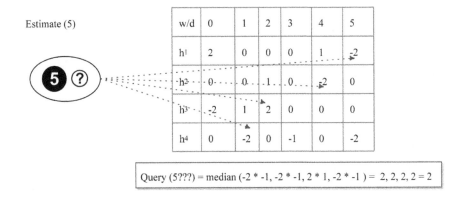

FIGURE 12.8
Estimate operation in count-sketch.

TABLE 12.3

Results of elements after passing through two hash functions h and g.

Element	h_1	h_2	h_3	h_4	g_1	g_2	g_3	g_4
12	0	0	0	5	+1	-1	-1	-1
5	5	4	2	1	-1	-1	+1	-1
16	4	2	1	5	+1	-1	+1	-1
6	0	0	0	3	+1	+1	-1	-1

FIGURE 12.9

Estimate operation in count-sketch representing over-estimate.

12.4   Count-Min with Conservative Update Sketch

The main logic behind the conservative update is "Minimal Increase" which only increment count with the minimum amount required to ensure that accuracy of the estimate remains. Counservative update (CU) can be applied to Count-Min-sketch and also to spectral BF. CM-CU sketch was introduced by authors of [76] with an aim to reduce the false positive error in the result. Specifically, the authors of [88] concluded that CMS with conservative update minimizes the over-estimation error by a factor of 1.5. Similar to CMS, CM-CU also uses a 2-D table of size $w*d$ where, w is the width and d is the depth of the table. Also, k hash functions equal to the depth of the table are used. For any incoming item, only the count by minimal amount will be incremented. However, the CM-CU sketch does not support deletion. The operations that are supported by CM-CU sketch are discussed as follows:

- Update (q, c): This operation adds an element q with count c to the sketch. To perform this operation, first, compute the approximate frequency of the element q from the existing state of the sketch by using the $Estimate(q)$ procedure explained for CMS, (i.e., by taking a minimum of the values returned from values indexed by d hash functions. Let's call this value f_q.

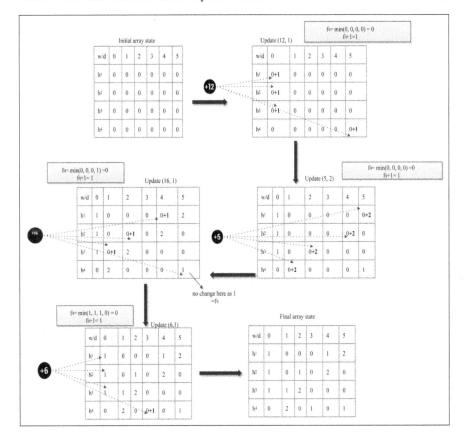

FIGURE 12.10
Update operation in CM-CU sketch.

Next, compare the values at k locations corresponding to k hash functions. Here, in CMS, the values at k locations are only incremented if the existing value in the sketch is less than $f_q + 1$, otherwise, the value won't get changed. This type of conditional updation ensures that unnecessary updation and reduces over-estimation error. In order to update q with the count, c first compute f_q using:

$$f_q = min_k \, sketch[k, h_k(q)] \; \forall \, 1 \le k \le d \qquad (12.4)$$

and update the count according o following equation:

$$sketch[k, h_k(q)] \leftarrow max\{sketch[k, h_k(q)], f_q + c\} \qquad (12.5)$$

- *Estimate(q)*: It follows the same procedure *Estimate(q)* as explained for CMS in section 12.2.

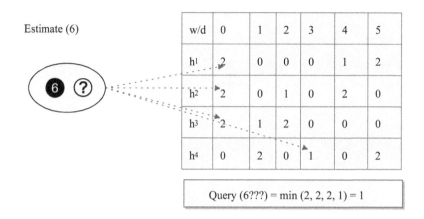

FIGURE 12.11
Estimate operation in CM-CU sketch.

The example for update operation has been represented in Fig. 12.10. Here, the operations $update(12, 1)$, $update(5, 2)$, $update(16, 1)$, $update(6, 1)$ in shown in series. The hash outputs for all these element has been shown in Table 12.2. Similarly the operation Estimate(6) has been shown in Fig. 12.11. Experiments concluded that error rate is proportional to $\frac{1}{M}$ where M is the available memory.

Activity

Multiple Choice Questions

1. What is the main idea behind count-min with conservative update?

    A Minimal increase

    B Minimal decrease

    C Maximal increase

    D Maximal decrease

2. If a sketch employs a table of size $t * b$ where t is number of rows and b is the number of columns, then how many hash functions are required in order to implement CMS?

    A. $O(t + b)$ B. $O(b)$ C. $O(t)$ D. $O(t * b)$

3. Which measure of central tendency is used in order to execute query by count-sketch ?

    A. Mode   B. Median   C. Average   D. Range

4. What is the impact on error rate with increase in width of 2-D array of CMS ?

    A. Error rate will become high

    B. Error rate will get reduced

    C. Error could be high or low

    D. No relation between error rate and width of table

5. Which of the following mentioned BF does not support deletion?

    A. Counting BF B. DBF   C. Stable BF   D. Compressed BF

6. Which among the following is the deterministic algorithm for frequency estimation?

    A CMS

    B HLL

    C Majority algorithm

    D All of the above

7. What is the time complexity for updation operation in CMS?

    A. $O(d)$ B. $O(w)$ C. $O(logd)$ D. $is\_shifted$

8. What is the space requirement for CMS?

     A. Linear   B. Sub-linear   C. Super-linear D. logarithmic

    1. a   2. b   3. b   4. b   5. c   6. c   7. a
8. b

13

Approximate Similarity Search Query Probabilistic Data Structures

---

13.1   Introduction

Large datasets generated from a system may contain duplicates or near duplicates. Applying brute force technique to probe all possible combination can give exact nearest neighbor match, but this way is no scalable. Over and above, the traditional cluster analysis techniques (e.g., k-nearest neighbor) take quadratic or cubic time which seems unpractical for large datasets. Moreover, tree structure methods, such as- kd-trees, BDD trees etc. demands enough space and time as these methods compare given query with each record while searching to identify similar records [83], [106]. Hence, there is a demand for efficient similarity search method that can solve desired queries in low cost. To address this problem, researchers proposed using approximation techniques for high dimensional similarity search.

The data structure under this category approximates similarity search for high dimensional data. Sometimes, similarity search is also referred to as approximate nearest neighbor search or proximity search. In such type of problem, different features of interest e.g., text document, images are treated as points and a distance metric is used to identify similarity between two objects. The similarity search measure maps a pair of set to a similarity score in range [0,1]. Specifically, the aim here is to find duplicates or cluster of similar points in high dimensional attribute space. The use-cases for approximate similarity search includes finding similarity between web pages in the Internet, locating similar image or audio/video files, data deduplication, identifying plagiarism cases, identify variations in malware family etc. Mathematically, the problem is defined as: For a query q, the aim is to locate item x such that $dis(q,x) \leq (1+\epsilon)\, dis(q,x)^*$ where, ϵ is the at most estimated expected error [212].

The fundamentals of approximate similarity also rely on hashing as hashing converts the data points to a low dimensional representation. Hash table lookup and fast distance approximation are two techniques of hashing to perform approximate nearest neighbor search. The former method uses a hash table as data structure that is comprised of buckets. Each item x is hashed to a bucket $h(x)$. However, different from conventional hashing algorithm, here hash table aims to maximize probability of neighbor item collision. In contrast, the later computes the distance between given query and hash code of the reference item. Subsequently, the reference item having smallest distance are the candidates of nearest neighbor. Next, we will present the different types of approximate similarity search PDS.

13.2 Minhashing

Andrie Border introduced minhashing to detect duplicacy in web pages of AltaVista search engine [53], [54]. Minhash is based on the jaccard similarity notion to identify similarity between two sets. Jaccard similarity for two sets is the ratio of intersection to the union of two sets and is given by:

$$JS(S_1, S_2) = |S_1 \cap S_2| / |S_1 \cup S_2|. \tag{13.1}$$

For example, take two small sets, $setA = 10, 113, 2, 55, 12$ and $setB = 10, 3, 56, 7, 9$. It can be noticed that there are 2 items in common between sets and there are total of 10 unique items in two sets. Therefore, the set A and B have a jaccard similarity of $\frac{2}{9}$. Although computing intersection and union between two set is an expensive operation. However, to compute similarity between documents, documents can also be represented as sets. Shingling is one of the popular way to convert a document into set. k-shingles is defined as set of all possible k size non repeatable substrings of the given document. A document with n words, having set of k-shingles consumes $O(kn)$ space. Suppose a document is made up of a small sentence "Clustering large number of binary program is a difficult task". So, 5 word long shingles are:

- Clustering large number of binary

- large number of binary program

- number of binary program is

- of binary program is a

- binary program is a difficult

- program is a difficult task

Therefore, the document as a set is: ("Clustering large number of binary", "large number of binary program", "number of binary program is", "of binary program is a", "binary program is a difficult", "program is a difficult task"). Time complexity to compute jaccard similarity is $O(n_2)$ as there are total of $\frac{n(n-1)}{2}$ comparisons.

Moreover, the large collection of set can also be represented by a single boolean matrix. To represent set as boolean matrix, rows of the matrix contain elements of universal set whereas column of the matrix contains all sets. The entry in row r and column c is 1 if and only if set of row r is a member of column c, otherwise the entry is zero. In this case, column similarity is the jaccard similarity of the set having rows with column value 1. To understand this, consider three columns C_1, C_2, C_3 with values: From table 13.1 $Sim(C_1, C_2) =$

TABLE 13.1
Understanding minhashing.

C_1	C_2	C_3
0	1	1
1	1	0
1	0	1
0	0	0
1	1	0
0	1	1

$\frac{2}{5}$ as there are two rows in column C_1 and C_2 where both entries 1. Therefore, intersection of set that column C_1 and C_2 represent is 2. Also, there are rows where atleast one column has 1. So, the union of represented set is 5. Hence, the jaccard similarity is $\frac{2}{5}$ which is 40%. Similarly, $Sim(C_1, C_3) = \frac{1}{5}$. Notably, this matrix is not sparse and calculating jaccard similarity for this case is quite simple. However, with this representation the resultant matrix is sparse, i.e., it has more zeros than one which is a overhead for the memory. From Table 13.1 $Sim(C_1, C_2) = \frac{2}{5}$ as there are wo rows in column C_1 and C_2 where both entries 1. Therefore, intersection of set that column C_1 and C_2 represent is 2. Also, there are rows where atleast one column has 1. So, the union of represented set is 5. Hence, the jaccard similarity is $\frac{2}{5}$ which is 40%. Similarly, $Sim(C_1, C_3) = \frac{1}{5}$. Notably, this matrix is not sparse and calculating jaccard similarity for this case is quite simple. However, with this representation the resultant matrix is sparse, i.e., it has more zeros than one which is a overhead for the memory. Minhash algorithm provides a way for fast approximation to jaccard similarity of two sets. In order to implement minhashing, for each set minhash signature is computed and saved in signature matrix. The computed minhash signature has a fixed length and it is independent to the size of set. Signature matrix of minhash is made up of h rows that signifies number of hash functions and c columns which is equal to total number of sets. The signature matrix is useful as it provides almost same similarity as that of boolean matrix but with quite less storage space.

- Randomly permute rows.

- Compute minhash value, $MH(C)$=index of first row (after permutation) with 1 in column C.

- Similarly, use multiple independent hash function and create a signature for each column so that signature matrix has h rows. These minhash functions are selected once and same set of minhash functions is applied to each column. Notably, large matrix produce less errors.

- $\text{Sim}(C_1, C_2) = \text{Sim}(\text{Sig}(C_1), \text{Sig}(C_2))$, i.e., similarity between two sets is fraction of permutations where minhash value agree.

Lets understand this concept with an example. Consider a input matrix with 5 columns and 7 rows as shown in Fig. 13.1. These columns are permuted thrice in order P_1, P_2, P_3. So, resultant signature matrix has 3 rows (each corresponding to one permutation) and 5 column. The minhash value for permutation 1 has value $2 - 1 - 2 - 3 - 4$ for each 5 column respectively and the reason is discussed as follows: The row 5 is first in order and row 4 is second and so on. Clearly, row 5 has 1 in second column and hence column second has got its first minhash value, next row 4 is analyzed. As row 4 has 1 for columns 1 and 3 and neither of these column has been assigned a value yet. So, both of these columns get a value of 2 in signature matrix. Next, row 2 is scanned and it has 1 for columns 2 and 4. As, column 2 is already having a minhash value, so only column 4 will get a value of 3 in signature matrix. Similarly, column 5 gets value 4. Notably, we have discovered minhash value for each column so there is no point of moving further.

Surprising property
If we consider all possible permutations of the rows then it is observed that:
$$P[MH(C_1)MH(C_2)] = JS(C_1, C_2)$$

Unfortunately, with large dataset, its difficult to pick random permutation. Moreover, representing random permutations for large entries require huge amount of space. Also, accessing rows in order of any of these permutations requires many disc access to get each row which is clearly time consuming.

Lets look at a better implementation of minhashing. The idea is to simulate permutations without actually permuting rows. Here in this implementation, a normal hash function (h) for each minhash function is chosen that hashes integer to some bucket. We assume that position of row r in the permutation is $h(r)$. Following steps are taken to obtain a signature matrix.

- Rather than permuting rows, pick some number of ordinary hash functions, one corresponding to each minhash function we want to simulate.

- For each column C and each hash function h_i, keep a slot $M(i, c)$. For example, number of slots is $100 * number\ of\ columns$.

- Initialize all slots $M(i, c)$ to infinity.

- To compute minhash signature, $M(i, c)$ should alwayz contain the smallest value of $h_i(r)$ for those column C has 1 in row r.

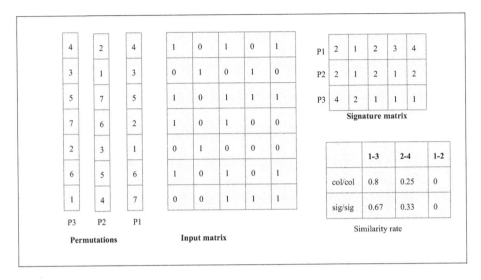

FIGURE 13.1
Understanding minhashing.

Algorithm 4 Minhash algorithm

The algorithm for above discussed method has been shown in algorithm 4.

1: **for** each row r **do**
2:   **for** each hash function **do**
3:     compute $h_i(r)$;
4:     **for** each column c **do**
5:       **if** c has 1 in row r **then**
6:         **for** each hash function h_i **do**
7:           **if** $h_i(r) ¡ M(i,c)$ **then** $M(i,c) \leftarrow h_i(r)$;
8:           **end if**
9:         **end for**
10:       **end if**
11:     **end for**
12:   **end for**
13: **end for**

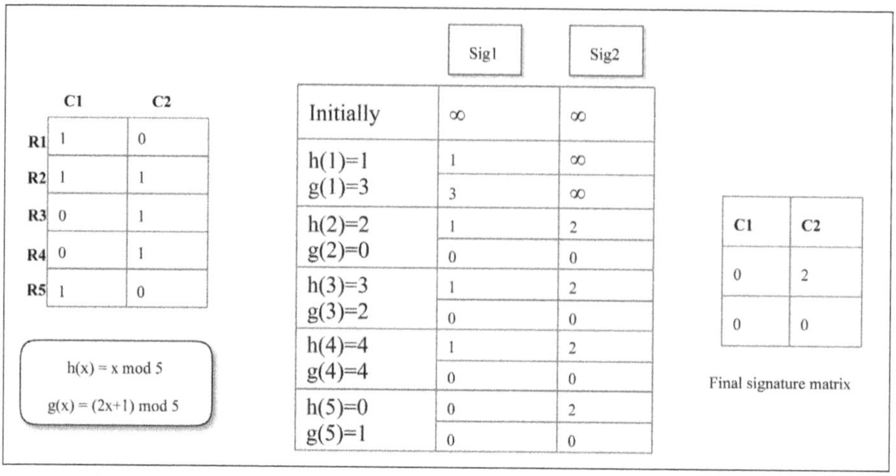

			Sig1		Sig2
		Initially	∞		∞
		h(1)=1	1		∞
		g(1)=3	3		∞
		h(2)=2	1		2
		g(2)=0	0		0
		h(3)=3	1		2
		g(3)=2	0		0
		h(4)=4	1		2
		g(4)=4	0		0
		h(5)=0	0		2
		g(5)=1	0		0

	C1	C2
R1	1	0
R2	1	1
R3	0	1
R4	0	1
R5	1	0

h(x) = x mod 5

g(x) = (2x+1) mod 5

C1	C2
0	2
0	0

Final signature matrix

FIGURE 13.2
Understanding minhashing.

This implementation is fast as well as uses fixed memory footprint. Although signature matrix consumes comparatively less space to represent document signature but it still takes $\binom{n}{2}(O(n^2))$ approximate time for finding similar pair of comparison. To understand this concept with example, consider a matrix with 2 columns and 5 rows as represented in Fig. 13.2. Two hash functions are used here, i.e., $h(x) = x mod 5$ and $g(x) = (2x+1) mod 5$. Hence, final signature matrix will be of length 2.

Initially all slots are infinity. The first row has 1 for column 1 and 0 in column 2. So, both of the component for column 2 has not changed and it remains infinity but first column value will get changed to values of $h(1)$ and $g(1)$ i.e., 1 and 3. Now, consider second row where both columns has 1 and $h(2) = 2$ and $g(2) = 0$. Simply for column 2, infinity values are replaced with hash values whereas for column 1 $h(2) > h(1)$ so, this value will not changed and $g(2) < g(1)$ so, second component here will get changed to 0. As minhash function uses minimum value encountered for each hash function. Hence, the name minhash is defendable. Likewise, other rows are observed and final signature matrix for both columns are shown in Fig. 13.2. Code 13.4 presents Python implementation using built-in hash function and h bitwise XOR masks for doing hashing.

Listing 13.1
Python implementation to convert documents to sets of shingles

```
print "Shingled documents"

# Whenever a new shingle gets added to the dictionary, current
shingle ID is increamented.
currentShingleID = 0
```

```
# Defining a dictionary of the documenent that maps documet
identifier  to the list of shingle IDs.
documentsAsShingleSets = {};

# Open the file having all data.
f = open(File , "U")

documentsNames = []

t0 = time.time()

totalShingles = 0

for i in range(0, numberDocs):

# Reading all words of documents and split them by white space.
word = f.readline().split(" ")

# Retrieve the article ID, which is the first word on the line.
documentID = word[0]

# Maintaining list of each document IDs.
documentNames.append(documentID)

del words[0]

shinglesInDocument = set()

# For every word in the document...
for index in range(0, len(word) - 2):
# Construct 3-word shingle
shingle = word[index] + " " + word[index + 1] + " " + word[index + 2]

# Hash the shingle to a 32-bit integer.
hash = binascii.crc32(shingle) & 0xffffffff

shinglesInDocument.add(hash)

# Store all shingles for this document in the dictionary.
documentsAsShingleSets[documentID] = shinglesInDocument

# Counting total number of shingles across whole documents.
totalShingles = totalShingles + (len(word) - 2)

# Closing thefile.
f.close()
```

Listing 13.2
Python implementation to calculate generate minhash signature

```
t0 = time.time()

print 'Generating hash functions...'

# Note down the maximum shingle ID that we assigned.
```

```
maximumShingleID = 2**32−1
nextPrime = 4294967311
```

```
# Taking hash function as:  h(i) = (x*i + y) % z   Where 'i' is the
input value, 'x' and 'y' are random coefficients, and 'z' is a
prime number just greater than maxShingleID.

# Generate a list of 'k' random coefficient,
def pickRandomCoefficients(k):
# Create a list of 'k' random values.
randomList = []

while k > 0:
# Generate a random shingle ID.
randomIndex = random.randomint(0, maximumShingleID)

# Ensure that each random number is unique.
while randomIndex in randomList:
randomIndex = random.randomint(0, maximumShingleID)

# Adding random number to the list.
randomList.append(randomIndex)
k = k − 1

return randomList

# For each of the 'numHashes' hash functions, generate a different
coefficient 'a' and 'b'.
coeffP = pickRandomCoefficients(numHashes)
coeffQ = pickRandomCoefficients(numHashes)

print '\nGenerating MinHash signatures for all documents...'

signatures = []

# For each and every document...
for documentID in documentNames:

# Get the shingle set for this document.
shingleIDSet = documentsAsShingleSets[documentID]

# The resulting minhash signature for this document.
signature = []

# For each of the random hash functions...
for i in range(0, numberHashes):

# For each of the shingles actually in the document, calculate its
hash code

# Track the mimumum hash ID seen.
minimumHashCode = nextPrime + 1
```

```
# For each and shingle in the document...
for shingleID in shingleIDSet:
# Compute the hash function.
hashCode = (coeffP[i] * shingleID + coeffQ[i]) % nextPrime

# Track the minimum hash code.
if hashCode < minimumHashCode:
minimumHashCode = hashCode

# Append the smallest hash code value,
signature.append(minimumHashCode)

# Save the MinHash signature for this document.
signatures.append(signature)
```

Listing 13.3
Python implementation to compare minhash signatures

```
# Define matrices to hold the similarity values
numberElementss = int(numberDocs * (numberDocs - 1) / 2)

# Initialize two empty lists to store the similarity values.
# 'JSim' for the actual Jaccard Similarity values.
# 'estJSim' for the estimated Jaccard Similarities found by
comparing the MinHash signatures.
JSim = [0 for x in range(numberElementss)]
estJSim = [0 for x in range(numberElementss)]

# Define a function to map a 2D matrix coordinate into a 1D index.
def getTriangleIndex(i, j):

    if i == j:
        sys.stderr.write("Can't access matrix with i == j")
        sys.exit(1)
# If j < i just interchange the values.
    if j < i:
        temp = i
        i = j
        j = temp

        k = int(i * (numberDocs - (i + 1) / 2.0) + j - i) - 1

    return k
#Comparing minhash signatures
t0 = time.time()

# For each of the test documents...
for i in range(0, numberDocs):
# Retrieve the MinHash signature for document i.
        signature1 = signatures[i]

# For each of the other test documents...
for j in range(i + 1, numDocs):

# Retrieve the MinHash signature for document j.
signature2 = signatures[j]
```

```
count = 0
# Compute the number of positions in the minhash signature
which are equal.
for k in range(0, numberHashes):
count = count + (signature1[k] == signature2[k])

# Record the percentage of positions which matched.
estJSim[getTriangleIndex(i, j)] = (count / numberHashes)
```

13.3   Locality Sensitive Hashing

Locality Sensitive Hashing (LSH) aims to find nearest data points to the given query. Here, also hash tables are utilized to find close enough match. Detecting plagiarism, classifiaction by topic, recommendation systems, entity resolution, genome-wide association study, audio-video fingerprinting , etc. are some of the key areas where LSH is used. The idea that LSH uses is "repurpose collisions" which states rather than avoiding collisions, make collisions happen for nearly data points. So, in LSH nearby or close enough data points are made to be fall in same bucket and distant data points in different buckets. More formally, the algorithm selects a hash family H and this hash family is locality sensitive if:

$Pr[h(A) = h(B)]$ is high if A is close enough to B

$Pr[h(A) = h(B)]$ is low if A is far away from B

LSH is an idea of hashing items many times and comparing only those that fall into same bucket even atleast once. However, LSH doesn't guarantee to provide exact answers but they give a good approximation. In order to implement LSH,

- First step is to perform shingling on the set of given documents.

- Second step is to perform minhashing that outputs short integer represen- tation of sets in form of signatures.

> Notably, minhashing converts large sets to short signatures using hashing, while preserving similarity whereas LSH further finds pairs of signature that are likely to be similar.

- Third step is to perform locality sensitive hashing that aims to find a small list of candidate pairs of signatures that are only evaluated for similarity check. Rather than probing all pair of a set for similarity check, only a list of candidate pairs are evaluated. To the minhash signature matrix, columns are hashed to different buckets using several hash functions and the documents that hashes to same bucket even for once are referred to as candidate pair.

Rather than detecting completely similar documents, LSH finds similarity greater than t between documents. So, two columns C_1 and C_2 of min-hash signatures matrix are candidate pairs if their signatures agree for atleast fraction t of their signatures of rows. to perform hashing of a single column,

- First partition signature matrix into b bands, having r rows per band.
- Hash each band of each column in any of k buckets. For better efficiency, take k as large as possible.
- Identify the candidate pair that hashes to same bucket for atleast 1 band.
- b and r should be selected to achieve most similar pairs and few non-similar pairs and also to eliminate false positives and false negatives. The more insight on choosing b and r is discussed next.

The concept of band partition and hash function computation of one band is represented in Fig. 13.3 and 13.4.

- Finally, main memory is accessed to test whether candidate pairs have really similar signatures.

> **Observation**
> For a 100 row signature matrix, if we choose 25 bands of 4 signature per band then there is higher probability for two given documents to fall in same hash buckets as the two documents will be hashed 20 times (one for each band) and only few signatures are getting compared in each band, i.e., only 5 as compared to another case with 10 bands of 10 signatures per band. Hence, there is higher chance for false positives if higher number of bands are selected. In contrast, chances of false negatives increases if we chose a lower value of number of bands.

Suppose there are 100,000 column and 100 rows in signature matrix which implies size of signature matrix is 100*100000. Lets assume number of bands chosen are 20 with 5 signature per band. To understand existence of false positives and false negatives consider two cases:

Case 1

Assume similarity threshold to be 80%, i.e., we want to retrieve all documents that are 80%similar pairs.

Probability that two columns C_1, C_2 are identical in one particular band: $(0.8)^5 = 0.32768$.

Probability that two columns C_1, C_2 are not identical in any of the 20 bands: $(1 - 0.328)^{20} = 0.00035$. which implies about $\frac{1}{3000}$th of truly 80% similar sets

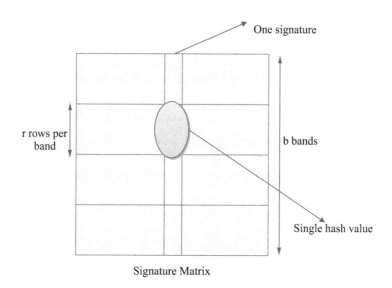

Signature Matrix

FIGURE 13.3
Band partition in LSH.

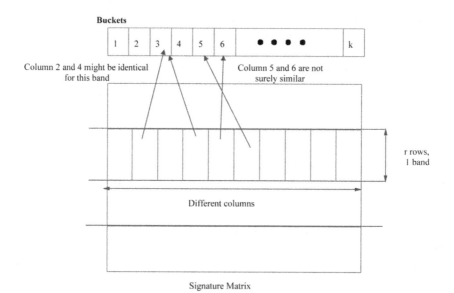

Signature Matrix

FIGURE 13.4
Hash function for one band.

are false negatives.

Case 2

Take another case for two documents to be 40% similar.

Probability that two columns C_1, C_2 are identical in one particular band: $(0.4)^5 = 0.01$.

So, probability that two columns C_1, C_2 are identical in atleast one of 20 bands: $(1-(1-0.01)) = 0.19$. which implies that there is about 20% probability of false positives.

Therefor b and r should be selected to achieve minimum rate of false positives and false negatives.

Listing 13.4

Python implementation to compare minhash signatures

```python
class Cache(object):
    def __init__(self, hasher, number_bands=10, **kwargs):
      each fingerprint is divided into n (bands) and duplicate
        self.bins = [defaultdict(set) for _ in range(number_bands)]
        self.hasher = hasher
        msg = 'The number of seeds in the fingerprint must ' \
        'be divisible by the number of bands'
        assert hasher.num_seeds % number_bands == 0, msg
        self.bandwidth = hasher.num_seeds
        self.number_bands = numbr_bands

        self.fingerprints = dict()
    def bins_(self, fingerprint):
        yield from enumerate(np.array_split(fingerprint,
        self.num_bands))
    def clear(self):
        self.bins = [defaultdict(set) for _ in range(self.num_bands)]
        self.hasher.fingerprint.cache_clear()
    def add_doc(self, document, document_id):
        fingerprint = self.hasher.fingerprint(document.encode('utf8'))
        self.add_fingerprint(fingerprint, document_id)
    def add_fingerprint(self, fingerprint, document_id):
        self.fingerprints[document_id] = fingerprint
        for bin_i, bucket in self.bins_(fingerprint):

            bucket_id = hash(tuple(bucket))

            self.bins[bin_i][bucket_id].add(document_id)
    def filter_candidates(self, candidate_id_pairs, min_jaccard):
        logging.info('Computing Jaccard sim of %d pairs',
        len(candidate_id_pairs))

        res = set()
        for id1, id2 in candidate_id_pairs:
            jaccard = self.hasher.jaccard(self.fingerprints[id1],
            self.fingerprints[id2])
            if jaccard > minimum_jaccard:
                res.add((id1, id2))
        logging.info('Keeping %d/%d candidate duplicate pairs',
        len(res),
        len(candidate_id_pairs))
```

```
            return res
    def remove_id(self, document_id):
            fingerprint = self.fingerprints[document_id]
            for bin_i, bucket in self.bins_(fingerprint):
                bucket_id = hash(tuple(bucket))
                self.bins[bin_i][bucket_id].remove(document_id)
            del self.fingerprints[document_id]
    def remove_document(self, document):
            fingerprint = self.hasher.fingerprint(document.encode
            ('utf8'))
            doc_ids = {id for id, finger in self.fingerprints.items()
                if all(a == b for a, b in zip(finger, fingerprint))}
            for i in doc_ids:
                self.remove_id(i)
    def get_all_duplicates(self, minimum_jaccard=None):
            candidate_pairs = set()
            for b in self.bins:
                for bucket_id in b:
                    if len(b[bucket_id]) > 1:
                        pairs_ = set(itertools.combinations(b[bucket_id],
                        r=2))
                        candidate_pairs.update(pairs_)
            if minimum_jaccard is None:
                    return candidate_pairs
            return self.filter_candidates(candidate_pairs,
            minimum_jaccard)
    def get_duplicates_of(self, document=None, document_id=None,
    minimum_jaccard=None):
            if doc_id is not None and doc_id in self.fingerprints:
                    fingerprint = self.fingerprints[doc_id]
            elif doc is not None:
                    fingerprint = self.hasher.fingerprint(doc.encode
                    ('utf8'))
            else:
                    raise ValueError('Must provide a document or a
                    known document id')
            candidates = set()
            for bin_i, bucket in self.bins_(fingerprint):
                bucket_id = hash(tuple(bucket))
                candidates.update(self.bins[bin_i][bucket_id])
            if minimum_jaccard is None:
                return candidates
            else:
                    return {x for x in candidates
                            if self.hasher.jaccard(fingerprint,
                            self.fingerprints[x]) > minimum_jaccard}
    def is_duplicate(self, document, document_id=None):
            return len(self.get_duplicates_of(document,
            document_id=document_id)) > 0
```

13.3.1   Simhash

Simhash is a variant of LSH and unlike typical cryptographic algorithm, simhash also tries to maximize the probability of collision for almost similar item [62]. It was proposed by Moses Chankar in order to detect near duplicate documents. Simhashing is based on the concept of sign random projection [34]. It basically reduces dimensionality of data and maps highly dimensional data to f-bit fingerprint (f is very small generated from hashing).

Simhash fingerprint is usally generated from any feature of document. The document feature is generally k-word shingles or frequency of word. To compute simhash fingerprint, follow the steps below:

- Generate the features of documents.

- Select a hash size f (8,16, 32.. etc.) and maintain a f-dimensional vector V and initialize all dimensions of vector to 0.

- Hash each feature to f-bit hash value (These unique f-bits of each feature increments/decrements the final f value of vector).

- For each unique f-bit hash value:
  $if bit_i of hash is set then, add 1 to final f - bitvector(V[i])$
  $elsif bit i of hash is not set, substract 1 from V[i]$

- Final simhash bit vector has
  bit_i as 1 if $V[i] > 0$ and 0 otherwise.

For example, take a sentence "Data Structures".

- First, convert all higher case word to lower case word and divide into 3-word shingles, i.e., 'dat', 'ata', 'tas', 'ast', 'str', 'tru', 'ruc', 'uct', 'ctu', 'tur', 'ure', 'res'.

- Hash each shingle
  $h(dat) = 10110000$
  $h(ata) = 10100001$
  $h(tas) = 10110010$
  $h(ast) = 01100011$
  $h(str) = 10110100$
  $h(tru) = 00100101$
  $h(ruc) = 10110110$
  $h(uct) = 10111000$
  $h(tur) = 01101001$
  $h(ure) = 10111010$
  $h(res) = 01101011$

- $if\ shingle.h[i] == 1$, $V[i]$ is incremented by 1
  $if\ shingle.h[i] == 0$, $V[i] =$ is decremented by 1
  The V vector is represented by Fig. 13.5.

1	0	1	1	0	0	0	0
1	0	1	0	0	0	0	1
1	0	1	1	0	0	1	0
0	1	1	0	0	0	1	1
1	0	1	1	0	1	0	0
0	0	1	0	0	1	0	1
1	0	1	1	0	1	1	0
0	0	0	1	0	1	1	1
1	0	1	1	1	0	0	0
0	1	1	0	1	0	0	1
1	0	1	1	1	0	1	0
0	1	1	0	1	0	1	1
V +2	-6	+10	+2	-4	-4	0	0

FIGURE 13.5

Simhash example.

- To compute final simhash fingerprint:
  if $V[i]>0$, $simhash[i] = 1$
  else $simhash[i] = 0$
  So, simhash fingerprint is (10110000).
  To detect similarity of document d with a given set of document. One solution is to take hamming distance of simhash fingerprint of fingerprint of d with all other documents simhash fingerprint value. However, with growing problem size this method is not efficient. In another approach, rather than comparing all simhash bits of document d with all bits in simhash value of document set, only compare some specific bit position. If they matches, only then hamming distance of two simhash fingerprint is computed.

Activity

Multiple Choice Questions

1. Which one of the following is not a type of similarity search PDS?

    A. Minhash   B. Maxhash   C. LSH   D. Simhash

2. The space consumed by set of k-shingles with total of n words in a documents is?

    A. $O(k^2)$ B. $O(k+n)$ C. $O(n^3)$ D. $O(k*n)$

3. The time consumed by signature matrix for comparing similar pairs is?

    A. $\binom{n}{2}(O(n^2))$ B. $O(n^4)$ C. $O(n)$ D. $O(logn)$

4. In general, probability of signature not to agree on any of the bands for two columns C_1 and C_2 is given by ?

    A. $(1-s^b)^r$ B. $(1-s^b)^r$ C. $(1-r^s)^b$ D. $(1-b^r)^s$

5. Which among the following is not a distance metric ?

    A. Euclidean distance

    B. Hamming distance

    C. Cosine distance

    D. Signature distance

6. What is the time complexity to compute jaccard similarity for n given document?

    A. $O(n^2)$ B. $O(logn)$ C. $O(n^3)$ D. $O(n)$

7. Higher number of bands in LSH implies:

    A Lower false positives

    B Higher false negatives

    C Higher false positive

    D Lower false negatives

8. Locality sensitive hashing generates:

    A False positives only

    B False negatives only

    C Both false positives and false negatives

    D Neither of false positive and false negatives

Part IV

Integration of Probabilistic Data Structures with Blockchain

14

Applicability of Membership Query PDS with Blockchain

14.1 Full Blockchain Client vs Lightweight Blockchain Client

As discussed in subsection 6.1.3, blockchain supports two types of clients. A full blockchain node stores a full copy of the digital ledger. The entire history of blocks has to be downloaded and stored. As it is time-consuming and requires high space to download the entire blockchain. This poses a heavy requirement on resources, memory, bandwidth, and computing of blockchain nodes. Along with disk space consumption, another concern is overhead of verifying the correctness of broadcasted block due to growth of Bitcoin volume. So, blockchain supports another type of client to solve the problem of resource and memory-constrained devices. In contrast to a full client, a lightweight client can transact without downloading full copy of the blockchain. Nevertheless, the lightweight client only stores block header in order to achieve the PoW blockchain concept. However, a lightweight client has to reference a trusted full client's copy of the blockchain. The full client only forwards the copy of the transactions requested by lightweight client.

In this context, SPV is a method used by lightweight client to verify whether a transaction is included in a block or not without downloading the entire blockchain. The process of verification has been described in subsection 6.1.3. Readers may refer to that subsection. Along with checking the existence of a transaction in a block, Lightweight clients can also verify the block's difficulty. To verify, the lightweight client checks whether a block has successful cryptographic ink to the previous block. Also, the lightweight client checks whether PoW solution meets the block difficulty or not. The difference between full blockchain client and lightweight blocchain client is shown in Table 14.1.

> **Key point**
> A full client can fool a lightweight client by simply not providing interested transaction. This is a case of DoS attack. However, by connecting to more than one full nodes, this problem can be solved.

TABLE 14.1
Full blockchain client vs lightweight blockchain client.

Full blockchain client	Lightweight blockchain client
Stores entire history (full copy) of blockchain distributed ledger	No need to download full copy of blockchain ledger
No reference to any other node required	References one or more full client for performing operations
Provides greater privacy	Lightweight client has to specify transaction to full nodes. Hence, privacy risks exists
Mostly consists of computer system	Mobile consists of mobile wallets
Nodes have mining rights	No mining rights are given to lightweight clients
Contributes to full functionality of a network	No contribution in functionality og the network
No dependency on third-party or any other node	Dependency on light wallet provider
Full control over your own money	No guarantee that referenced full node is online when required
Full clients maintenance is highly complex	Provides ease of use
These nodes have to verify the correctness of each transaction of the network	These nodes doesn't have rights to verify blocks to be added in blockchain network

14.2   BF with probabilistic data structures

14.2.1   Bitcoin using BF

Notably, SPV client does not need to list every transaction in which they are interested in (this could be thousand in number). In this context, a BF can be used with SPV clients. Rather than directly sending an interested transaction's address list, BF can be used with SPV clients to achieve a space-efficient means to acquire the transaction of interest. All the addresses required by SPV client are embedded in BF and is forwarded to associated full client. The step by step sequence of this process is described as follows:

- Here, client forms a BF by inserting addresses of all interested transaction.

- When referenced full client comes online, the lightweight client establishes a connection with the full client and upon a successful connection, formulated BF is transferred over a secure channel.

- For every received block of transaction, the full client will first check it against BF received from SPV/lightweight clients.

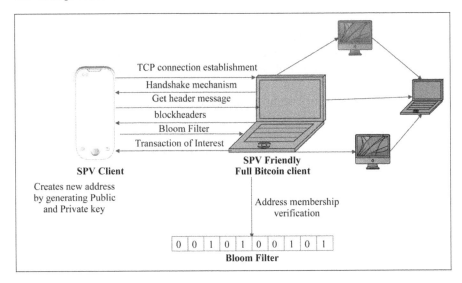

TCP connection establishment

Handshake mechanism

Get header message

blockheaders

Bloom Filter

Transaction of Interest

SPV Client

**SPV Friendly
Full Bitcoin client**

Creates new address
by generating Public
and Private key

Address membership
verification

0	0	1	0	1	0	0	1	0	1

Bloom Filter

FIGURE 14.1
Sequence of steps between SPV client and Full Client.

- In case of positive results matched transactions along with some Merkle branch required to achieve Merkle hash is sent to SPV client. The sequence steps between SPV client and full client is represented in Fig. 14.1.

Issues with SPV client

- A full node now knows all public addresses of the transaction received by the requesting light client, this fact obviously violates the client's privacy. Information such as- purchase habits may get released with this privacy threat. Also, it can lead to DoS attack.

- A full node may get compromised by attacker and steals BF pertaining to SPV client. Moreover, in case of Sybil attack (where attacker intentionally generates lots of malicious nodes) launched by attacker, the chances of picking any malicious node as full client increases.

- Unfortunately, the false positive probability exists in this case as well which implies may be an unwanted transaction can be transferred to the lightweight client. However, this property creates difficulty to recognize Bitcoin address owned by users as it is hard to identify what positive addresses are actually inside BF. Nevertheless, authors of [86] suggested that false positive of BF is not enough to preserve privacy of SPV client. Also, high false positive rate waste more network bandwidth. However, a SPV client with enough bandwidth may choose high positive rate. This implies full client can't accurately judge the interested transaction of SPV client.

Infact, a BF with much high false positive rate would result in downloading almost entire blockchain. In contrast, by setting a low FP rate, full node would know exactly the transaction of interest for a SPV client as specific transactions would be downloaded only. Moreover, low FP rates would result in faster synchronization for SPV clients whereas high FPR rate leads to high synchronization time as large number of transactions are downloaded

---

Key point: BF represents a tradeoff between privacy and network bandwidth.

- The size of memory request gets increased with the increase in number of addresses possessed by SPV client.

Research on preserving privacy of SPV client using BF

- Authors of [86] discussed the issue of addresses information leakage with BF used by SPV client. The authors have concluded and observed the following points:

  - It is shown by experiment that address information leakage depends on number of addresses used by SPV client to form BF. It has been concluded that if an SPV client constructs BF with ¡20 addresses, the risk of information leakage is high as compared to case if 20 plus addresses are embedded in BF.

  - If an adversary is able to collect more than one BF from same SPV client, this situation leaks considerable more number of addresses. Hence, construction of more than one BF by same SPV client should be avoided. Moreover, BF should be formed with different elements and different seeds in order to avoid much information leakage by adversary.

  - Information leakage is worsen if SPV client is restarted and a adversary can link two different BF with same elements but different parameters. Hence, SPV client should remember state for their outsourced BF in order to avoid recomputing a new filter with same elements but different parameters.

- Notably, for a fixed false positive rate of BF, privacy level preserved depends on total number of unique addresses in the block. As these total number of unique addresses in a block may increase steadily, so it is important to decide a strategy for privacy preservation while designing BF. In this context, authors of [114] proposed a privacy metric, i.e., γ-deniability to determine how truly involved addresses are hidden by false positive rate of BF. Basically, γ is a parameter to control privacy level while designing SPV client's BF. γ-deniability depicts measure of how much addresses inserted in BF are kept balanced by false positive Bitcoin addresses. However to create a BF that specify a particular γ, it is required to have information about the number of unique addresses from the last checkpoint to latest block (N_u). To calculate N_u, without accessing the entire blockchain, linear regression model s suggested by authors. To check the mathematics behind estimation scheme of N_u, readers may refer to [114]. After computing N_u using linear regression model and target γ, the array size of BF can be constructed. It has been shown in results that as compared to conventional scheme, achieved privacy level is high in the proposed scheme.

- Authors of [163] explained that there is another implementation of SPV client where this client downloads whole Bitcoin blockchain from full node to verify a single transaction of interest. However, client will only keep the interested transactions from block and discard rest other transactions. This approach is privacy preserving as no other node on the network can determine the transaction of interest for SPV client. Unfortunately, this way there is lots of bandwidth wastage. Here, authors used the concept of private information retrieval (PIR) to create fully private queries with low bandwidth and low latency cost. PIR enable users to query a database in a way that database doesnot learn anything about user's query. The system model of this proposal involves different PIR servers that responds to PIR queries of SPV client and provides required data to perform operations. PIR server don't learn anything about user-centric transaction data. PIR server actually first downloads whole blockchain and stores it in PIR database. For every database, a description file named manifest file is created by PIR server. SPV client still downloads BF from associated full client and fetches manifest file to query PIR database afterwards.

- To integrate BF with BC, a similar approach in [23], presents a method that leverages fast chain synchronization by not sending any irrelevant transaction to SPV Client. Three messages perform operations between lightweight client and full client: *filterload* message initializes and set current BF on connection, *filteradd* message updates current BF by adding data elements to current BF, *filterclear* message deletes current BF in use. Also, authors concluded that compact size of BF enables fast membership which consequently open up risk for DoS attack. Moreover, SPV approach can lead to privacy issue as full client has information regarding bitcoin address used by SPV client. However, false positive generated by BF makes it difficult for a full client to identify actual addresses but it cannot completely hide the anonymity of addresses of SPV Client. Besides, high FPR can lead to wastage of network bandwidth [153].

14.2.1.1   PoW using BF

In addition to SPV implementation, PoW mechanism of Bitcoin uses BF to avoid nonce reuse attack. To realize In addition to SPV implementation, PoW mechanism of Bitcoin uses BF to avoid nonce reuse attack [24]. To realize this each verifier employs two BF's: current and previous. Before computing PoW, each nonce is checked against both BF's and for positive membership results, reject the nonce value and compute $SHA-256(SHA-256(++n||h))$ (where, n is nonce and h is previous header) to check whether MSB bits of results match with the given target. Finally, add nonce value n to update current BF. Also, the verifier can reset current BF by copying current BF to previous BF.

14.2.2   Ethereum using BF

Other than *Bitcoin, Ethereum* also integrates BF to achieve better space efficiency. Parameters in Ethereum storage are indexed, to filter the event logs for specific value/address [215]. Receipt of each transaction is encoded in Ethereum. Each transaction receipt is denoted as $BR[i]$ where i represents i^{th} transaction. This receipt consists of 4 items, i.e., (R, R_u, R_l, R_b) where R signifies post transaction state, R_u signifies the amount of cumulative gas consumed in block holding the transaction receipt just immediately after the transaction has been executed, R_l signifies set of logs created while execution of transactions and R_b signifies BF constructed from information in each log entries. The BF is of 2048 bits. With BF entire Ethereum blockchain can be scanned in seconds to find logs matching specific topic.

Whenever a new block is created, the address of any logging contract and indexed fields of logs generated when transaction has happened are inserted in BF and this BF is added to the block header. Indexed fields mostly consists of address fields of transaction including "to, from and smart contract address" and other log topics (e.g., transfer). Nevertheless, actual logs are not added to the block header in order to save space. If an application requires to find log entries of a given contract or having specific indexed fields, it just need to scan each block header to retrieve BF to check for relevant logs it contains or not. In case of positive results, the node again executes the transaction from that block, regenerates logs, and return the relevant ones. However, direct indexing of the transaction by addresses can put a high burden on target machine. In this context, the authors in [166] proposed a method using BF that extracts account wise information of individual account in an improvised way. Also, authors in [90] proposed a cuckoo filter to check address membership. It has been concluded that cuckoo filter performs fast membership search over SBF.

14.2.3 Integration of blockchain and BF for certificate revocation

Authors of [64] proposed to use blockchain for a certificate management system which is the core component of public key infrastructure. Here. All the associated operations to certificates are stored on the blockchain for public audit. However, the authors described some of the concerns with blockchain for certificate management.

- Centralization in practice: Due to privileged nodes which possess high stakes or better computational capability in consensus algorithm including PoW, PoS, etc., there is a risk of centralization in the network.

- Block size management: As discussed earlier, the current block size of the blockchain is specific and limited. However, in some case certification revocation list size can reach up to 76 MB which clearly does not get fit to one block. Hence more than one block is required to store CRL information. Therefore, to check information regarding certificate revocation becomes insufficient.

To maintain the brevity of this book, we will not discuss the solution to the first problem. We are just discussing the integration of blockchain and Bitcoin. Readers may refer to the original paper for detailing.

In order to solve the later issue, i.e., block size limitation, authors have presented a revocation checking method using Dual Counting Bloom Filter (DCBF). DCBF provides efficient query processing and economic storage. The whole certificates of the system are divided into two sets, i.e., valid certificate set and revoked certificate set. To store two different varieties of sets two counting BF's are employed, i.e., CBF1 and CBF2. The updated or newly created certificates are stored in CBF1 and a revoked certificate is first deleted from CBF1, then stored in CBF2. When a block is created, both CBF1 and CBF2 are stored in one block. To check for a revoked certificate, first, the certificate in question is passed through CBF2. If this BF returns negative, the certificate is marked as a valid certificate. Otherwise, in case of positive results, the certificate is matched in CBF1. If the result is negative in this case, the certificate is revoked definitely whereas, for positive results, related operations of certificates are then checked in the block. Comparing results in two BF's ensures the accurate status of certificate without any false positive.

14.2.4 Integration of blockchain and BF in smart grid sector

In research work [91], the authors have presented solutions to achieve privacy in the smart grid. Here, authors employ blockchain for data aggregation rather than relying on trusted third-party. The system architecture divides all users of smart grid in different groups as per their electricity consumption type. The keys of all users are initialized by a key management center (KMC). KMC basically allocates multiple public and private keys to each user and the

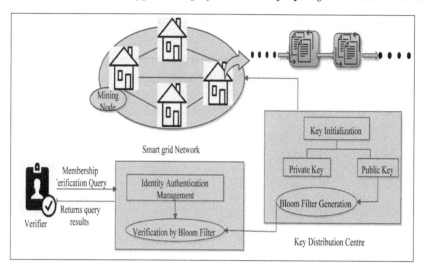

FIGURE 14.2
Identity Authentication Management System using BF.

public key is used as a user's pseudonym. In each time slot, a new miner node is chosen according to electricity consumption data. The selected miner node aggregates nodes data and records this data in private blockchain to ensure message integrity. To select a miner node, a random procedure is followed. The node whose electricity consumption data is nearest to average electricity consumption data for a time slot, that node is selected as the miner node. A user of the network can create multiple pseudonyms to submit their electricity generation/consumption information. This way users true identity can't be revealed.

Moreover, to ensure fast authentication in the blockchain-based system, BF is used. BF probes the existence of fake pseudonyms using zero-knowledge proof. The bloom filter is constructed for each different group by using pseudonyms for that group and the constructed BF is sent to all nodes in the corresponding group. To authenticate the validity of a user, the registered pseudonym of the user is passed through BF. If there is a positive match, the user is authenticated otherwise not. Notably, identity authentication is done using zero-knowledge proof. In case an unregistered user uses a pseudonym and sends wrong information to the system, BF can validate a user's pseudonym with efficient space consumption. Therefore is a user without registration at KMC tries to send false information to the network, this attempt will get fail as mapping value in BF will contain at least one zero. To avoid false positive, authors have suggested that the array size of BF should be sufficiently large so that the probability of hash collisions ca be decreased. Fig. 14.2 shows the identity management system using bloom filter.

14.2.5 Integration of blockchain and Bitcoin for bodyworn sensing devices

Health issuers are developing strategies to collaborate with bodyworn devices with their policies. Although bodyworn IoT devices generate quite private information about patient's routine and this information should not be tampered with in any sense [209]. In order to address the concern of secure data logging, authors of [172] presented a lightweight solution. Here, all smart devices that lie in same broadcast domain serve as witnesses for neighboring devices by logging all data conversation in a chain like structure. However, a gateway is employed for detailed logging of all information that it conducts with sensor devices. Basically, sensor devices record all conversations they overhear in the network and maintain a record and forward it to the gateway. Notably, there is heavy traffic in the network with this approach which uses large memory and imposes high communication overhead for witnesses. As a solution, rather than recording the whole conversation, these devices use BF to store fingerprints of conversation in chronological order instead. Hence, using BF reduces space complexity. After a certain time, witnesses upload their signed BF to the gateway. The digital signing ensures integrity and non-repudiation in the system. Moreover, to reduce false positive probability authors have suggested using different hash functions.

14.2.6 Graphene: Block propagation protocol

In distributed systems, it is always required to minimize the network bandwidth for efficient synchronization among replicas. Clearly, the efficiently designed network protocol for synchronization of newly mined block and newly created transactions provides may benefits. For example, if blocks are passed on consuming less network data, consequently maximum block size can be increased. Additionally, there will be an increase in processing of overall number of transactions per second. Many researchers are trying to invent techniques that transmits block with less bandwidth. The lesser the bandwidth is used, faster the blocks or messages will be propagated in the network. Blocks transferred with less bandwidth not only increases synchronization among peers but also reduces forks in the chain. Graphene protocol in blockchain is believed to be a protocol which transmits block with minimum amount of bandwidth possible.

Moreover, Bitcoin miners aim to broadcast the newly founded block fast as delay of even milliseconds increases the probability of other blocks to be added into the BC. This motivates a miner to cut the number of transactions to be added in a block. Miners in Bitcoin network keep a memory pool for all unconfirmed transactions. Miners choose some transaction from memory pool and construct a new candidate block. If mining pool of all the miners are ideally synchronized and they use same protocol for selecting the transactions to be added to their candidate block. This eliminates the need to include transactions in blocks and enables each miner to reconstruct a block from memory pool. In real scenarios, memory pool of miners are not perfectly synchronized, thus it leads to inefficiency in block propagation. To address this issue, authors in [159] presented a protocol named Graphene to design new blocks for a BC based network. It integrates BF with a Inverse Bloom Lookup Table (IBLT) to solve the issue of set reconciliation in P2P network. IBLT [25] solves the problem of calculating difference in two data sets which helps in determining what data sets share in common. To synchronize the blocks, sender first constructs a IBLT from transaction ID's in block. Also, it constructs a BF using same transaction ID's. The receiver utilizes BF to strain transactions ID's from memory pool and construct its own IBLT. Finally, receiver decodes the difference between two blocks. This way network bandwidth can be decreased significantly. Simulation results proved that with Graphene, network traffic decreases dramatically.

14.2.7   Anti-malware software using BF and blockchain

With the increase in Internet usage, the threats of viruses and malwares also gets increased. Mostly, anti-malware programs work by matching signatures of attack to arbitrary input stream. Nevertheless, its important to update these pattern matching mechanism in order to protect users from all types of new malwares. The idea of deploying a centralized update server is obviously a target for malicious attacker.

Authors of [156] provides a architecture named "BitAV" that scans the input with less memory usage and fast speed. Along with this, BitAV provides decentralized updates and maintenance by relying on blockchain based system. Systems can distribute the novel virus pattern on blockchain which increases the fault tolerance. Moreover, the blockchain enabled P2P maintenance mechanism that improves end-to-end performance and it is comparatively less susceptible to DoS attack. The blockchain structure of BitAV blockchain is similar to Bitcoin implementation. The only difference comes in the way transaction fields works. BitAV stores two information in place of transaction field, i.e, identifier and invalidation fields. The identifier field enables addition of new malware identifiers. The rest metadeta section is same as the Bitcoin header section to ensure verifiability. Every new identifier on blockchain holds format: $[Identifier][Publickey][Signature]$. Over and above, the scanning mechanism of BitAV uses a BF to enable constant time key value queries. Instead of storing signatures of malwares or their updates, BF stores them in hash format to save space and to reduce query time.

14.2.8   Transaction execution in disaster prone area using BF and blockchain

Authors of [157] utilizes a BF and blockchain to enable mobile based transaction mechanism in a disaster prone area. Here, it is assumed that there is no or limited access to bank in a disaster prone area as there is no Internet connectivity to this area. Endorsers supports absolute payment security for transactions between customer and merchant. Similar to Bitcoin, here also transactions are stored in blockchain like structure. Nevertheless, in this approach computing PoW by Miners is not required. Users computes hash of transactions log and other neighboring nodes add this signature to the log after verification to form an event chain. An event chain is a use case of cryptographic hash function on block. Rather than signing entire log, endorser computes hash value of previous block and sends it to monitor. Furthermore, monitor signs on the integration of hash value, GPS co-ordinate, spending of coin and sends back to endorser. Each user on the network stores event chain as their transaction log. Whenever a new event happens, a new block is cryptographically linked to last event chain. In case a mobile phone is switched off, the event chain is considered broken as the device is not able to ping messages with neighboring monitor nodes. Therefore, restricting a new event from being added to the event chain.

Additionally, in order to depict all spent e-coin from the beginning, a BF is used. All spent e-coins are mapped using hash function to BF. Rather than storing all ID's of spent e-coins, only the hashes of ID's are recorded in event chain. To check double spending of a certain e-coin, BF is probed. Clearly, communication overhead is reduced by using a BF.

14.2.9 Non-equivocation with BF and blockchain

Authors of [197] discussed their concerns on non -equivocation by a Certificate authority. If a CA equivocates different contradicting certificates for the same identity, it can compromise user's privacy. Hence, non-revocation is indeed an important necessity in security system today including blockchain based transparency and public key distribution. However with online trusted parties non-equivocation is difficult again because of privacy concerns and single point of failure.

To address this issue, authors have used Bitcoin witness approach, mainly due to three reasons:

- Bitcoin witnesses scheme is resistant to forking attacks.

- It involves a single global witnesses, i.e., Bitcoin blockchain and other multiple trusted entities for example, log providers and auditors are not allowed.

- Bitcoin blockchain provides open, decentralized and transparent environment to provide a efficient witnesses system.

Authors present their scheme with name Catena that reduces auditors bandwidth and provides tamper-evident log on the top of Bitcoin blockchain. Also, with Catena, forking is not allowed. Each Catena transaction consists of exactly one statement and previous catena transaction is suspended, thus creating a chain of transactions. Along with prevention of equivocation attack, Man-in-the-Middle (MITM) attacks are also prevented with Catena. Here, Bitcoin blockchain employs a trustworthy witnesses that can confirm for directory digest. For instance, in certificate transparency a log server can be employed to directly witness signed heads via a Catena log. Additionally, auditors who are running client interface can check for non-equivocation via SPV method. Similar to SPV verification, clients only have to download Bitcoin block headers and some pieces of Merkle hash to check for non-equivocation. Here also, thin clients relies on BF in order to avoid downloading whole data. Thin nodes insert only transactions of interest or its relevant connections in BF to filter out irrelevant transactions. Therefore, with using BF, Catena clients only receive relevant Catena transactions. Notably, authors of this scheme also pointed out that thin nodes have less security than full nodes.

14.2.10   Outdoor health monitoring using blockchain and BF

A popular application of IoT is in health care system [149] [214]. In this context, Unmanned aerial vehicle (UAV) can provide help to body wearable sensors in outdoor by alarming unpredictable problems for example, natural disaster and traffic hotspot. (UAV also known as drones is a type of aircrraft without a pilot on board and it has capability to provide efficient solutions in military, civil, and commercial sectors for audio and video surveillance [138].) Notably, UAV collaborated with mobile edge computing (MEC) can enable real-time support to users to store their health related information to MEC server. MEC brings cloud storage services near to user proximity [45]. Nevertheless, communication link between UAV and MEC suffers lots of cyber threats such as- MITM etc. Also, MEC server is prone to data integrity attack.

Authors of [110] suggested to blockchain as a solution for resolving security issues existing among UAV and MEC server. This is the first attempt when outdoor health monitoring system is proposed using blockchain. Here, health information that is collected from via UAV from users and stored on MEC server is protected with blockchain based architecture. To validate users, authors have used BF and health data is only stored in blockchain if blockchain validators them. Every user first registers on the network and for that user first generate a public and private key pair by using ECC. Next, user requests MEC server for registration. The health data collected from wearable devices and this data is transferred to MEC server via UAV. Before sending health care data, user encrypt this data using public key of UAV. Next, after decrypting health data UAV users using BF. Finally after successful validation, MEC encrypts health data and forwards to nearest MEC server. However before forwarding data, UAV validates identity of user with BF. Hence, using a BF in this case reduces data transmission. MEC server decrypts this data and checks this data for finding abnormalities. In case of any issue it is reported to the hospital. To validate the results parameters, i.e., processing time of MEC server, UAV validation time, UAV energy consumption, transmission of data for MEC server are used. It has been proved in experiments expected size of transmission data increases at much lower rate with BF over non-BF. With increase in number of users, data increases exponentially for non-BF.

14.2.11 Multi-domain collaboration for MEC in 5G and beyond based on blockchain and BF

The rapid growth of IoT and 5G systems accelerates the concept of Internet of everything [145], [55]. Clearly, this increase in number of devices lead to high growth of data. However, this high data growth possess challenge for the computing power of 5G systems and cloud computing models [58]. To solve this problem, heterogeneous MEC system were designed [132], [220]. Heterogeneous MEC is designed as a distributed computing platform integrating more than one MEC server, cloud server, and computing storage that provides intelligent edge services near the data source. As these systems have short transmission link, edge computing responds quickly to the service request. Nevertheless, in order to accomplish a heterogeneous MEC system, multiple MEC servers needs to integrate their resources so as to complete large scale computing tasks. Unfortunately, this multi-server collaboration involves trust and security issues as these server belongs to different domains and they are managed by different organization. MEC server contacts other MEC servers via cross-domain routing enabled by SDN controller. However, to ensure cross-domain routing among multiple server, SDN controller demands topology information of other domain. Notably, this information of different domain should be confidential to each other and this privacy leakage can harm MEC system.

Authors in [218] resolves privacy leakage issue using blockchain. Here, blockchain enables trusted data sharing between MEC servers to achieve trusted collaboration of multi-domain MEC network. Also, this system adopts accommodative BF as a carrier to help multi-domain collaborative routing consensus without revealing topology privacy.

First, a cross-domain MEC request arrives at controller A through domain 1. As per this request, controller A computes intra domain path for domain 1 and choses the optimal one with minimized sum of weights. While a new request is also send to controller of subsequent domain having virtual topology of domain 1. Also, controller A constructs BF containing the routing results from the controller. Here, BF maintains distributed ledger and efficient routing mechanism. In specific, BF are also used as a carrier of routing verification. Tables 14.2, and 14.3 represents tabular comparison of above discussed scheme.

TABLE 14.2

Comparison between different schemes integrating blockchain with BF.

Reference	Year	PDS used	Application	Metrics Evaluated	Purpose of using BF	Characteristics	Platform	Public/Private	Consensus Mechanism	Ensures privacy
[23]	2014	SBF	Financial	• Memory requirements • Time complexity • Privacy	Enables SPV client to specify transaction of interest in a compact manner	• Fast synchronization • Less memory consumption	Bitcoin	Public	PoW	×
[86]	2014	SBF	Financial	• Privacy • Number of addresses in a wallet • False positive rate	Enables SPV client to specify transaction of interest in a compact manner	• Easily integrated with existing SPV Client • No additional computational load	Bitcoin	Public	PoW	✓
[114]	2017	SBF	Financial	• Average error rate in estimating distinct addresses	Enables SPV client to download transaction of interest in a compact way	• Good accuracy	Bitcoind and block-parser	—	PoW	✓
[172]	2017	SBF	Healthcare	• False positive rate • Size of BF • Optimal Hash functions • Memory requirements • Processing time • Epoch Length	Maintains logs for bodyworn sensing devices	• Ensures Data integrity and Non-repudiation	MicaZ mote, Python	Private	—	×
[91]	2018	SBF	Smart Grid	• Data Privacy • Authentication • Computation Cost • Time Complexity	To authenticate users without revealing actual identity	• Ensures Privacy, authentication • Less time complexity and computation cost	—	Private	—	✓
[215]	2014	SBF	Financial	• Computation Cost • Storage requirements	To store indexed enteries from logs of transaction	• Flexible but less optimized	Solidity, Ethereum	Public	PoW	×
[157]	2017	SBF	Financial	• Impersonation attack • Colluding attack • Double spending • Non-repudiation • Reset and recovery attack • Transaction Completion Ratio • Communication Overhead • Event chain Validity • Transaction Completion Time	To ensure no double spending	• Less Computational cost • Prevents impersonation and Non-repudiation	–	–	–	×

SBF: Standard Bloom Filter, ABF: Adaptive Bloom filter, IBLT: Inverse Bloom Lookup table, –: Not specified

TABLE 14.3

Comparison between different schemes integrating blockchain with BF.

Ref	Year	Scheme	Domain	Parameters	Purpose	Benefits	Platform	Type	Consensus		Valid
[166]	2017	ABF	Financial	• Storage requirements	To identify account wise list of transactions of interest	• Comparatively less false positive rate • Minimal storage requirements	Ethereum	Public	Quick-Blocks	–	✓
[159]	2017	SBF and IBLT	Financial	• Transaction rate • Network bandwidth consumed	Set reconciliation	• Higher saving if blocks are mined after every 15 seconds	Any cryptocurrency platform	Public	PoW		✗
[90]	2018	Cuckoo Filter	Financial	• Lookup time	Enables SPV client to specify transaction of interest	• Fast membership search over SBF	Ethereum	Public		–	✓
[110]	2019	SBF	Healthcare	• Processing time of MEC server • UAV validation time • UAV energy consumption • Transmission of data for MEC server	To validate user's identity	• BF reduces data transmission for validating user	Ethereum	Public		—	✓
[218]	2020	Accommodative BF	Mobile edge computing	• Average mistrust rate • Resource utilization • Path provisioning latency	For efficient routing mechanism	• Improves credibility and efficiency of MEC collaboration	—	—	—		✗

SBF: Standard Bloom Filter, ABF: Adaptive Bloom filter, IBLT: Inverse Bloom Lookup table, –: Not specified

14.3 Integration of QF with Blockchain

QF serves the same purpose as BF. However, BF fails if data does not fit inside main memory. Literature does not support any work integrating QF and blockchain. Nevertheless, the above mentioned work using BF can be replaced with QF specially if the filter size is too large to get fit inside main memory.

14.4 Integration of Skiplist with Blockchain

One of the worth mentioning use case for blockchain is in notarizing document for example, academic degrees. The tamper proof and transparent property of blockchain makes the document on blockchain harder to forge and modify. However, being a promising application the notarization use case suffers from some limitations. One of such challenge is to verify the presence of a document on blockchain even if that document is very old with respect to a reference point. There may be a case when a user has not updated his/her blockchain, then verifiers reference point on the blockchain may be behind in time with the block in question. Notably, this problem becomes even more worse for a low powered device.

One solution to this problem is to use SPV client that is discussed in previous chapters. Additionally, SPV introduces security weakness; if SPV client acquires transaction from a single full node, which may become prone to single point of failure. Moreover, SPV and full client are prone to isolation attack (for example, a fork from public blockchain with vey less work) and routing based hijacking attacks [37]. Also, if a SPV client connects with more than one full node, it may lead to consumption of more bandwidth and power. Hence it is not scalable for large number of thin clients. Importantly, it is necessary that an SPV client should remain online in order to check whether the transaction is committed to blockchain or not. Infact for any verifier to verify, device needs to be online with a good Internet connection. Verification of a transaction without a well connected network is either impossible or insecure.

Other solution to this problem is to use collective signing (CoSi) [183], an efficient digital signatures technique offered by ByzCoin. ByzCoin constructs a consensus group from recently successful proof of work miners from past few days or weaks. In order to commit transactions securely, this consensus group formed runs PBFT algorithm. However, rather than using all-to-all communication, CoSi is used during each of these phases CoSi produces a single efficiently verifiable compact and collective signature cryptographically signed revealing that a fraction of consensus group has verified. To check CoSi on a transaction, verifier should know the public keys of miners in the consensus group in time when the transaction was committed. Clearly, this consensus group continuously gets changed. To address this problem, on change of a consensus group, some nodes of previous consensus group collectively forms and signs a forward link have two important information. The architecture of CoSi protocol is represented in Fig. 14.3.

- A hash pointer to the very first block committed by next consensus group.

- A description telling how consensus group is changed which specifying which miners public keys are inserted or removed.

Also, all committed block has backward links using hashes. Hence, a verifier with no Internet connection can verify using forward and backward link of the chain. However, with his method it is required that prover should send all intervening block headers and forward link. Clearly, this puts bandwidth, power and storage bandwidth on low powered devices.

To solve this problem, Chainiac used Skipchains, a cryptographic blockchain variant of skiplist integrated with blockchain to provide secure P2P verification. *Skipchains* were originally introduced in context of updating softwares by a framework called *CHAINIAC* [154]. It uses *skipchains* to validate integrity and authenticity of software update provided by the vendors. Also, this proposal eliminates a single point of failure. Skipchain contains both long distance forward and backward links to the blockchain. With *skipchains*, the verifier can traverse both in forward and backward directions to track the timeline from any reference point. Whenever a new block is created in Chainiac, that block contains the hash link to point farther backward in time along with having link to immediate prior block. This backward link can prove integrity of old transaction anywhere in the blockchain. Also, Chainiac provides long distance forward links along with CoSi. The long distance forward links contains information of public key changes in consensus group. With this technique, instead of a single authority to validate the documents, document is validated by a leader as well as by a group of decentralized witnesses. It is implemented in 4 rounds of communication and after each round, signature is generated and verified by witnesses. It gives assurance that if central authority key gets compromised, client can not validate the document unless it is signed by multiple witnesses. Additionally, it reduces communication overhead in PBFT. As each node no longer requires individual node signature. So, *CoSi* reduces the data size of message that is to be broadcasted in network during prepare and commit phase [72]. With having both long distance forward and long distance backward links, the cryptographic chain is traversable in both direction so that verifier can verify the correctness of a block anywhere in time having others participants reference to a point on blockchain. This verification can be performed in logarithmic number of steps. Hence this offline and P2P verification with skipchain can be extended in future blockchain technology

Skipchains is denoted as S_b^h where h and b, define height and basis of *skipchain* respectively; if $0<b<1$ skipchain is randomized and if $b>1$ (integer) it is defined to be deterministic. The tuples of *skipchains* contain $(id_t, D_t, h_t, F_t, B_t)$ which denotes block identifier, payload data, block height, list of forward and backward link respectively.

In BC, *Skipchains* is used by resource-constrained devices to verify the correctness of a transaction. In order to verify, instead of downloading all BC data, *skipchains* only downloads some logarithmic number of blocks. Fig. 14.4 shows forward and backward links in skipchain. Verification process in *skipchain* is also similar to verification process using Merle tree. All committed blocks contain backward hash link to not only immediate prior block, but also it points farther backward. Forward links are formed using *CoSi* which ensures that a certain number of miners have verified and committed a block.

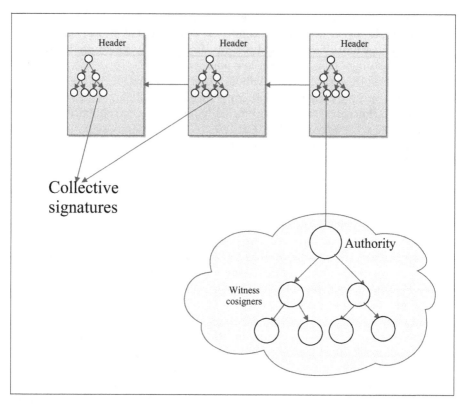

FIGURE 14.3
CoSi protocol architecture [121].

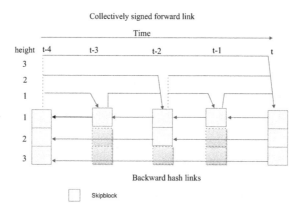

FIGURE 14.4
Structure of S_2^3 deterministic Skipchains.

Activity

Multiple Choice Questions

1. What are the characteristics of a lightweight blockchain client?

    A. Lightweight client is also known as SPV client

    B. Lightweight client only downloads block header of a blockchain network.

    C. Lightweight client downloads full copy of a blockchain distributed ledger

    D. Lightweight client has to refer to a trusted full client for performing operations

2. The method used by lightweight client to verify inclusion of a transaction in a block is called?

    A. Complex payment verification

    B. Simplified payment verification

    C. Blockchain payment verification

    D. None of these

3. What are the characteristics of a full blockchain client?

    A. Stores entire history of blockchain distributed ledger

    B. Provides better security over lightweight client

    C. Refers to lightweight client for performing operations

    D. None of these

4. Integrating BF with SPV client provides?

    A. Protection from DoS attack

    B. Space efficient way to acquire transaction of interest

    C. Protection from sybil attack

    D. BF can't be used with SPV client

5. Which of the following is the main issue with SPV client?

    A. SPV client can't download block header easily

    B. SPV client can't be run on a mobile device

    C. SPV client privacy is threatened

    D. None of these

6. Explain how Ethereum uses BF for better space efficiency?

7. Explain how Bitcoin is using BF for implementing SPV client?

8. Explain how BF can be used for blockchain based certificate revocation system?

9. Explain working of Graphene protocol.

10. How anti-malware softwares are using BF and blockchain in integration?

11. Explain the concept of Skipchains.

1. a, b, d   2. b   3. a, b   4. b   5. c

15

Applicability of Cardinality Estimation PDS with Blockchain

15.1 DDoS Attack in Blockchain

DDoS stands for distributed denial of service attack. This attack is used to create a complete shutdown for a machine. Here, the target machine is overloaded with bogus traffic so that legitimate requests cannot be processed. The term distributed is used as this attack is delivered by a network of computers called botnets. Particularly, attackers launch this attack for fun and profit purpose. One reason that DDoS is hard to tackle is that it is difficult to differentiate between legitimate and malicious requests.

However, the decentralized nature of blockchain prevents this attack to be launched [164], [173], [174]. In particular, attacks on single blockchain machine are known in a blockchain network (such as sybil attack, routing attack). Nevertheless, if some nodes fail to be active, the blockchain network still operates. Later when attacked system manged to recover, they re-sync and updates with recent data collected from the nodes. The degree of protection in blockchain network depends on number of nodes and hash rate of the network. In order to compromise the whole system, attacker needs to attack 51% of the total number of nodes of the network or in other words attacker needs to have more computational power over combination of other participants.

For a blockchain based cryptocurrency system this attack include targeting transaction processes, i.e., disabling a machine so as to refrain the generation of new transactions. One way to launch this attack is by creating various transaction to transfer asset between malicious attacker's pre created wallet's. By creating multiple transactions miners involve themselves solving proof for these transactions. The denial of service is caused by requirement to process legitimate transactions. Notably, in Bitcoin blockchain network, a transaction fee is charged but this fees is not much high to be payed by an attacker.

For example, when cryptocurrency named Bitcoin gold [26] was launched, it immediately got effected by DDoS leading to website down for four hours. Bitcoin gold hard fork noticed 10 million hits per minute. Later the twitter statement reveals that most of the hits involve IP addresses routed via china.

An another effort to launch DDoS attack on blockchain is discussed by the authors of [143] and the attack is named as **blockchain denial of ser-**

vice **(BDoS)**. This is based on the fundamental that blockchain protocol distributes incentives for security as miners get reward for mining a block successfully. BDoS exploits rationality of miners by giving them higher profit for playing against system. Compared to traditional DoS attack, BDoS can disrupt the blockchain with significantly less resources. Unlike selfish mining, here aim of attacker is not to provide revenue to adversary but to disrupt the blockchain network. Lets understand BDoS attack.

If more than one miner mines block concurrently, it results in fork (if block have same parent) and in that case chain got different branches. As per Bitcoin rules, to prevent ambiguity, only a single chain is extended, i.e., the miner should extend the longest chain in the main chain. Then the rewards of blocks diverged from that chain are ignored. However, to avoid reward loss, miners usually start mining even before the current block is validated. Notably, they start mining on the latest block once its metadata of the header is received. Therefore by avoiding wasting resources on block, miners try to increase their mining chance of next block . This approach of mining using only header is called SPV mining described earlier in chapter 7. To launch an attack, attacker creates a block and publishes its header only. With a given header, miner tries to extend that block. However, attacker never publishes full block and that block tried by rational miner never gets included in the blockchain's main chain and it comes with zero expected reward from that block. Hence, the attacker created a situation where honest miner ends up in loosing reward. Also, miners can't process legitimate requests that leads to a situation where honest miner gives up with mining and leads to wastage of resources.

Countermeasure of DDoS attack include identifying source of flooding and then to design filter in order to block that source. Allow the outgoing and incoming traffic from a source only if the source address is in the range of expected IP addresses.

> **Note:**
> DDoS attack is not directly effecting the security of data stored in blockchain network but the ode being attacked can't take part in consensus mechanism and its computation power and resources are therefore wasted.

15.2 Mempool Transaction Count

All transactions waiting to be confirmed is stored in memory pool(mempool) of Bitcoin network. To get confirmed, transaction first needs to be in block from mempool. Notably, there is no global memory pool in blockchain network. Every node on Bitcoin network constructs its own version of mempool by connecting to Bitcoin network. Each transaction in mempool pays a fees and has a size. Clearly, transaction having high fees are picked with priority by miners. Mempool is cleared whenever the node is rebooted. Nodes pay fees to miners for mining transactions. The maximum number of transaction in a block varies as all transaction doesn't have same size. The more the number of transactions in mempool, the more is the congestion in traffic that leads to longer confirmation time. Also, transaction fees of network is determined by network congestion and size of transaction. The size of Bitcoin block size is 1 MB which implies a miner can take and process 1 MB of transactions per block roughly around every 10 minutes. For a Bitcoin network, if number of transactions exceeds 1 MB, it leads to network congestion and miners then prioritize transaction having higher fees. In this context, the mempool transaction count metric [27] of Bitcoin reveals number of transactions causing the congestion. (In contrast, mempool size will specify for how long congestion will last long.)

15.3 Interation of Linear Counting, LogLog and Hyper-LogLog with Blockchain

Although there is no existing work in literature that integrates HLL, LogLog or linear counting in blockchain. But these PDS can be used for counting purpose in blockchain network as discussed below. Notably, we have presented our view in context of HLL as this the most popular and efficient algorithm among all three.

15.3.1 Counting transaction in mempool

This cardinality estimation PDS can be used to count transactions in mempool. Mempool transaction count tells how many transactions causes the congestion. As each system on blockchain network has different storage capacity for these unconfirmed transactions. In this context, HLL can be used to count number of transactions in each nodes mempool. To implement this logic, whenever a new transaction is added to mempool, it is first hashed and this resultant hash is stored in the bucket as per the value of longest zero sequence. Finally, the values in buckets are combined using harmonic mean of the values in bucket. Moreover, using programming an upper limit can be set on mempool specifying maximum transactions to be added in mempool to avoid congestion. To set a limit, concept of smart contract can also be used where a contract with logic specifying maximum transaction in mempool is developed. The usage of HLL to check congested traffic in blockchain network is show in Fig. 15.1.

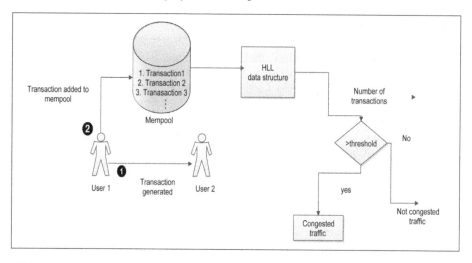

FIGURE 15.1
HLL to check congested traffic in Bitcoin network.

15.3.2   HLL to prevent DoS attack

An interesting area where HLL can be implemented is to prevent DDoS in blockchain. Here, the intention of an attacker is to overwhelm victim machine with bulk of non-sense traffic to consume resources and bandwidth. As discussed earlier, DDoS attack can be launched in blockchain by sending lots of transaction simultaneously. Another way, adversary can also send an extra large size opcode so as to process the block, time taken by miners also gets high. Consequently, miners cannot process legitimate request. Another way of performing DoS on blockchain is by filling up orphan blocks with unlimited bogus transactions as orphan transactions blocks are provided with unlimited storage. So, when new transaction arrives, all transactions in orphan blocks are verified and validated if not validated earlier which consequently makes miner node so busy that it is unable to process normal transactions [28]. In this context, HLL can be employed in the network to notify if the source IP of the incoming packet extends a predefined threshold. For example, authors in [60] proposed an algorithm that uses sliding HLL and BF to detect port scan attack. Port Scan attack is a form of DoS attack where an attacker targets to find some services on victims machine. Sliding HLL is almost similar to original HLL which was proposed by [61] to approximate cardinality over a changeable bounded interval using sliding window model. Also, smart contracts can be employed for the same purpose. For example, Rodrigues et al. [164] used smart contract to mitigate DoS. Here, smart contract reports blacklisted IP address across multiple domains. Notably, techniques of blocking IP address only works for static IP addresses and this fails for dynamic IP address. Smart contracts are programmed with logic to block IP address in the

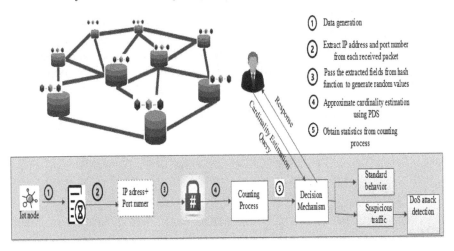

FIGURE 15.2
Approximate cardinality estimation in blockchain based IoT environment.

blockchain. However, authors used traditional data structures to count number of transactions from same IP address. Instead of using traditional data structures, probabilistic data structure can be used in order to save space and to perform the operation of counting in constant time. The process of handling DoS in blockchain based IoT network is shown in Fig. 15.2 To obtain unique count of addresses within a block, extract IP address and port number from data/transaction generated by IoT node. Pass the extracted fields from SHA-256 hash function to estimate cardinality.

> **Note** The above discussion can be applicable to IoT based environment as this environment involves financial services like exchanging payments, paying bills etc. for smart grid environment or V2G environment. Also, blockchain network is applicable to many other IoT fields such as agriculture, medical line etc.

15.3.3 IoT chain

A project named, IoT chain [29] is designed using blockchain and PDS to make IoT network better. IoT chain (ITC) was introduced to solve challenges such as data privacy, DDoS attack, overhead cost of centralized environment, data acquisition, data processing etc. in IoT. This technology is a combination of asymmetric encryption, semi-homomorphic encryption and distributed ledgers powered by blockchain technology. With a private-public key pair of asymmetric algorithm, private data of users cannot be seen by the adversary.

Blockchain technology reduces the cost incurred by the centralized architecture, besides it ensures that data is not shared with any third party. Homomorphic encryption enables operations to be performed on an encrypted data. In addition to this, ITC uses BF and HLL in the decentralized environment to perform real-time analysis of data where it becomes necessary to process the data before a certain time period.

Activity

Multiple Choice Questions

1. What does mempool transaction count reveals?

    A. Number of transactions that are causing congestion.

    B. For how long congestion will last?

    C. Block size

    D. None of these

2. What does mempool size metric tells?

    A. Number of transactions that are causing congestion.

    B. For how long congestion will last?

    C. Block size

    D. None of these

3. What is IoT chain?

    A. Integration of blockchain and IoT

    B. Integration of IoT and PDS

    C. Integration of IoT and homonorphic encryption

    D. None of these

4. What is Bitcoin gold?

    A. Gold version of Bitcoin

    B. A variant of Ethereum

    C. Consensus algorithm

    D. Hard fork of Bitcoin

5. There is a global memory pool for a blockchain network.

    A. True

    B. False

6. To compromise the whole blockchain network, attacker needs to attack ....% of total nodes?

    A. 51%

    B. 30%

    C. 33%

D. 1%

7. What are the main characteristics of homomorphic encryption?

    A. Operations can be performed on encrypted data.

    B. It resolves encryption issues

    C. Its process involves a third party service provider

    D. All of the above

8. BDoS stands for?

    A. Blockchain Denial of Service

    B. Base Denial of Service

    C. Bloated Denial of Service

    D. None of these

1. a   2. b   3. a   4. d   5. b   6. c   7. d
8. a

16

Applicability of Frequency Estimation PDS with Blockchain

16.1 RFID Tag Cloning

Radio frequency identification (RFID) is latest auto-identification technology based on radio waves for identification and tracking of object without line of sight [31]. Unlike conventional barcode, RFID tag is a reusable, readable or writable and less likely to be error prone. RFID use case includes shipping, port operation, supply chain management, banknotes etc. to name a few. Enhanced operational efficiency, better accuracy, lower operational cost, improved service are some of the benefits of RFID. RFID tag reading are in form of data stream. For example, say $S = S_1, S_2, \ldots, S_m$ is a data stream of tag readings divided into batches of t seconds. Despite having various technology, security issues of RFID are a matter of concern among which RFID cloning attack is one of the malicious attack. RFID cloning attack implies fabricating more than one replicas of genuine tag. A cloned tag is generally the duplicate copy of Electronic Product Code (EPC) against a genuine tag. Whenever a reader reads the tag, it is hard to differentiate among two tags. Additionally, using same hash function against same EPC results in hash collision. Cloning of RFID can lead to financial loses. However, cryptography based authentication method assures security and privacy but also impose requirements of high memory and computational power [80].

16.2 Understanding Heavy Hitters

Network traffic monitoring is very important for secure network operation. In this context, detecting heavy hitters is one of the process for traffic measurement applications. Detecting heavy hitters can be used for network operations such as traffic accounting and anomaly detection. Heavy hitter is defined as a flow that has a particular fraction of total link capacity. In other words it is detecting flow whose size is more than given threshold. According to Zhou et al., detecting heavy hitter is the process of determining the frequency of same element belonging to network data stream [221]. Notably, network flow is determined by 5 tuples, i.e., source IP address, destination IP address, source port, destination port and protocol. Generally, the data stream is defined as $S=p_1, p_2,....,p_n$ where, p_i that is made up of IP address, port number etc. Detecting heavy hitters has been studied in many domains such as- network traffic and IP calling.

To detect heavy hitters with PDS, first step is packet processing stage which extracts network data stream from network packet. Second, each element of data stream is updated to probabilistic sketch. In third step, flow size is calculated by probabilistic counting. Finally, heavy hitters are detected as the estimation of flow size in measurement interval. If the value of a element is greater than or equal to a threshold then the corresponding IP address is identified as heavy hitter.

16.3 Integration of CMS with Blockchain

Literature lacks work supporting integration of CMS and blockchain. However, we could use CMS for various ways in blockchain.

16.3.1 Detecting DoS attack

As discussed above detecting DoS attack, anomaly detection, QoS management are important use-cases of detecting heavy hitters in real-time. Apart from HLL, DoS attack can also be handled by CMS by setting a threshold ϕ for any time slot t and if the frequency of counter in CMS is greater than predefined threshold $\phi * N$ (N is overall count) then that node can be identified as malicious node. Also, by using frequency count PDS, a verifier can check frequency of address in a block or to count frequency of same source and destination address pair to generate real-time response. This way by using CMS, each streaming update can be processed in logarithmic number of steps. Another advantage of CMS is that legitimate connection can be deleted from the pool of observation [118].

Inspired from the work of [179], an idea to detect heavy hitter in real-time for private blockchain based IoT network is presented in Fig. 16.1. Although authors in [179] have not used PDS to detect heavy hitters. As the number of participants in private blockchain are usually less, therefore it is necessary to ensure the availability of nodes in order to operate correctly. Clearly, the nodes of the private blockchain network should be available all time while being protected from DoS attack. The proposal used an Software Defined

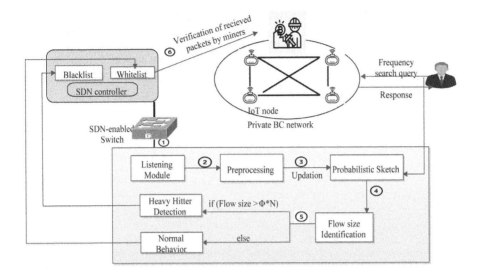

FIGURE 16.1
Heavy hitter detection in blockchain based IoT environment.

Network (SDN)-enabled switch to protect nodes within private blockchain against DDoS attack. Within a network, this attack refrains nodes participation in consensus mechanism which can lead to wastage of computational power. However, DDoS is detected based on flow statistics by usage of Count-Sketches [135, 134, 84]. SDN-enabled switch filters out remote nodes that generate heavy hitters and tries to send data within network. It listens to all incoming packets $(p_1, p_2, \ldots, p_n)$ and extracts source-destination pair from each packet to compute statistics for flow entries. The SDN switch is configured with information (IP address and port number) of registered blockchain nodes of private network. SDN network controller checks probabilistic count sketch periodically to detect heavy hitters. It places heavy hitter flow and normal flow in blacklist and whitelist respectively. Finally, packets from whitelist are forwarded to be verified by miner nodes within the network.

16.3.2 Detecting RFID tag cloning

In IoT environment, Count-sketches can be used to detect RFID clone tagging in applications, such as supply chain management, shipping and port operations, water level monitoring etc. In this context, Hazalila *et al.* [113] proposed a lightweight anti-cloning approach based on CMS vector and consistency of dual hash collisions. CMS uses two independent hash functions to probe identical EPC. While hashing the identical EPC, the same hash function results in hash collisions which implies high chance of tag cloning. Implementation results show that the proposed method performs better than baseline approaches and achieves a better accuracy in detecting clone ratio. Although, this proposal does not implement blockchain technology but the CMS could be extended to a blockchain based IoT network. The sketch is a accumulation of tag reading spread out for multiple RFID readers. Each sketch has tag readings received during batch interval.

Activity

Answer the following questions

1. What does EPC stand for in context to RFID?

2. Explain how integration of CMS and blockchain helps in preventing RFID tag cloning?

3. Explain what is meant by heavy hitter?

4. How RFID tag cloning can be performed?

5. Explain how count-sketch can prevent DoS attack.

17

Applicability of Approximate Similarity Search PDS with Blockchain

17.1 Approximate Nearest Neighbor Binary Search Algorithm for Wireless Multimedia Sensor Network

Storing massive IoT data on blockchain requires a large space of memory. Also, existing similarity search methods take space even more than that for an actual dataset for creating indexed structure. In view of this problem, similarity search PDS in blockchain allows a verifier or user to retrieve similar data for a given query in real time. ASS based PDS performs computations with minimum number of distance evaluations. In literature [136] authors have combined LSH and blockchain with IPFS to manage data generated by Wireless multimedia sensor network (WMSN). Blockchain based system protects highly sensitive data from tampering.

17.2 A Blockchain of Image Copyrights Using Locality Sensitive Hashing

For proving copyrights on digital asset, A. Zhuvikin [222] proposed a blockchain based image copyright registry based on robust image features. As discussed above, LSH searches easily on high dimensional data sets by ensuring that similar objects has high probability for collision over dissimilar objects. Rather than using LSH, cross-polytop LSH is used that also maps similar data to same index value [35]. However, compared to original LSH, cross-polytope significantly reduces space and time complexity. It uses LSH to retrieve images with similar content even if they are changed by content-preserving operations, such as- JPEG compression, shrinking, zooming etc. To share original image with copyright, first robust image features vector is calculated by performing LSH and signing using private key of the owner. In the next step, obtained signature is multiplied with a random integer called blinding factor to generate blind signatures which is broadcasted to all miner nodes on network for verification. Finally, image index item is constructed using LSH and blind signatures to ease locating copyright owner. Moreover, a hybrid data query method named One Permutation with rotation and cross-polytope locality sensitive hashing (OPRCP) is proposed which approximates nearest neighbour search in WMSN hybrid data (audio, image, text) along with constructing a query data structure. OPRCP first extracts feature vector of multimedia data using TF-IDF method followed by constructing a hash table data structure from obtained feature vector. When a verifier or a user has to map query object to data structure, then after feature vectorization query undergoes same hash calculation process. Authors have also analyzed relationship between query time and accuracy of query from LSH nearest neighbor search. Compared to original LSH, OPRCP improves similarity search in terms of space and time.

Activity

Answer the following questions

1. Explain how integration of blockchain and locality sensitive hashing can help to preserve image copyrights.

2. According to you, what are the possible fields where minhashing can be integrated with blockchain?

Bibliography

[1] Internet of Things (IoT) connected devices installed base worldwide from 2015 to 2025. Available: `https://www.statista.com/statistics/471264/iot-number-of-connected-devices-worldwide/`, [Accessed: Jan. 2020].

[2] IDC predicts ten-fold increase in data by 2025. Available: `https://inform.tmforum.org/data-analytics-and-ai/2017/04/idc-predicts-ten-fold-increase-data-2025/`, [Accessed: Jul. 2020].

[3] Edge computing promises near real-time insights and facilitates localized actions. Available: `https://www.gartner.com/smarterwithgartner/what-edge-computing-means-for-infrastructure-and-operations-leaders/`, [Accessed: Feb. 2020].

[4] World population projected to reach 9.8 billion in 2050, and 11.2 billion in 2100. Available: `https://www.un.org/development/desa/en/news/population/world-population-prospects-2017.html`, [Accessed: March 2020].

[5] Agriculture IoT Market. Available: `https://www.marketsandmarkets.com/Market-Reports/iot-in-agriculture-market-199564903.html`, [Accessed: March 2020].

[6] Smart gets cheaper & four other predictions for global manufacturing. Available: `https://www.smartindustry.com/assets/Uploads/2019-Crystal-Ball-Report.pdf`, [Accessed: March 2020].

[7] Worldwide Global DataSphere IoT Device and Data Forecast, 2019–2023. Available: `https://www.idc.com/getdoc.jsp?containerId=US45066919`, [Accessed: March 2020].

[8] Blockchain. Available: `https://en.wikipedia.org/wiki/Blockchain`, [Accessed: March 2020].

[9] Size of the Bitcoin blockchain from 2010 to 2020, by quarter. Available: `https://www.statista.com/statistics/647523/worldwide-bitcoin-blockchain-size/#:~:text=The%20size%20of%20the%20Bitcoin,the%20end%20of%20March%202020`, [Accessed: May 2020].

[10] Remaining challenges of blockchain adoption and possible solutions. Available: `https://www.finextra.com/blogposting/18496/ remaining-challenges-of-blockchain-adoption-and-possible- solutions`, [Accessed: April 2020].

[11] Blockchain is here. What's your next move? Available: `https://www.pwc.com/gx/en/issues/blockchain/blockchain- in-business.html`, [Accessed: April 2020].

[12] Developer Hub Build, Contribute & Earn with ARK. Available: `https: //ark.io/developers`, [Accessed: April 2020].

[13] Litecoin - Open source P2P digital currencylitecoin.org. Available: `https://litecoin.org/`, [Accessed: May 2020].

[14]

[15] Tor Project , Anonymity Online. Available: `https://www.torproject. org/`, [Accessed: June 2020].

[16] IPFS powers the Distributed Web. Available: `https://ipfs.io/`, [Accessed: May 2020].

[17] Delegated Proof-of-Stake Consensus. Available: `https://bitshares. org/technology/delegated-proof-of-stake-consensus/`, [Accessed: April 2020].

[18] wiki/Proof-of-Authority-Chains.md. Available: `https://github.com/ openethereum/wiki/blob/master/Proof-of-Authority-Chains.md`, [Accessed: June 2020].

[19] Building a Proof of Authority network with Parity. Available: `https://medium.com/quantstamp/building-a-proof-of- authority-network-with-parity-654d18bce321`, [Accessed: June 2020].

[20] Setup your own private Proof-of-Authority Ethereum network with Geth. Available: `https://hackernoon.com/setup-your-own- private-proof-of-authority-ethereum-network-with-geth- 9a0a3750cda8`, [Accessed: June 2020].

[21] Proof of burn. Available: `https://en.bitcoin.it/wiki/Proof_of_ burn#:~:text=Proof%20of%20burn%20is%20a,Work%20and%20Proof% 20of%20Stake.&text=The%20idea%20is%20that%20miners,to%20a% 20verifiably%20unspendable%20address`, [Accessed: Jul. 2016].

[22] Bitcoin Blockchain Size. Available: `https://ycharts.com/ indicators/bitcoin_blockchain_size`, [Accessed: March 2020].

[23] Connection Bloom filtering. Available: `https://github.com/bitcoin/bips/blob/master/bip-0037.mediawiki`, [Accessed: Sep. 2019].

[24] Proof of Work with SHA256 and Bloom filter. Available: `https://github.com/indutny/proof-of-work`, [Accessed: May 2020].

[25]

[26] Bitcoin Gold Website Down Following DDoS Attack. Available: `https://www.coindesk.com/bitcoin-gold-website-following-massive-ddos-attack`, [Accessed: June 2020].

[27] Mempool Transaction Count. Available: `https://www.blockchain.com/charts/mempool-count`, [Accessed: June 2020].

[28] CVE-2012-3789. Available: `https://en.bitcoin.it/wiki/CVE-2012-3789`, [Accessed: June 2020].

[29] IoT Chain—A High-Security Lite IoT OS. Available: `https://steemit.com/blockchain/@ansteadm/iot-chain-or-a-high-security-lite-iot-os`, [Accessed: June 2020].

[30] World energy outlook 2017. Accessed: 30, March 2019.

[31] Jemal Abawajy. Enhancing rfid tag resistance against cloning attack. In *2009 Third International Conference on Network and System Security*, pages 18–23. IEEE, 2009.

[32] Shaik V. Akram, Praveen K. Malik, Rajesh Singh, Gehlot Anita, and Sudeep Tanwar. Adoption of blockchain technology in various realms: Opportunities and challenges. *Security and Privacy*, n/a(n/a):e109.

[33] Fadele Ayotunde Alaba, Mazliza Othman, Ibrahim Abaker Targio Hashem, and Faiz Alotaibi. Internet of things security: A survey. *Journal of Network and Computer Applications*, 88:10–28, 2017.

[34] Noga Alon, Yossi Matias, and Mario Szegedy. The space complexity of approximating the frequency moments. *Journal of Computer and system sciences*, 58(1):137–147, 1999.

[35] Alexandr Andoni, Piotr Indyk, Thijs Laarhoven, Ilya Razenshteyn, and Ludwig Schmidt. Practical and optimal lsh for angular distance. In *Advances in neural information processing systems*, pages 1225–1233, 2015.

[36] Leonardo Aniello, Roberto Baldoni, Edoardo Gaetani, Federico Lombardi, Andrea Margheri, and Vladimiro Sassone. A prototype evaluation of a tamper-resistant high performance blockchain-based transaction log for a distributed database. In *2017 13th European Dependable Computing Conference (EDCC)*, pages 151–154. IEEE, 2017.

[37] Maria Apostolaki, Aviv Zohar, and Laurent Vanbever. Hijacking bitcoin: Routing attacks on cryptocurrencies. In *2017 IEEE Symposium on Security and Privacy (SP)*, pages 375–392. IEEE, 2017.

[38] Morton M. Astrahan, Mario Schkolnick, and Whang Kyu-Young. Approximating the number of unique values of an attribute without sorting. *Information Systems*, 12(1):11–15, 1987.

[39] S. Banerjee, V. Odelu, A. K. Das, S. Chattopadhyay, N. Kumar, Y. Park, and S. Tanwar. Design of an anonymity-preserving group formation based authentication protocol in global mobility networks. *IEEE Access*, 6:20673–20693, 2018.

[40] Michael A. Bender, Martin Farach-Colton, Rob Johnson, Russell Kraner, Bradley C. Kuszmaul, Dzejla Medjedovic, Pablo Montes, Pradeep Shetty, Richard P. Spillane, and Erez Zadok. Don't thrash: How to cache your hash on flash. *Proceedings of the VLDB Endowment*, 5(11):1627–1637, 2012.

[41] Abishek Bhat. Use the bloom filter, luke!, 2016. Accessed: 17, August 2019.

[42] Jitendra Bhatia, Ridham Dave, Heta Bhayani, Sudeep Tanwar, and Anand Nayyar. Sdn-based real-time urban traffic analysis in vanet environment. *Computer Communications*, 149:162–175, 2019.

[43] Jitendra Bhatia, Yash Modi, Sudeep Tanwar, and Madhuri Bhavsar. Software defined vehicular networks: A comprehensive review. *International Journal of Communication Systems*, 32(12):e4005, 2019. e4005 dac.4005.

[44] P. Bhattacharya, S. Tanwar, U. Bodke, S. Tyagi, and N. Kumar. Bindaas: Blockchain-based deep-learning as-a-service in healthcare 4.0 applications. *IEEE Transactions on Network Science and Engineering*, pages 1–1, 2019.

[45] Pronaya Bhattacharya, Sudeep Tanwar, Rushabh Shah, and Akhilesh Ladha. Mobile edge computing-enabled blockchain framework—a survey. In Pradeep Kumar Singh, Arpan Kumar Kar, Yashwant Singh, Maheshkumar H. Kolekar, and Sudeep Tanwar, editors, *Proceedings of ICRIC 2019*, pages 797–809, Cham, 2020. Springer International Publishing.

[46] Burton H Bloom. Space/time trade-offs in hash coding with allowable errors. *Communications of the ACM*, 13(7):422–426, 1970.

[47] U. Bodkhe, P. Bhattacharya, S. Tanwar, S. Tyagi, N. Kumar, and M. S. Obaidat. Blohost: Blockchain enabled smart tourism and hospitality management. In *2019 International Conference on Computer, Information and Telecommunication Systems (CITS)*, pages 1–5, Aug 2019.

[48] U. Bodkhe, D. Mehta, S. Tanwar, P. Bhattacharya, P. K. Singh, and W. Hong. A survey on decentralized consensus mechanisms for cyber physical systems. *IEEE Access*, 8:54371–54401, 2020.

[49] U. Bodkhe, S. Tanwar, K. Parekh, P. Khanpara, S. Tyagi, N. Kumar, and M. Alazab. Blockchain for industry 4.0: A comprehensive review. *IEEE Access*, 8:79764–79800, 2020.

[50] Umesh Bodkhe and Sudeep Tanwar. Secure data dissemination techniques for iot applications: Research challenges and opportunities. *Software: Practice and Experience*, n/a(n/a):1–23.

[51] Flavio Bonomi, Michael Mitzenmacher, Rina Panigrahy, Sushil Singh, and George Varghese. An improved construction for counting bloom filters. In *European Symposium on Algorithms*, pages 684–695. Springer, 2006.

[52] Robert Stephen Boyer. *Automated reasoning: Essays in honor of woody bledsoe*, volume 1. Springer Science & Business Media, 2012.

[53] Andrei Z Broder. On the resemblance and containment of documents. In *Proceedings. Compression and Complexity of SEQUENCES 1997 (Cat. No. 97TB100171)*, pages 21–29. IEEE, 1997.

[54] Andrei Z Broder, Moses Charikar, Alan M Frieze, and Michael Mitzenmacher. Min-wise independent permutations. *Journal of Computer and System Sciences*, 60(3):630–659, 2000.

[55] I. Budhiraja, S. Tyagi, S. Tanwar, N. Kumar, and M. Guizani. Cr-noma based interference mitigation scheme for 5g femtocells users. In *2018 IEEE Global Communications Conference (GLOBECOM)*, pages 1–6, Dec 2018.

[56] I. Budhiraja, S. Tyagi, S. Tanwar, N. Kumar, and J. J. P. C. Rodrigues. Diya: Tactile internet driven delay assessment noma-based scheme for d2d communication. *IEEE Transactions on Industrial Informatics*, 15(12):6354–6366, 2019.

[57] I. Budhiraja, S. Tyagi, S. Tanwar, N. Kumar, and J. J. P. C. Rodrigues. Tactile internet for smart communities in 5g: An insight for noma-based solutions. *IEEE Transactions on Industrial Informatics*, 15(5):3104–3112, 2019.

[58] Ishan Budhiraja, Sudhanshu Tyagi, Sudeep Tanwar, Neeraj Kumar, and Mohsen Guizani. Cross layer noma interference mitigation for femtocell users in 5g environment. *IEEE Transactions on Vehicular Technology*, PP, 02 2019.

[59] Miguel Castro, Barbara Liskov, et al. Practical byzantine fault tolerance. In *OSDI*, volume 99, pages 173–186, 1999.

[60] Yousra Chabchoub, Raja Chiky, and Betul Dogan. How can sliding hyperloglog and ewma detect port scan attacks in ip traffic? *EURASIP Journal on Information Security*, 2014(1):5, 2014.

[61] Yousra Chabchoub and Georges Heébrail. Sliding hyperloglog: Estimating cardinality in a data stream over a sliding window. In *2010 IEEE International Conference on Data Mining Workshops*, pages 1297–1303. IEEE, 2010.

[62] Moses Charikar, Kevin Chen, and Martin Farach-Colton. Finding frequent items in data streams. In *International Colloquium on Automata, Languages, and Programming*, pages 693–703. Springer, 2002.

[63] K. Chauhan, S. Jani, D. Thakkar, R. Dave, J. Bhatia, S. Tanwar, and M. S. Obaidat. Automated machine learning: The new wave of machine learning. In *2020 2nd International Conference on Innovative Mechanisms for Industry Applications (ICIMIA)*, pages 205–212, 2020.

[64] Jing Chen, Shixiong Yao, Quan Yuan, Kun He, Shouling Ji, and Ruiying Du. Certchain: Public and efficient certificate audit based on blockchain for tls connections. In *IEEE INFOCOM 2018-IEEE Conference on Computer Communications*, pages 2060–2068. IEEE, 2018.

[65] Saar Cohen and Yossi Matias. Spectral bloom filters. In *Proceedings of the 2003 ACM SIGMOD international conference on Management of data*, pages 241–252. ACM, 2003.

[66] Graham Cormode and Shan Muthukrishnan. An improved data stream summary: the count-min sketch and its applications. *Journal of Algorithms*, 55(1):58–75, 2005.

[67] Li Da Xu, Wu He, and Shancang Li. Internet of things in industries: A survey. *IEEE Transactions on industrial informatics*, 10(4):2233–2243, 2014.

[68] Stefano De Angelis, Leonardo Aniello, Roberto Baldoni, Federico Lombardi, Andrea Margheri, and Vladimiro Sassone. Pbft vs proof-of-authority: applying the cap theorem to permissioned blockchain. 2018.

[69] Fan Deng and Davood Rafiei. Approximately detecting duplicates for streaming data using stable bloom filters. In *Proceedings of the 2006 ACM SIGMOD international conference on Management of data*, pages 25–36, 2006.

[70] Fan Deng and Davood Rafiei. New estimation algorithms for streaming data: Count-min can do more, 2007.

[71] Vijay Deshmukh, Kiyoshi Komatsu, and Prashant Saraswat. System and method for storing and accessing data using a plurality of probabilistic data structures, October 16 2012. US Patent 8,290,972.

[72] Tien Tuan Anh Dinh, Rui Liu, Meihui Zhang, Gang Chen, Beng Chin Ooi, and Ji Wang. Untangling blockchain: A data processing view of blockchain systems. *IEEE Transactions on Knowledge and Data Engineering*, 30(7):1366–1385, 2018.

[73] Benoit Donnet, Bruno Baynat, and Timur Friedman. Retouched bloom filters: allowing networked applications to trade off selected false positives against false negatives. In *Proceedings of the 2006 ACM CoNEXT conference*, page 13. ACM, 2006.

[74] Marianne Durand and Philippe Flajolet. Loglog counting of large cardinalities. In *European Symposium on Algorithms*, pages 605–617. Springer, 2003.

[75] Stefan Dziembowski, Sebastian Faust, Vladimir Kolmogorov, and Krzysztof Pietrzak. Proofs of space. In *Annual Cryptology Conference*, pages 585–605. Springer, 2015.

[76] Cristian Estan and George Varghese. *New directions in traffic measurement and accounting*, volume 32. ACM, 2002.

[77] Ittay Eyal, Adem Efe Gencer, Emin Gün Sirer, and Robbert Van Renesse. Bitcoin-ng: A scalable blockchain protocol. In *13th {USENIX} symposium on networked systems design and implementation ({NSDI} 16)*, pages 45–59, 2016.

[78] Bin Fan, Dave G. Andersen, Michael Kaminsky, and Michael D. Mitzenmacher. Cuckoo filter: Practically better than bloom. In *Proceedings of the 10th ACM International on Conference on Emerging Networking Experiments and Technologies*, CoNEXT '14, pages 75–88, New York, NY, USA, 2014. ACM.

[79] Li Fan, Pei Cao, Jussara Almeida, and Andrei Z Broder. Summary cache: A scalable wide-area web cache sharing protocol. In *ACM SIGCOMM Computer Communication Review*, volume 28, pages 254–265. ACM, 1998.

[80] Mohammad Sabzinejad Farash, Omer Nawaz, Khalid Mahmood, Shehzad Ashraf Chaudhry, and Muhammad Khurram Khan. A provably secure rfid authentication protocol based on elliptic curve for healthcare environments. *Journal of medical systems*, 40(7):165, 2016.

[81] Wu-chang Feng, Kang G Shin, Dilip D Kandlur, and Debanjan Saha. The blue active queue management algorithms. *IEEE/ACM transactions on networking*, 10(4):513–528, 2002.

[82] Philippe Flajolet, Éric Fusy, Olivier Gandouet, and Frédéric Meunier. Hyperloglog: the analysis of a near-optimal cardinality estimation algorithm. 2007.

[83] Jerome H Friedman, Jon Louis Bentley, and Raphael Ari Finkel. An algorithm for finding best matches in logarithmic expected time. *ACM Transactions on Mathematical Software (TOMS)*, 3(3):209–226, 1977.

[84] Sumit Ganguly, Minos Garofalakis, Rajeev Rastogi, and Krishan Sabnani. Streaming algorithms for robust, real-time detection of ddos attacks. In *27th International Conference on Distributed Computing Systems (ICDCS'07)*, pages 4–4. IEEE, 2007.

[85] Abdullah Gani, Aisha Siddiqa, Shahaboddin Shamshirband, and Fariza Hanum. A survey on indexing techniques for big data: taxonomy and performance evaluation. *Knowledge and information systems*, 46(2):241–284, 2016.

[86] Arthur Gervais, Srdjan Capkun, Ghassan O Karame, and Damian Gruber. On the privacy provisions of bloom filters in lightweight bitcoin clients. In *Proceedings of the 30th Annual Computer Security Applications Conference*, pages 326–335, 2014.

[87] M. Gor, J. Vora, S. Tanwar, S. Tyagi, N. Kumar, M. S. Obaidat, and B. Sadoun. Gata: Gps-arduino based tracking and alarm system for protection of wildlife animals. In *2017 International Conference on Computer, Information and Telecommunication Systems (CITS)*, pages 166–170, July 2017.

[88] Amit Goyal and Hal Daumé III. Approximate scalable bounded space sketch for large data nlp. In *Proceedings of the Conference on Empirical Methods in Natural Language Processing*, pages 250–261. Association for Computational Linguistics, 2011.

[89] Amit Goyal, Hal Daumé III, and Graham Cormode. Sketch algorithms for estimating point queries in nlp. In *Proceedings of the 2012 joint conference on empirical methods in natural language processing and computational natural language learning*, pages 1093–1103. Association for Computational Linguistics, 2012.

[90] Damian Gruber, Wenting Li, and Ghassan Karame. Unifying lightweight blockchain client implementations.

[91] Zhitao Guan, Guanlin Si, Xiaosong Zhang, Longfei Wu, Nadra Guizani, Xiaojiang Du, and Yinglong Ma. Privacy-preserving and efficient aggregation based on blockchain for power grid communications in smart communities. *IEEE Communications Magazine*, 56(7):82–88, 2018.

[92] D. Guo, Y. Liu, X. Li, and P. Yang. False negative problem of counting bloom filter. *IEEE Transactions on Knowledge and Data Engineering*, 22(5):651–664, 2010.

[93] Deke Guo, Jie Wu, Honghui Chen, and Xueshan Luo. Theory and network applications of dynamic bloom filters. In *Proceedings IEEE INFOCOM 2006. 25TH IEEE International Conference on Computer Communications*, pages 1–12. IEEE, 2006.

[94] Divya Gupta, Sahil Garg, Amritpal Singh, Shalini Batra, Neeraj Kumar, and MS Obaidat. Proids: Probabilistic data structures based intrusion detection system for network traffic monitoring. In *GLOBECOM 2017-2017 IEEE Global Communications Conference*, pages 1–6. IEEE, 2017.

[95] R. Gupta, S. Tanwar, F. Al-Turjman, P. Italiya, A. Nauman, and S. W. Kim. Smart contract privacy protection using ai in cyber-physical systems: Tools, techniques and challenges. *IEEE Access*, 8:24746–24772, 2020.

[96] R. Gupta, S. Tanwar, S. Tyagi, and N. Kumar. Tactile-internet-based telesurgery system for healthcare 4.0: An architecture, research challenges, and future directions. *IEEE Network*, 33(6):22–29, Nov 2019.

[97] R. Gupta, S. Tanwar, S. Tyagi, N. Kumar, M. S. Obaidat, and B. Sadoun. Habits: Blockchain-based telesurgery framework for healthcare 4.0. In *2019 International Conference on Computer, Information and Telecommunication Systems (CITS)*, pages 1–5, Aug 2019.

[98] Rajesh Gupta, Aparna Kumari, and Sudeep Tanwar. A taxonomy of blockchain envisioned edge-as-a-connected autonomous vehicles. *Transactions on Emerging Telecommunications Technologies*, n/a(n/a):e4009.

[99] Rajesh Gupta, Sudeep Tanwar, Neeraj Kumar, and Sudhanshu Tyagi. Blockchain-based security attack resilience schemes for autonomous vehicles in industry 4.0: A systematic review. *Computers & Electrical Engineering*, 86:106717, 2020.

[100] Rajesh Gupta, Sudeep Tanwar, Sudhanshu Tyagi, and Neeraj Kumar. Tactile internet and its applications in 5g era: A comprehensive review. *International Journal of Communication Systems*, 32(14):e3981, 2019. e3981 dac.3981.

[101] Rajesh Gupta, Sudeep Tanwar, Sudhanshu Tyagi, and Neeraj Kumar. Machine learning models for secure data analytics: A taxonomy and threat model. *Computer Communications*, 153:406 – 440, 2020.

[102] J. Hathaliya, P. Sharma, S. Tanwar, and R. Gupta. Blockchain-based remote patient monitoring in healthcare 4.0. In *2019 IEEE 9th International Conference on Advanced Computing (IACC)*, pages 87–91, Dec 2019.

[103] Jigna J. Hathaliya and Sudeep Tanwar. An exhaustive survey on security and privacy issues in healthcare 4.0. *Computer Communications*, 153:311 – 335, 2020.

[104] Jigna J. Hathaliya, Sudeep Tanwar, and Richard Evans. Securing electronic healthcare records: A mobile-based biometric authentication approach. *Journal of Information Security and Applications*, 53:102528, 2020.

[105] Jigna J Hathaliya, Sudeep Tanwar, Sudhanshu Tyagi, and Neeraj Kumar. Securing electronics healthcare records in healthcare 4.0 : A biometric-based approach. *Computers & Electrical Engineering*, 76:398 – 410, 2019.

[106] Kaiming He and Jian Sun. Computing nearest-neighbor fields via propagation-assisted kd-trees. In *2012 IEEE Conference on Computer Vision and Pattern Recognition*, pages 111–118. IEEE, 2012.

[107] Qingqiang He, Nan Guan, Mingsong Lv, and Wang Yi. On the consensus mechanisms of blockchain/dlt for internet of things. In *2018 IEEE 13th International Symposium on Industrial Embedded Systems (SIES)*, pages 1–10. IEEE, 2018.

[108] Yun Heo, Xiao-Long Wu, Deming Chen, Jian Ma, and Wen-Mei Hwu. Bless: bloom filter-based error correction solution for high-throughput sequencing reads. *Bioinformatics*, 30(10):1354–1362, 2014.

[109] Luiz C Irber and C Titus Brown. Efficient cardinality estimation for k-mers in large dna sequencing data sets: k-mer cardinality estimation. *BioRxiv*, page 056846, 2016.

[110] Anik Islam and Soo Young Shin. Bhmus: Blockchain based secure outdoor health monitoring scheme using uav in smart city. In *2019 7th International Conference on Information and Communication Technology (ICoICT)*, pages 1–6. IEEE, 2019.

[111] M. Jariso, B. Khan, S. Tanwar, S. Tyagi, and V. Rishiwal. Hybrid energy system for upgrading the rural environment. In *2018 IEEE Globecom Workshops (GC Wkshps)*, pages 1–6, Dec 2018.

[112] Naman Kabra, Pronaya Bhattacharya, Sudeep Tanwar, and Sudhanshu Tyagi. Mudrachain: Blockchain-based framework for automated cheque clearance in financial institutions. *Future Generation Computer Systems*, 102:574 – 587, 2020.

[113] Hazalila Kamaludin, Hairulnizam Mahdin, and Jemal H Abawajy. Clone tag detection in distributed rfid systems. *PloS one*, 13(3):e0193951, 2018.

[114] Kota Kanemura, Kentaroh Toyoda, and Tomoaki Ohtsuki. Design of privacy-preserving mobile bitcoin client based on γ-deniability enabled bloom filter. In *2017 IEEE 28th Annual International Symposium on Personal, Indoor, and Mobile Radio Communications (PIMRC)*, pages 1–6. IEEE, 2017.

[115] S. Kaneriya, D. Lakhani, H. U. Brahmbhatt, S. Tanwar, S. Tyagi, N. Kumar, and J. J. P. C. Rodrigues. Can tactile internet be a solution for low latency heart disorientation measure: An analysis. In *ICC 2019 - 2019 IEEE International Conference on Communications (ICC)*, pages 1–6, 2019.

[116] S. Kaneriya, S. Tanwar, S. Buddhadev, J. P. Verma, S. Tyagi, N. Kumar, and S. Misra. A range-based approach for long-term forecast of weather using probabilistic markov model. In *2018 IEEE International Conference on Communications Workshops (ICC Workshops)*, pages 1–6, May 2018.

[117] S. Kaneriya, S. Tanwar, A. Nayyar, J. P. Verma, S. Tyagi, N. Kumar, M. S. Obaidat, and J. J. P. C. Rodrigues. Data consumption-aware load forecasting scheme for smart grid systems. pages 1–6, Dec 2018.

[118] Santhosh Kumar Karre. Distributed detection of ddos attack. *International Journal of Future Computer and Communication*, 2(6):628, 2013.

[119] Sunny King and Scott Nadal. Ppcoin: Peer-to-peer crypto-currency with proof-of-stake. *self-published paper, August*, 19, 2012.

[120] Donald Ervin Knuth. *The art of computer programming: sorting and searching*, volume 3. Pearson Education, 1997.

[121] Eleftherios Kokoris Kogias, Philipp Jovanovic, Nicolas Gailly, Ismail Khoffi, Linus Gasser, and Bryan Ford. Enhancing bitcoin security and performance with strong consistency via collective signing. In *25th {usenix} security symposium ({usenix} security 16)*, pages 279–296, 2016.

[122] A Kosba, A Miller, E Shi, and ZW Hawk. The blockchain model of cryptography and privacy-preserving smart contracts on security and privacy. In *2016 IEEE symposium. Retrieved Apr*, volume 12, page 2017, 2016.

[123] R. Kumar, M. Kalra, S. Tanwar, S. Tyagi, and N. Kumar. Min-parent: An effective approach to enhance resource utilization in cloud environment. In *2016 International Conference on Advances in Computing, Communication, Automation (ICACCA) (Spring)*, pages 1–6, 2016.

[124] A. Kumari, S. Tanwar, S. Tyagi, N. Kumar, M. S. Obaidat, and J. J. P. C. Rodrigues. Fog computing for smart grid systems in the 5g environment: Challenges and solutions. *IEEE Wireless Communications*, 26(3):47–53, 2019.

[125] Aparna Kumari, Rajesh Gupta, Sudeep Tanwar, and Neeraj Kumar. Blockchain and ai amalgamation for energy cloud management: Challenges, solutions, and future directions. *Journal of Parallel and Distributed Computing*, 143:148 – 166, 2020.

[126] Aparna Kumari, Sudeep Tanwar, Sudhanshu Tyagi, and Neeraj Kumar. Fog computing for healthcare 4.0 environment: Opportunities and challenges. *Computers and Electrical Engineering*, 72:1 – 13, 2018.

[127] Aparna Kumari, Sudeep Tanwar, Sudhanshu Tyagi, Neeraj Kumar, Michele Maasberg, and Kim-Kwang Raymond Choo. Multimedia big data computing and internet of things applications: A taxonomy and process model. *Journal of Network and Computer Applications*, 124:169 – 195, 2018.

[128] Aparna Kumari, Sudeep Tanwar, Sudhanshu Tyagi, Neeraj Kumar, Reza M. Parizi, and Kim-Kwang Raymond Choo. Fog data analytics: A taxonomy and process model. *Journal of Network and Computer Applications*, 128:90 – 104, 2019.

[129] L Lamport, R Shostak, and M Pease. The byzantine generals problem acm transactions on progamming languages and syetems, vol. 4 no. 3 pp. 382-401, 1982.

[130] Daniel Larimer. Delegated proof-of-stake (dpos). *Bitshare whitepaper*, 2014.

[131] Kruti Lavingia and Sudeep Tanwar. *Augmented Reality and Industry 4.0*, pages 143–155. Springer International Publishing, Cham, 2020.

[132] Lei Lei, Zhangdui Zhong, Kan Zheng, Jiadi Chen, and Hanlin Meng. Challenges on wireless heterogeneous networks for mobile cloud computing. *IEEE Wireless Communications*, 20(3):34–44, 2013.

[133] Xiaoqi Li, Peng Jiang, Ting Chen, Xiapu Luo, and Qiaoyan Wen. A survey on the security of blockchain systems. *Future Generation Computer Systems*, 107:841–853, 2020.

[134] Zhichun Li, Yan Gao, and Yan Chen. Hifind: A high-speed flow-level intrusion detection approach with dos resiliency. *Computer Networks*, 54(8):1282–1299, 2010.

[135] Haiqin Liu, Yan Sun, and Min Sik Kim. Fine-grained ddos detection scheme based on bidirectional count sketch. In *2011 Proceedings of 20th International Conference on Computer Communications and Networks (ICCCN)*, pages 1–6. IEEE, 2011.

[136] Huakun Liu, Xin Wei, Ruliang Xiao, Lifei Chen, Xin Du, and Shi Zhang. Oprcp: Approximate nearest neighbor binary search algorithm for hybrid data over wmsn blockchain. *EURASIP Journal on Wireless Communications and Networking*, 2018(1):208, 2018.

[137] R. F. T. Martins, F. L. Verdi, R. Villaça, and L. F. U. Garcia. Using probabilistic data structures for monitoring of multi-tenant p4-based

networks. In *2018 IEEE Symposium on Computers and Communications (ISCC)*, pages 00204–00207, 2018.

[138] Parimal Mehta, Rajesh Gupta, and Sudeep Tanwar. Blockchain envisioned uav networks: Challenges, solutions, and comparisons. *Computer Communications*, 151:518 – 538, 2020.

[139] Sarah Meiklejohn, Marjori Pomarole, Grant Jordan, Kirill Levchenko, Damon McCoy, Geoffrey M Voelker, and Stefan Savage. A fistful of bitcoins: characterizing payments among men with no names. In *Proceedings of the 2013 conference on Internet measurement conference*, pages 127–140, 2013.

[140] Ralph C Merkle. A digital signature based on a conventional encryption function. In *Conference on the theory and application of cryptographic techniques*, pages 369–378. Springer, 1987.

[141] A. Mewada, S. Tanwar, and Z. Narmawala. Comparison and evaluation of real time reservation technologies in the intelligent public transport system. In *2018 Fifth International Conference on Parallel, Distributed and Grid Computing (PDGC)*, pages 800–805, Dec 2018.

[142] Mitar Milutinovic, Warren He, Howard Wu, and Maxinder Kanwal. Proof of luck: An efficient blockchain consensus protocol. In *proceedings of the 1st Workshop on System Software for Trusted Execution*, pages 1–6, 2016.

[143] Michael Mirkin, Yan Ji, Jonathan Pang, Ariah Klages-Mundt, Ittay Eyal, and Ari Jules. Bdos: Blockchain denial of service. *arXiv preprint arXiv:1912.07497*, 2019.

[144] Jayadev Misra and David Gries. Finding repeated elements, 1982.

[145] Ishan Mistry, Sudeep Tanwar, Sudhanshu Tyagi, and Neeraj Kumar. Blockchain for 5g-enabled iot for industrial automation: A systematic review, solutions, and challenges. *Mechanical Systems and Signal Processing*, 135:106382, 2020.

[146] M. Mitzenmacher. Compressed bloom filters. *IEEE/ACM Transactions on Networking*, 10(5):604–612, 2002.

[147] Saraju P Mohanty, Uma Choppali, and Elias Kougianos. Everything you wanted to know about smart cities: The internet of things is the backbone. *IEEE Consumer Electronics Magazine*, 5(3):60–70, 2016.

[148] Joanna Moubarak, Eric Filiol, and Maroun Chamoun. On blockchain security and relevant attacks. In *2018 IEEE Middle East and North Africa Communications Conference (MENACOMM)*, pages 1–6. IEEE, 2018.

[149] Ammar Awad Mutlag, Mohd Khanapi Abd Ghani, Net al Arunkumar, Mazin Abed Mohammed, and Othman Mohd. Enabling technologies for fog computing in healthcare iot systems. *Future Generation Computer Systems*, 90:62–78, 2019.

[150] Ashley I Naimi and Daniel J Westreich. Big data: A revolution that will transform how we live, work, and think, 2014.

[151] Satoshi Nakamoto et al. Bitcoin: A peer-to-peer electronic cash system.(2008), 2008.

[152] Muqaddas Naz, Nadeem Javaid, and Sohail Iqbal. *Research based data rights management using blockchain over ethereum network*. PhD thesis, MS thesis, COMSATS University Islamabad (CUI), Islamabad 44000, Pakistan, 2019.

[153] Jonas David Nick. Data-driven de-anonymization in bitcoin. Master's thesis, ETH-Zürich, 2015.

[154] Kirill Nikitin, Eleftherios Kokoris-Kogias, Philipp Jovanovic, Nicolas Gailly, Linus Gasser, Ismail Khoffi, Justin Cappos, and Bryan Ford. {CHAINIAC}: Proactive software-update transparency via collectively signed skipchains and verified builds. In *26th {USENIX} Security Symposium ({USENIX} Security 17)*, pages 1271–1287, 2017.

[155] Akhilesh Arvind Nimje, Akhilesh Baliram Panwar, Annima Gupta, and Sudeep Tanwar. *Capacity Estimation of Electric Vehicle Aggregator for Ancillary Services to the Grid*, pages 235–257. Springer Singapore, Singapore, 2019.

[156] Charles Noyes. Bitav: Fast anti-malware by distributed blockchain consensus and feedforward scanning. *arXiv preprint arXiv:1601.01405*, 2016.

[157] Babatunde Ojetunde, Naoki Shibata, and Juntao Gao. Secure payment system utilizing manet for disaster areas. *IEEE Transactions on Systems, Man, and Cybernetics: Systems*, 2017.

[158] Jitendra Oza, Zunnun Narmawala, Sudeep Tanwar, and Pradeep Kr Singh. Public transport tracking and its issues. *International Journal of Computer Sciences and Engineering*, 5:192–197, 11 2017.

[159] A Pinar Ozisik, Gavin Andresen, George Bissias, Amir Houmansadr, and Brian Levine. Graphene: A new protocol for block propagation using set reconciliation. In *Data Privacy Management, Cryptocurrencies and Blockchain Technology*, pages 420–428. Springer, 2017.

[160] S. B. Patel, P. Bhattacharya, S. Tanwar, and N. Kumar. Kirti: A blockchain-based credit recommender system for financial institutions.

IEEE Transactions on Network Science and Engineering, pages 1–1, 2020.

[161] Ripon Patgiri, Sabuzima Nayak, and Samir Kumar Borgohain. Preventing ddos using bloom filter: A survey. *arXiv preprint arXiv:1810.06689*, 2018.

[162] Vivek Prasad, Madhuri Bhavsar, and Sudeep Tanwar. Influence of monitoring: Fog and edge computing. *Scalable Computing*, 20:365–376, 05 2019.

[163] K. Qin, H. Hadass, A. Gervais, and J. Reardon. Applying private information retrieval to lightweight bitcoin clients. In *2019 Crypto Valley Conference on Blockchain Technology (CVCBT)*, pages 60–72, 2019.

[164] Bruno Rodrigues, Thomas Bocek, Andri Lareida, David Hausheer, Sina Rafati, and Burkhard Stiller. A blockchain-based architecture for collaborative ddos mitigation with smart contracts. In *IFIP International Conference on Autonomous Infrastructure, Management and Security*, pages 16–29. Springer, Cham, 2017.

[165] Christian Esteve Rothenberg, Carlos AB Macapuna, Fábio L Verdi, and Mauricio F Magalhaes. The deletable bloom filter: a new member of the bloom family. *IEEE Communications Letters*, 14(6), 2010.

[166] Thomas Jay Rush. Adaptive enhanced bloom filters for identifying transactions of interest in a blockchain. 2017.

[167] Stuart Schechter, Cormac Herley, and Michael Mitzenmacher. Popularity is everything: A new approach to protecting passwords from statistical-guessing attacks. In *Proceedings of the 5th USENIX conference on Hot topics in security*, pages 1–8. USENIX Association, 2010.

[168] Kulesh Shanmugasundaram, Hervé Brönnimann, and Nasir Memon. Payload attribution via hierarchical bloom filters. In *Proceedings of the 11th ACM conference on Computer and communications security*, pages 31–41. ACM, 2004.

[169] Priyanka Sharma, Manish K Nunia, Madhushree Basavarajaish, and Sudeep Tanwar. Tree-based ant colony optimization algorithm for effective multicast routing in mobile adhoc network. *Recent Advances in Computer Science and Communications (Formerly: Recent Patents on Computer Science)*, 13(2):120–127, 2020.

[170] Mike Sharples and John Domingue. *Chapter:'The Blockchain and Kudos: A Distributed System for Educational Record, Reputation and Reward'from Book: Adaptive and Adaptable Learning: 11th European Conference on Technology Enhanced Learning, EC-TEL 2016, Lyon, France, September 13-16, 2016*. Springer, 2016.

[171] Nir Shavit and Itay Lotan. Skiplist-based concurrent priority queues. In *Proceedings 14th International Parallel and Distributed Processing Symposium. IPDPS 2000*, pages 263–268. IEEE, 2000.

[172] Muhammad Siddiqi, Syed Taha All, and Vijay Sivaraman. Secure lightweight context-driven data logging for bodyworn sensing devices. In *2017 5th International Symposium on Digital Forensic and Security (ISDFS)*, pages 1–6. IEEE, 2017.

[173] Rajeev Singh, Sudeep Tanwar, and Teek Parval Sharma. Utilization of blockchain for mitigating the distributed denial of service attacks. *Security and Privacy*, 3(3):e96, 2020.

[174] Rajeev Singh, Sudeep Tanwar, and Teek Parval Sharma. Utilization of blockchain for mitigating the distributed denial of service attacks. *Security and Privacy*, 3(3):e96, 2020.

[175] Y. Singh, J. A. Lone, P. K. Singh, Z. Polkowski, S. Tanwar, and S. Tyagi. Deployment and coverage in wireless sensor networks: A perspective. In *2019 11th International Conference on Electronics, Computers and Artificial Intelligence (ECAI)*, pages 1–7, 2019.

[176] Yonatan Sompolinsky and Aviv Zohar. Accelerating bitcoin's transaction processing. fast money grows on trees, not chains. *IACR Cryptology ePrint Archive*, 2013(881), 2013.

[177] Daniel Sperling and Deborah Gordon. Two billion cars: transforming a culture. *TR news*, (259), 2008.

[178] A. Srivastava, S. K. Singh, S. Tanwar, and S. Tyagi. Suitability of big data analytics in indian banking sector to increase revenue and profitability. In *2017 3rd International Conference on Advances in Computing, Communication Automation (ICACCA) (Fall)*, pages 1–6, Sep. 2017.

[179] Mathis Steichen, Stefan Hommes, and Radu State. Chainguard—a firewall for blockchain applications using sdn with openflow. In *2017 Principles, Systems and Applications of IP Telecommunications (IPTComm)*, pages 1–8. IEEE, 2017.

[180] Sumit Kumar Gupta Neeraj Kumar Sudhanshu Tyagi, Sudeep Tanwar and Joel J. P. C. Rodrigues. Selective cluster-based temperature monitoring system for homogeneouswireless sensor networks. *ZTE Communications*, 12(3):22, 2014.

[181] Håkan Sundell and Philippas Tsigas. Scalable and lock-free concurrent dictionaries. In *Proceedings of the 2004 ACM symposium on Applied computing*, pages 1438–1445. ACM, 2004.

[182] Melanie Swan. *Blockchain: Blueprint for a new economy.* "O'Reilly Media, Inc.", 2015.

[183] Ewa Syta, Iulia Tamas, Dylan Visher, David Isaac Wolinsky, Philipp Jovanovic, Linus Gasser, Nicolas Gailly, Ismail Khoffi, and Bryan Ford. Keeping authorities "honest or bust" with decentralized witness cosigning. In *2016 IEEE Symposium on Security and Privacy (SP)*, pages 526–545. Ieee, 2016.

[184] Amir Taherkordi and Frank Eliassen. Data-centric iot services provisioning in fog-cloud computing systems. In *2017 IEEE/ACM Second International Conference on Internet-of-Things Design and Implementation (IoTDI)*, pages 317–318. IEEE, 2017.

[185] S. Tanwar, Q. Bhatia, P. Patel, A. Kumari, P. K. Singh, and W. Hong. Machine learning adoption in blockchain-based smart applications: The challenges, and a way forward. *IEEE Access*, 8:474–488, 2020.

[186] S. Tanwar, P. Patel, K. Patel, S. Tyagi, N. Kumar, and M. S. Obaidat. An advanced internet of thing based security alert system for smart home. In *2017 International Conference on Computer, Information and Telecommunication Systems (CITS)*, pages 25–29, July 2017.

[187] S. Tanwar, S. Tyagi, I. Budhiraja, and N. Kumar. Tactile internet for autonomous vehicles: Latency and reliability analysis. *IEEE Wireless Communications*, 26(4):66–72, August 2019.

[188] S. Tanwar, S. Tyagi, N. Kumar, and M. S. Obaidat. La-mhr: Learning automata based multilevel heterogeneous routing for opportunistic shared spectrum access to enhance lifetime of wsn. *IEEE Systems Journal*, 13(1):313–323, March 2019.

[189] S. Tanwar, J. Vora, S. Kaneriya, and S. Tyagi. Fog-based enhanced safety management system for miners. In *2017 3rd International Conference on Advances in Computing,Communication Automation (ICACCA) (Fall)*, pages 1–6, Sep. 2017.

[190] Sudeep Tanwar, Neeraj Kumar, and Jian-Wei Niu. Eemhr: Energy-efficient multilevel heterogeneous routing protocol for wireless sensor networks. *International Journal of Communication Systems*, 27(9):1289–1318, 2014.

[191] Sudeep Tanwar, Neeraj Kumar, and Joel J.P.C. Rodrigues. A systematic review on heterogeneous routing protocols for wireless sensor network. *Journal of Network and Computer Applications*, 53:39 – 56, 2015.

[192] Sudeep Tanwar, Aparna Kumari, Sudhanshu Tyagi, and Neeraj Kumar. Verification and validation techniques for streaming big data analytics in internet ofthings environment. *IET Networks*, November 2018.

[193] Sudeep Tanwar, Karan Parekh, and Richard Evans. Blockchain-based electronic healthcare record system for healthcare 4.0 applications. *Journal of Information Security and Applications*, 50:102407, 2020.

[194] Sudeep Tanwar, Tilak Ramani, and Sudhanshu Tyagi. Dimensionality reduction using pca and svd in big data: A comparative case study. In Zuber Patel and Shilpi Gupta, editors, *Future Internet Technologies and Trends*, pages 116–125, Cham, 2018. Springer International Publishing.

[195] Sudeep Tanwar, Sudhanshu Tyagi, and Sachin Kumar. The role of internet of things and smart grid for the development of a smart city. In Yu-Chen Hu, Shailesh Tiwari, Krishn K. Mishra, and Munesh C. Trivedi, editors, *Intelligent Communication and Computational Technologies*, pages 23–33, Singapore, 2018. Springer Singapore.

[196] Sudeep Tanwar, Jayneel Vora, Sudhanshu Tyagi, Neeraj Kumar, and Mohammad S. Obaidat. A systematic review on security issues in vanet. *Security and Privacy*, 1(5):e39, 2018.

[197] Alin Tomescu and Srinivas Devadas. Catena: Efficient non-equivocation via bitcoin. In *2017 IEEE Symposium on Security and Privacy (SP)*, pages 393–409. IEEE, 2017.

[198] Hardik Trivedi, Sudeep Tanwar, and Priyank Thakkar. Software defined network-based vehicular adhoc networks for intelligent transportation system: Recent advances and future challenges. In Pradeep Kumar Singh, Marcin Paprzycki, Bharat Bhargava, Jitender Kumar Chhabra, Narottam Chand Kaushal, and Yugal Kumar, editors, *Futuristic Trends in Network and Communication Technologies*, pages 325–337, Singapore, 2019. Springer Singapore.

[199] S. Tyagi, S. K. Gupta, S. Tanwar, and N. Kumar. Ehe-leach: Enhanced heterogeneous leach protocol for lifetime enhancement of wireless sns. In *2013 International Conference on Advances in Computing, Communications and Informatics (ICACCI)*, pages 1485–1490, Aug 2013.

[200] S. Tyagi, S. K. Gupta, S. Tanwar, and N. Kumar. Ehe-leach: Enhanced heterogeneous leach protocol for lifetime enhancement of wireless sns. In *2013 International Conference on Advances in Computing, Communications and Informatics (ICACCI)*, pages 1485–1490, Aug 2013.

[201] Sudhanshu Tyagi, Sudeep Tanwar, Sumit Kumar Gupta, Neeraj Kumar, and Joel J. P. C. Rodrigues. A lifetime extended multi-levels heterogeneous routing protocol for wireless sensor networks. *Telecommunication Systems*, 59(1):43–62, May 2015.

[202] Sudhanshu Tyagi, Sudeep Tanwar, Neeraj Kumar, and Joel J.P.C. Rodrigues. Cognitive radio-based clustering for opportunistic shared spectrum access to enhance lifetime of wireless sensor network. *Pervasive*

and Mobile Computing, 22:90 – 112, 2015. Special Issue on Recent Developments in Cognitive Radio Sensor Networks.

[203] Hrishikesh Vachhani, Mohammad S. Obiadat, Arkesh Thakkar, Vyom Shah, Raj Sojitra, Jitendra Bhatia, and Sudeep Tanwar. Machine learning based stock market analysis: A short survey. In Jennifer S. Raj, Abul Bashar, and S. R. Jino Ramson, editors, *Innovative Data Communication Technologies and Application*, pages 12–26, Cham, 2020. Springer International Publishing.

[204] Rakeshkumar Vanzara, Priyanka Sharma, Haresh S. Bhatt, Sudeep Tanwar, Sudhanshu Tyagi, Neeraj Kumar, and Mohammad S. Obaidat. Adytia: Adaptive and dynamic tcp interface architecture for heterogeneous networks. *International Journal of Communication Systems*, 32(2):e3855, 2019. e3855 dac.3855.

[205] Jai Prakash Verma, Sudeep Tanwar, Sanjay Garg, Ishit Gandhi, and Nikita H. Bachani. Evaluation of pattern based customized approach for stock market trend prediction with big data and machine learning techniques. *International journal of business*, 6:1–15, 2019.

[206] J. Vohra, S. Tanwar, S. Tyagi, N. Kumar, and J. J. P. C. Rodrigues. Hridaay: Ballistocardiogram-based heart rate monitoring using fog computing. In *2019 IEEE Global Communications Conference (GLOBECOM)*, pages 1–6, 2019.

[207] J. Vora, P. Italiya, S. Tanwar, S. Tyagi, N. Kumar, M. S. Obaidat, and K. Hsiao. Ensuring privacy and security in e-health records. In *2018 International Conference on Computer, Information and Telecommunication Systems (CITS)*, pages 1–5, July 2018.

[208] J. Vora, A. Nayyar, S. Tanwar, S. Tyagi, N. Kumar, M. S. Obaidat, and J. J. P. C. Rodrigues. Bheem: A blockchain-based framework for securing electronic health records. In *2018 IEEE Globecom Workshops (GC Wkshps)*, pages 1–6, Dec 2018.

[209] J. Vora, S. Tanwar, S. Tyagi, N. Kumar, and J. J. P. C. Rodrigues. Faal: Fog computing-based patient monitoring system for ambient assisted living. In *2017 IEEE 19th International Conference on e-Health Networking, Applications and Services (Healthcom)*, pages 1–6, Oct 2017.

[210] J. Vora, S. Tanwar, S. Tyagi, N. Kumar, and J. J. P. C. Rodrigues. Home-based exercise system for patients using iot enabled smart speaker. In *2017 IEEE 19th International Conference on e-Health Networking, Applications and Services (Healthcom)*, pages 1–6, Oct 2017.

[211] J. Vora, D. Vekaria, S. Tanwar, and S. Tyagi. Machine learning-based voltage dip measurement of smart energy meter. In *2018 Fifth*

International Conference on Parallel, Distributed and Grid Computing (PDGC), pages 828–832, Dec 2018.

[212] Jingdong Wang, Heng Tao Shen, Jingkuan Song, and Jianqiu Ji. Hashing for similarity search: A survey. *arXiv preprint arXiv:1408.2927*, 2014.

[213] Kyu-Young Whang, Brad T Vander-Zanden, and Howard M Taylor. A linear-time probabilistic counting algorithm for database applications. *ACM Transactions on Database Systems (TODS)*, 15(2):208–229, 1990.

[214] Min Woo Woo, JongWhi Lee, and KeeHyun Park. A reliable iot system for personal healthcare devices. *Future Generation Computer Systems*, 78:626–640, 2018.

[215] Gavin Wood. Ethereum: A secure decentralised generalised transaction ledger. *Ethereum project yellow paper*, 151:1–32, 2014.

[216] Jeff Yan and Pook Leong Cho. Enhancing collaborative spam detection with bloom filters. In *2006 22nd Annual Computer Security Applications Conference (ACSAC'06)*, pages 414–428. IEEE, 2006.

[217] Zheng Yan and Silke Holtmanns. Trust modeling and management: from social trust to digital trust. In *Computer security, privacy and politics: current issues, challenges and solutions*, pages 290–323. IGI Global, 2008.

[218] Hui Yang, Yongshen Liang, Jiaqi Yuan, Qiuyan Yao, Ao Yu, and Jie Zhang. Distributed blockchain-based trusted multi-domain collaboration for mobile edge computing in 5g and beyond. *IEEE Transactions on Industrial Informatics*, 2020.

[219] F. Zhao and L.J. Guibas. *Wireless Sensor Networks: An Information Processing Approach*. Morgan Kaufmann, 2004.

[220] Tianchu Zhao, Sheng Zhou, Xueying Guo, Yun Zhao, and Zhisheng Niu. A cooperative scheduling scheme of local cloud and internet cloud for delay-aware mobile cloud computing. In *2015 IEEE Globecom Workshops (GC Wkshps)*, pages 1–6. IEEE, 2015.

[221] Aiping Zhou, Huisheng Zhu, Lijun Liu, and Chengang Zhu. Identification of heavy hitters for network data streams with probabilistic sketch. In *2018 IEEE 3rd International Conference on Cloud Computing and Big Data Analysis (ICCCBDA)*, pages 451–456. IEEE, 2018.

[222] ALEKSEI ZHUVIKIN. A blockchain of image copyrights using robust image features and locality-sensitive hashing. *International Journal of Computer Science & Applications*, 15(1), 2018.

[223] Guy Zyskind, Oz Nathan, and Alex Pentland. Enigma: Decentralized computation platform with guaranteed privacy. *arXiv preprint arXiv:1506.03471*, 2015.

Index